MW00579440

WHY MATERIALISM IS BALONEY

Bernardo Kastrup's book is another nail in the coffin of the superstition of materialism. With elegant clarity he explains that mind, brain & cosmos are what consciousness does.
Deepak Chopra, M.D. Pioneer in the field of mind-body medicine. Author of over sixty-five books with twenty New York Times best sellers.

Bernardo Kastrup takes a bold and brilliant step in the collective movement of humanity beyond the confines of current materialism and everything that it entails. Truly speaking, alternative worldviews to the current paradigm of a material universe and associated ontologies, including various religious kinds, classical Newtonian physics, economic systems based on external consumption, etc., are easily dismissed as they don't fit current modern societal values. Yet, these ontologies may be rapidly leading us to major problems, including perhaps the demise of current 'Western' societies. The hidden ontologies of an external, material universe, devoid of the dynamical, evolutionary role of consciousness are prevalent, all-consuming, and insidious. It is time to abandon them or at least see them as an aspect of reality but not the true reality. Bernardo Kastrup is brave and a true pioneer to show us why and how we should.
Menas Kafatos, Ph.D. Fletcher Jones Professor of Computational Physics, Chapman University. Author of *The Conscious Universe: Parts and Wholes in Physical Reality*.

Bernardo takes us on a journey to an alternative worldview, one that makes a great deal more sense than the scientistic one we are being spoon-fed through academia and the media. He expresses his ideas lucidly and constructively in a manner that does not lose their scientific and logical force. ... I challenge you to read Bernardo Kastrup's prescription for what metaphysically ails you. You will be a wiser being for it. *(from the Foreword)*

Shogaku Zenshin Stephen Echard Musgrave Roshi. Director of the Zen Institute of San Diego, California. Author of *Zen Buddhism, Its Practice and the Transcendental Mind.*

[Bernardo Kastrup is a] remarkable, intellectually diverse and energetic thinker. ... [A] turnabout in the way scientists conceive and interpret natural phenomena requires new interdisciplinary thinkers like Bernardo. ... [He] has brought a brand new way of seeing the ancient idea of 'infinite mind.' Although written in a personal and breezy tone, this book is a vast philosophical endeavor. It captures 'big picture' ideas in a manner accessible to a wider audience. *(from the Afterword)*

Rick Stuart, Ph.D. Practicing psychotherapist.

Why Materialism Is Baloney

Is Baloney

How *true* skeptics know there is no death
and fathom answers to life, the universe
and everything

Why Materialism Is Baloney

How *true* skeptics know there is no death
and fathom answers to life, the universe
and everything

Dr. Bernardo Kastrup

BOOKS

Winchester, UK
Washington, USA

First published by iff Books, 2014
iff Books is an imprint of John Hunt Publishing Ltd., No. 3 East Street, Alresford,
Hampshire SO24 9EE, UK
office1@jhpbooks.net
www.johnhuntpublishing.com
www.iff-books.com

For distributor details and how to order please visit the 'Ordering' section on our website.

Text copyright: Dr. Bernardo Kastrup 2013, 2017

ISBN: 978 1 78279 362 5
978 1 78279 361 8 (ebook)

A CIP catalogue record for this book is available from the British Library.

Figure 1 © 2013 by Bernardo Kastrup. Created by Karolina Rodrigues (karolrodrigues.com).
Figure 2 © 2013 by Bernardo Kastrup. Figure 9 is in the Public Domain. Figure 10 is reproduced
from *Popular Science Monthly*, Volume 3 (1873). It is in the Public Domain because its copyright
has expired (published before 1923).

All quotations in this book are either from works in the
Public Domain or are believed, in good faith, to fall well within Fair Use provisions.

Design: Lee Nash

UK: Printed and bound by CPI Group (UK) Ltd, Croydon, CR0 4YY
US: Printed and bound by Thomson Shore, 7300 West Joy Road, Dexter, MI 48130

We operate a distinctive and ethical publishing philosophy in all
areas of our business, from our global network of authors to
production and worldwide distribution.

CONTENTS

Other books by Bernardo Kastrup

Rationalist Spirituality:
An exploration of the meaning of life and existence informed by logic and science

Dreamed up Reality:
Diving into mind to uncover the astonishing hidden tale of nature

Meaning in Absurdity:
What bizarre phenomena can tell us about the nature of reality

Brief Peeks Beyond:
Critical essays on metaphysics, neuroscience, free will, skepticism and culture

More Than Allegory:
On religious myth, truth and belief

Coming March 2019
The Idea of the World:
A multi-disciplinary argument for the mental nature of reality

Every book is a journey into the bottomless ocean of mind, not only for its readers but, and perhaps foremost, for its writer. This book is the diary of the most important journey of my life thus far. In it, I wasn't alone. Those who walked next to me will always live within me: Natalia Vorontsova, Rick Stuart, Guiba Guimarães, Rob van der Werf, Snoes and... the Other.

Foreword

'The mind is the brain'
Scientistic materialism consensus

'What certainty can there be in a Philosophy which consists in as many Hypotheses as there are Phenomena to be explained. To explain all nature is too difficult a task for any one man or even for any one age. 'Tis much better to do a little with certainty, & leave the rest for others that come after you, than to explain all things by conjecture without making sure of anything.'
Sir Isaac Newton

Bernardo Kastrup has articulated a much-needed corrective to the metaphysical illness of our age, scientistic materialism. Scientism is the belief that science is the most valuable part of human learning because it supposedly is the most authoritative, or serious, or beneficial. But science itself is merely a particular method for dousing the tools at hand to propose hypotheses, do experiments, and come to conclusions based on the information derived. As such, it is regrettable that some practitioners of science – and even some philosophers of science – have now taken on the attitude that scientism is the only valid approach to human knowledge. The idea that science, and science alone, exhausts the human potential has grown into a boy too big for his britches. Behind this monstrous presumption is the highly metaphysical view of materialism. One should make no mistake here: metaphysical beliefs distort science, for any kind of metaphysics is, in and of itself, contradictory to science's own purposes as an open-ended search for truth. That does not mean a scientist cannot have a metaphysical view; but this view cannot impinge on the interpretation of observations. Scientism today is doing what the Church did in the fifteenth century: forcing theory to fit a predetermined metaphysics.

In the pursuit of an external truth, scientistic materialism has forgotten the internal, most fundamental reality of human existence: we can know nothing but that which appears in our own mind. Our mind is our reality and, when we attempt to reify either the subject or the object, we chase our own tail at light speed. The ontological vertigo produced by this exercise has extended to the point where materialist philosophers, such as Daniel Dennett, Owen Flannigan, and Patricia and Paul Churchland, tell us that consciousness itself does not exist. And, as if this were not enough, they utter this pronouncement with the smugness and self-assuredness of a Pat Robertson or Jerry Falwell.

How can anyone of us take seriously someone who stands up and pronounces that his or her own mind does not exist? Truly, this is a kōan worthy of a Zen Patriarch. It is, in fact, the very opposite of not only Buddhist thinking, but also common sense. And not a common sense based merely on the obvious, but on the most primal reality of the human condition.

Two thousand five hundred years ago, philosophers in India and Greece struggled with articulating the nature of mind and reality. Over the millennia, there have been many approaches to this articulation by many schools of Buddhism, but none of them became so confused as to assert that mind itself does not exist or is not primary. Many people who learn of Zen and the teachings of Nagarjuna stumble over the words of the Heart Sutra: form is emptiness; emptiness is not different from form. They believe erroneously that this is a sort of nihilistic formula, when it is quite the opposite: form (matter) and emptiness (mind) interpenetrate each other as one single reality, like water and sea. This is a monist expression *par excellence,* and it flows from the depth of the experiences of meditation and mindfulness before it is ever articulated into words.

Zen teachers use every weapon in our arsenal to force the student to confront this reality him or herself, and not to hide in the words of dualistic thinking. The horse does not ride you; you ride the horse. To quote Bernardo:

'There are 'external' regions of the medium of mind, in the sense that there are regions that you do not identify yourself with. But this does not entail that there is an abstract 'shadow' universe outside mind; it does not entail an inflationary doubling of reality.'

He goes on to say:

'This way, unlike what materialism entails, a neural process isn't the subjective experience it correlates with, but merely a partial image of it.'

In many ways, this echoes the Zen perspective. In the words of Zen Master Soyen Shaku, as translated by Nyogen Senzaki:

'Make a thorough analysis of yourself. Realize that your body is not your body; it is part of the whole body of sentient beings. Your mind is not solely your mind; it is but a constituent of all mind.'

Bernardo takes us on a journey to an alternative worldview, one that makes a great deal more sense than the scientistic one we are being spoon-fed through academia and the media. He expresses his ideas lucidly and constructively in a manner that does not lose their scientific and logical force. The truly ironic thing is that, in attacking the pretenses of scientistic materialism, Bernardo grounds himself in the latest and deepest understanding produced by science; one that scientistic materialism refuses to accept philosophically.

I challenge you to read Bernardo Kastrup's prescription for what metaphysically ails you. You will be a wiser being for it.

Shogaku Zenshin Stephen Echard Musgrave Roshi. Director of the Zen Institute of San Diego, California. Author of *Zen Buddhism, Its Practice and the Transcendental Mind.*

Chapter 1

The Current Worldview and its Implications

A worldview is a set of ideas and beliefs on the basis of which one relates to oneself and to the world at large. It entails tentative answers to questions like: What am I? Where did I come from? What is the universe? What is the underlying nature of reality? What is the meaning of my role in the play of existence? And so on. One's worldview is probably *the* most important aspect of one's life. After all, our worldviews largely determine, given the circumstances of our lives, whether we are happy or depressed; whether our lives are rich in meaning or desperately vacuous; and whether there is reason for hope. It is thus very hard, if at all possible, to overestimate the relevance of the choices we make, with our minds and hearts, when it comes to defining our worldviews.

Society's worldview

Though worldviews are fundamentally individual, there is tight interplay between people's individual worldviews and society at large. While the majority worldview tends to influence how society organizes itself, society also largely influences the worldviews of individuals through education, the media, and the overall cultural zeitgeist. Indeed, it is nearly impossible for any person inserted in a modern cultural context to escape the haze of the zeitgeist and develop a truly unbiased, critical, and personal worldview. We are all bombarded daily with messages suggesting to us who we are, what reality is, what is possible or impossible, what is believable or unbelievable, what is meaningful or pointless and how we should live our lives. These messages come from the media in the form of advertisements, newscasts, documentaries, newspaper and magazine articles, political rhetoric, etc., but they also come from our own parents, family doctors, bosses, partners, friends and so on. The entire world around us is constantly pushing views regarding *what is going on* and *what to do about it.*

But just *what* is going on? Does anyone *really* know? Or do we simply live in a reality shaped by ephemeral best guesses? Either way, if we could escape the hysterical cacophony of culture so to develop a more authentic and unbiased worldview, grounded in direct experience and clear thinking, what would such a worldview be like? I will attempt to sketch answers to these questions in subsequent chapters. For now, though, we need to develop a more explicit understanding of what the mainstream worldview of our culture entails.

The influence of materialism

No society on Earth has a single worldview coordinating the lives of all its citizens, though many a dictator would like just that. Western societies, for instance, host myriad contradictory world-views: religious fundamentalism, material consumerism, showbiz hysteria, political activism, spirituality and New Age, scientism, militant skepticism and so on. Each of these general amalgamations of ideas and beliefs entails a particular way to relate to oneself and to reality at large. Their mutual contradic-toriness leads to all kinds of cultural conflicts that, ironically, help sustain and vitalize each faction by providing them with reasons to close ranks. For instance, from my own personal perspective, little did more to help galvanize religious fundamentalism than militant atheism, and vice-versa. And all these different factions operate simultaneously in our society.

Yet, it is quite clear to any diligent commentator on Western culture that there is, indeed, a subtle but irresistible core of ideas and beliefs – a core worldview – that holds more influence than any other in our society; even among those people who, outwardly, declare their allegiance to different belief systems. I am speaking, of course, of Western *metaphysical* materialism.

Materialism subtly pervades our expectations, value systems, goals, and nearly every aspect of our lives. Take, for instance, people who consider themselves deeply religious, holding beliefs about the immortality of the soul and the reality of heaven: they, too, often fear and resist death as if, deep inside, they actually believed that it represented oblivion. They will pray to a divinity to spare them and their loved ones an early demise. They will subject themselves to horrendous medical procedures to extend life for a few more weeks or months. They will weep in anguish at the loss of loved ones as if, deep inside, they believed the dead were lost forever.

One could argue that the fear of death is genetically programmed by evolution and, as such, should transcend any worldview. There is, of course, some validity to this. However, ethnography shows us that truly internalized belief systems can supplant this programming. Take, for instance, the Zuruahã tribe in the Brazilian Amazon: their worldview entails the belief that the soul (*'asoma'*) reunites with lost relatives after physical death. This belief is so deeply internalized that, in the period between 1980 and 1995, 84.4% of all deaths among adults – defined as people over 12 years old – in their society was caused by *suicide*. As a result, a population known for excellent health and very few diseases has an average life expectancy of only 35 years.[1] Faced with what you and I would consider completely ordinary crises and frustrations – like disputes of ownership, control of female sexuality, periods of low self-esteem, etc. – many Zuruahã simply choose to rejoin their lost loved ones in the afterlife. They don't do it for heroic status, or for religious and socio-political causes – like the phenomenon of martyrdom – but simply as an attempt to improve their personal situations. To you and me, it would be like choosing to move to another town.

Even though, from an anthropological perspective, it is silly to judge a different culture on the basis of our Western values, I find it hard not to disapprove of such disregard for the value of life. Be it as it may, when looked at coldly, the case of the Zuruahã is dramatically illustrative of the point I am trying to make: *unlike modern Christians, Jews, Muslims, Buddhists, Hindus, etc., the Zuruahã have never been exposed to an overwhelmingly materialist culture, which explains their ability to deeply internalize the alternative cultural notion that death is but a transition.* The example of the Zuruahã, as well as others, shows clearly that the way human beings relate to death is indeed largely a question of worldview, not only of genes.

Either way, materialism influences our 'subconscious' reactions, attitudes, and values in many other aspects of life as well, not only our beliefs regarding the after-death state. For instance, the implications of materialism lie directly behind the Western love affair with *things*. It is our often-'subconscious'[2] belief that only matter truly exists that drives our urge to achieve material success. After all, if there is only matter, what other goal can there conceivably be in life other than the accumulation of material goods? And this belief is highly symbiotic with our economic system, for it is the drive towards material success that motivates key people to work long hours, often having to tolerate unpleasant circumstances, in order to improve their status and financial condition well beyond otherwise acceptable levels. It is also this belief that motivates people to spend their hard-earned income on unnecessary goods and premature upgrades. The materialist worldview has caused many of us to project numinous value and meaning onto *things*.

The point I am trying to make is that, while acknowledging that there are many superficial worldviews operating simultaneously in society, there is a powerful *core* worldview that subtly pervades the deepest, often 'subconscious' levels of our minds, ultimately determining how we truly *feel* about ourselves and reality. This core worldview is materialism. Many of us absorb materialist beliefs from the culture without even being aware of it, all the while trusting that we hold *other* beliefs. Materialism suffuses the core of our being by a kind of involuntary osmosis. Like a virus, it spreads unnoticed until it's too late and the infection has already taken a firm hold. I include myself among those who have been victimized by this pernicious, yet natural, epidemic. The recent history of my life has been a diligent, yet very difficult, attempt to restore reason and lucidity to, and remove unexamined cultural biases and assumptions from, the 'subconscious' layers of my thinking. This book shares many of my insights and conclusions in this regard.

The role of the intellectual elite

The power of the core materialist worldview comes from its adoption by intellectual elites and its amplification by the mainstream media. Social *validation* is often crucial to our ability to truly hold onto a belief system, both consciously and 'subconsciously.' And no form of social validation is stronger than the validation provided by the segment of society that has become perceived as the learned elite. The reason for this is simple: our progress in understanding the complexities of nature is now so great, entailing such proliferation of evidence and details, that it has become completely impossible for any single person to study and evaluate all the relevant evidence on her own. *We fundamentally depend on a collective, distributed effort to develop a critical opinion regarding what is going on.* We need to share the task of studying and evaluating the relevant evidence. We have become dependent on others in the process of converging to a personal worldview. Intellectual specialization and a certain form of narrow-mindedness have become the norm in our epistemology in a way analogous to how the division of labor became the norm during the Industrial Revolution. In this sense, *trust* is now a crucial ingredient of the whole process, since we must be able to trust the conclusions of others in order to put together the whole jigsaw puzzle. And it is in this regard – trust – that the intellectual elite holds the cards, whether we admit it to ourselves or not. If we cannot trust the recognized specialists in different domains, who can we trust?

The problem is that the specialists in the intellectual elite – in our age, mostly scientists – are people like you and me. They, too, need the validation of a group to develop and hold onto a worldview. No specialist can hold the whole jigsaw puzzle in his mind so they, too, lack the all-important *overview*. But instead of receiving collective validation from the outside, the validation emerges organically and iteratively from within the group of specialists itself. This process is only partially guided by evidence, and largely by psychosocial dynamics, as Thomas Kuhn cogently showed.[3] Each person plays the dual role of, on the one hand, contributing personal insights to the emerging consensus and, on the other hand, calibrating her own opinions based on the validation (or lack thereof) she gets from the emerging consensus. Once the system has evolved to a point where a strong consensus has emerged, and all serious dissenting views have been purged, most members of the intellectual elite begin to see it as their job to *reinforce* and *promote* this reigning consensus. Individuals who attempt to question the consensus at this stage become traitors primed for debunking, for their efforts, if successful, could deprive *everyone* of the collective validation they need to ground their intellectual and emotional lives. Nobody fancies falling back into the dark abyss of intellectual chaos and uncertainty that, according to our modern account of history, characterized the pre-Enlightenment years.

Materialism and science

Having said all the above, it is important to keep in mind the difference between materialism as a *metaphysics* and scientific theories as *models*. Many people – including many scientists – easily confuse the two, mistakenly construing the empirical evidence collected from nature through the scientific method to lend direct support to the materialist metaphysics. Were that to be so, materialism wouldn't be a psychosocial phenomenon, as I argued above, but a scientific conclusion. However, that is *not* so. Empirical data proves the *models* of science under certain conditions, not the *metaphysical interpretation* of such models. Allow me to elaborate on this.

The scientific method allows us to study and model the observable *patterns and regularities* of nature. For instance, the observation that objects consistently fall when dropped – a *regularity* observed anywhere on the surface of the planet – allows us to infer the law of gravity. The observation that crystals form according to symmetrical shapes allows us to infer specific *patterns* of crystallization for different materials. By observing the consistency of these *patterns and regularities*, we can create mathematical models capturing them, run such models as computer simulations, and then *predict* how similar phenomena will unfold in the future. Such an ability to model and predict the phenomena of nature lies at the heart of the technological prowess of our civilization and represents the main social value-add of science.

But our ability to model the patterns and regularities of reality *tells us little about the underlying nature of things*. Scientific modeling is useful for informing us how one thing or phenomenon relates to another thing or phenomenon – this being precisely what mathematical equations do – but it cannot tell us what these things or phenomena fundamentally are in and by themselves. The reason is simple: *science can only explain one thing in terms of another thing;* it can only explicate and characterize a certain phenomenon in terms of its relative differences with respect to another phenomenon.[4] For instance, it only makes sense to characterize a positive electric charge relative to a negative electric charge; positive charges are defined in terms of their differences of behavior when compared to the behavior of negative charges, and the other way around. Another example: science can explain a body in terms of tissues; tissues in terms of cells; cells in terms of molecules; molecules in terms of atoms; and atoms in terms of subatomic particles. *But then it can only explain one subatomic particle in terms of another*, by highlighting their *relative differences*. Science cannot explain the fundamental nature of what a subatomic particle *is* in itself, since all scientific explanations need a frame of reference to provide contrasts.[5]

Capturing the observable patterns and regularities of the elements of reality, relative to each other, is an empirical and scientific question. *But pondering about the fundamental nature of these elements is not; it is a philosophical question.* The problem is that, in recent decades, scientists who have little or no under-standing of philosophy have begun to believe that science alone can replace philosophy.[6] This dangerous combination of ignorance and hubris has done our culture an enormous disservice, which was exacerbated by the fact that scientists are over-represented in our society's acknowledged intellectual elite, to the detriment of artists, poets, psychologists, philosophers, etc. Childishly emboldened by the technological success achieved by our civilization, many scientists have begun to believe that the scientific method suffices to provide us with a complete account of the nature of existence – that is, with a complete ontology. In doing so, they have failed to see that they are simply *assuming* a certain metaphysics – namely, materialism – without giving it due thought. They have failed to see that the ability to predict how things behave with respect to one another says little about what things fundamentally are.

We, as a society, are guilty, by ignorance or omission, of allowing science to outreach its boundaries on the basis of the equivocated assumption that technological prowess is proof of some deep scientific understanding of the underlying nature of reality. Let us put this in context with an analogy: one needs to know nothing about computer architecture or software in order to play a computer game well and even win; just watch a five-year-old kid. Playing a computer game only requires an ability to understand and predict how the elements of the game behave relative to one another: if your character shoots that spot, it scores points; if your character touches that wall, it dies; etc. It requires no understanding whatsoever of the underlying machine and code upon which the game runs. You can be a champion player without having a clue about Central Processing Units (CPU), Random-Access Memories (RAM), Universal Serial Buses (USB), or any of the esoteric computer engineering that makes the game possible. *All this engineering transcends the 'reality' accessible empirically from within the game.* Yet, the scientific method limits itself to what is empirically and ordinarily observed from within the 'game' of reality. *Scientific modeling requires little or no understanding of the underlying nature of reality in exactly the same way that a gamer needs little or no understanding of the computer's underlying architecture in order to win the game.* It only requires an understanding of how the elements of the 'game,' accessed empirically from within the 'game' itself, unfold relative to one another.

On the other hand, to infer things about what *underlies* the 'game' – in other words, to construct a *meta*physics about the fundamental nature of reality – demands more than the empirical methods of science. Indeed, *it demands a kind of disciplined introspection that critically assesses not only the elements observed, but also the observer, the process of observation, and the interplay between the three in a holistic manner; an introspection that, as such, seeks to see through the 'game.'* The construction of a metaphysics demands, thus, the methods of *philosophy.*

Our culture has become so blindly enamored with technology that we allowed science, on the basis of a misunderstanding, to be over-represented in our intellectual elite. The damaging consequences of this mistake are felt with increasing intensity in the culture, in the form of a materialist paradigm that, while unsubstantiated – as I will attempt to show in this and subsequent chapters – dissolves all meaning and hope out of human life. It is time we corrected this. It is time we understood that physics, while valuable and extremely important, just models the elements of the 'game': where to shoot, which wall to avoid, etc. The true underlying nature of reality – the inner workings of the computer running the game – is an issue of philosophy. It requires different methods to be properly assessed and understood. For as long as scientists like Stephen Hawking are allowed to make preposterous pseudo-philosophical pronouncements[7] and *not* be either ignored or thoroughly ridiculed by the mainstream media – in *exactly* the same way that, say, a famous artist would be ridiculed or ignored for making pseudo-scientific statements – our culture will fail to understand the nature of our predicament.

The goals of this book

It is an initial goal of this book to offer a sane, coherent, evidence-based criticism of the materialist consensus that has emerged among the intellectual elite of our society ever since the Enlightenment; a consensus that, through the amplification provided by the mainstream media and the natural psychosocial needs inherent to human beings, has deeply influenced the core belief system of society at large, including you and me. I hope to show you that much of what we are told to believe is based on unexamined and unjustified assumptions and biases, some of them preposterous. Much of what society at large takes to be the 'hard, cold facts of life' is, in reality, ungrounded supposition and abstraction, much of it flying in the face of reason, parsimony and lucid observation. To boil this down to a simple statement, my aim is to convince you that much of what you take to be true, even the most basic aspects of reality and of your own identity, is a fantasy that you couldn't sell to a five-year-old child. And *in lieu* of the madness that our materialist worldview has turned into, I

hope – as the main goal of this book – to offer you the foundations of a sane and simple alternative that easily stands to reason,
to all available evidence and to your personal experience of
reality.

But, before we can accomplish any of this, we first need to
summarize and make explicit *what is actually entailed by the
current materialist worldview.* Many people are profoundly
surprised when they actually grok what notions materialism
requires in order to work as a worldview. Below, I will try to
make the key aspects of materialism explicit and clear, as well as
their key implications. For some of you, making the implications
of materialism explicit will already suffice to permanently shake
your belief in it. For the others, the discussion in the next
chapters will provide plenty of additional substantiation.

The basics of materialism

The most basic assertion of materialism is that reality is, well,
exclusively material.[8] Materialism asserts that reality exists
outside your mind in the form of assemblies of material particles
occupying the framework of space-time. Even force fields are
imagined, in current physics, to be force-carrying material
particles.[9] The existence of this material reality is supposed to be
completely independent of your, or anyone else's, subjective
perception of it. Thus, even if there were no conscious beings
observing reality, it would supposedly still go merrily on: the
planets would still orbit the sun, the continents would still drift,
volcanoes would still erupt, crystals would still form in the
bowels of the Earth and so on. That there is such a thing as
consciousness is, according to materialism, a *product* of chance
configurations of matter, driven mechanically by the pressures of
natural selection. We are supposedly an accident of probabilities,
there being nothing more to a human being than an arrangement
of material particles – maintained rather precariously out of
thermodynamic equilibrium through metabolism – which will

eventually lose its integrity and dissipate into a gooey entropic soup. When you die, materialism states that your consciousness and everything it means to be you – your memories, your personality, your experiences, everything – will be lost. There is little, if any, room for meaning or purpose under a materialist worldview.

Indeed, materialism holds that consciousness is itself a phenomenon produced, and entirely explainable, by the assembly of material particles that we call a brain. There is supposedly *nothing* to consciousness but the movements and interactions of material particles inside a brain, so that consciousness *is* material brain processes at work. How the mechanical movements of particles are accompanied by inner life is a question left unanswered by materialism. After all, just like in the case of computers, all the 'calculations' taking place inside our brains could, in principle, just happen 'in the dark,' completely unaccompanied by inner experience. This question is known as the 'hard problem of consciousness,'[10] or the 'explanatory gap.'[11] In its 125th anniversary edition, *Science* magazine listed the 'hard problem' as the second most important unanswered question in science.[12] It should have been the first.

The hard problem of consciousness

Though much has been published on the 'hard problem,' I think it is appropriate that I quickly summarize here what it is all about. The problem is this: according to current state-of-the-art materialism, the primary element of reality is a relatively small set of fundamental subatomic particles described in the so-called 'Standard Model' of particle physics.[13] These particles are referred to as 'ontological primitives': they are materialism's basic building blocks for constructing *everything else* in nature, from galaxies to chairs, to you and me. In other words, we should be able to construct explanations for every object or phenomenon in nature in terms of the dynamics of these subatomic particles; how they move and interact with one another. The problem is that materialism ordinarily assumes these subatomic particles to lack consciousness. So how do you eventually get consciousness simply by arranging 'dead' subatomic particles together?

In principle, there is nothing mysterious about the emergence of higher-level properties as systems become more and more complex.[14] For instance, beautiful and highly complex sand ripples emerge in dunes when there are enough grains of sand and wind. So why can't consciousness emerge when there are enough subatomic particles arranged together in specific ways? The problem here is that, unless one is prepared to accept magic, the emergent properties of a complex system must be deducible from the properties of the lower-level components of the system.[15] For instance, we can deduce – and even predict – the shape of sand ripples from the properties of grains of sand and wind. We can put it all in a computer program and watch simulated sand ripples form in the computer screen that look exactly like the real thing. *But when it comes to consciousness, nothing allows us to deduce the properties of subjective experience – the redness of red, the bitterness of regret, the warmth of fire – from the mass, momentum, spin, charge, or any other property of subatomic particles bouncing around in the brain.* This is the hard problem of consciousness.

As a matter of fact, consciousness is a sore on the foot of materialism. The materialist understanding of the world would seem a lot more solid if there were no such a thing as subjective experience at all. It is conceivable – though not necessarily possible – that science could eventually explain all structure, function, and behavior of a human being on the basis of the positions and movements of the subatomic particles composing the human body. But how and why that structure, function, and behavior are accompanied by *inner experience* is deeply problematic for materialism. Your personal computer also has structure, function, and behavior. However, its internal calculations do not seem to be accompanied by any inner experience at all, otherwise we would need to think twice before turning our computers off. From a materialist perspective, the case of the computer makes perfect sense. But a human being whose internal 'calculations' are accompanied by inner experience is an uncomfortable anomaly.

Animism revived

Consciousness clearly is a problem for materialists, some of whom resort to ludicrous attempts to even deny its very existence![16] Here is what philosopher Galen Strawson wrote about this denial: *"I think we should feel very sober, and a little afraid, at the power of human credulity, the capacity of human minds to be gripped by theory, by faith. For this particular denial is the strangest thing that has ever happened in the whole history of human thought, not just the whole history of philosophy."*[17]

At the very moment he acknowledged the existence of consciousness Strawson had to confront the 'hard problem.' To do so, he proposed what seems to me to be a logical implication of materialism: *panpsychism*.[18] Panpsychism is the notion that all matter is conscious, even though the intensity or quality of consciousness may depend on the particular arrangement of matter at hand.[19] This way, as philosopher David Chalmers pointed out, the implication is that your home thermostat must be conscious; it must experience every single time it turns the heating system on or off.[20] If you play the piano, beware: the piano must be conscious of every keystroke you perform. Every electric appliance you own, from your home computer to the vacuum cleaner, is also supposedly conscious under panpsychism. Clearly, this is a kind of modern articulation of animism, the belief that inanimate objects, like statues or even rocks, are also 'alive.'

Under materialism, if you cannot explain consciousness in terms of emerging dynamics of unconscious subatomic particles, *you must then postulate that consciousness is itself a fundamental property – like electric charge, mass or spin – of all particles.*[21] This is another 'hidden' implication of materialism that most people are not aware of, and it entails an unfathomable explosion of conscious entities in nature.

The problem with panpsychism is, of course, that there is *precisely zero* evidence that any inanimate object is conscious. To resolve an abstract, theoretical problem of the materialist metaphysics one is forced to project onto the whole of nature a property – namely, circumscribed, individualized consciousness – which observation only allows to be inferred for a tiny subset of it – namely, living beings. *This is, in a way, an attempt to make nature conform to theory, as opposed to making theory conform to nature.*

You may claim that it is impossible to assess whether an inanimate object, like a thermostat, is really conscious or not. This is true: we cannot even know for sure whether other people are really conscious, since it is impossible for us to gain access to the inner life of someone or something else. For all you know, everyone else is just a kind of sophisticated biological robot, completely unconscious, but manifesting all the right conscious-like behaviors out of complex calculations.

Still, the point here is not what can be known for sure, *but what inferences can be justified on the basis of observation.* That's all we can hope to accomplish when developing a worldview. And we *can* infer that other people are conscious. After all, we observe in other people, and even in animals, behaviors that are entirely analogous to our own: they scream in pain, behave illogically when in love, sigh deeply when lost in thoughts, etc. We explain our own manifestations of these behaviors based on the firsthand knowledge that we are conscious: you know that you scream *because* you actually *feel* pain. So it is reasonable to infer that other people, who are physically analogous to you in every way, manifest those same behaviors *for the same reason that you do* – namely, that they are also conscious. Were it not to be so, we would need two different explanations for the same types of behavior in entirely analogous organisms, which is not the simplest alternative.

Therefore, there is indeed good empirical justification for the inference that other people and animals, and perhaps even all life forms, are conscious. But there is *no* empirical justification to infer that inanimate objects, which manifest no external behaviors that anyone could possibly relate to one's own inner experience, are individually conscious in any way or to any degree whatsoever. As such, the only possible reason to believe in panpsychism is to make materialism work. And here is where Strawson should have heeded his own advice: *"We should feel very sober, and a little afraid, at ... the capacity of human minds to be gripped by theory, by faith."*[22]

A 'hallucinated' reality

There is more. The current materialist view in neuroscience is that the ordinary, waking world we experience every day is in fact a brain-constructed 'hallucination' analogous in nearly every way to a dream. Indeed, the same neural mechanisms seem to underlie our experience of dreams *and* of the waking world. The difference between, on the one hand, the waking 'hallucination' you call your daily life and, on the other hand, your dreamed-up hallucination during sleep is, according to materialism, merely this: the former is believed to be modulated by electromagnetic signals emanating from a supposedly external reality that we can never have direct access to, for we're irremediably locked into our brain-generated hallucination.[23] It is this abstract, assumed external reality that, supposedly, explains why our waking experiences seem to be shared with other individuals, while our nightly dreams are highly individual and idiosyncratic.

According to materialism, *what we experience in our lives every day is not the world as such, but a kind of brain-constructed 'copy' of the world.* Everything we see, hear, or otherwise perceive is supposedly a complex amalgamation of electrochemical signals unfolding in a kind of theater inside our skulls.[24] The book or electronic reader you see and feel in your hands right now is supposed to be entirely inside your head, though it should *correspond* to a 'real book' that exists outside your head and to which you can never have *direct* access. When you look at your face in the mirror, the reflection you see is supposedly just a subjective 'copy' of your head inside your *actual* head. The latter you can *never* see. The outside, 'real world' of materialism is supposedly an amorphous, colorless, odorless, soundless, tasteless dance of abstract electromagnetic fields devoid of all qualities of experience. It's supposedly more akin to a mathematical equation than to anything concrete.

You may be thinking now that either I am misrepresenting the mainstream views of materialism or I am just very confused. I assure you, neither is the case. This is *really* what materialism entails. For instance, a formal academic paper has concluded that your real skull is actually *beyond* all the stars you see in the night sky.[25] After all, the stars you see are all *inside* your head. One must applaud materialists for their self-consistency and honesty in exploring the implications of their metaphysics, even when such implications are utterly absurd.

Why does materialism depart so drastically from everyday intuition? Because it *must*, if it is to remain internally consistent. If all that exists is matter, and if consciousness is somehow produced by the suitable arrangement of matter represented by the brain, then it *must* be the case that *all* subjective perception resides in the brain; and *in the brain only*. Thus, according to materialism, the only way you can experience a world *outside* your head is if signals from that outside world penetrate your brain via the sense organs and, then, somehow modulate the creation of a brain-constructed hallucination that *corresponds* to the outside world. Ergo, your whole life – all reality you can ever know directly – is but an internal 'copy' of the 'real reality.'

Nothing you see, touch, smell, feel, or hear around you right now is a direct apprehension of the 'real reality.' It is all, instead, an internal copy-of-sorts generated by your brain. Materialism, thus, requires a *doubling of all reality*: it presupposes an abstract and unprovable 'external' universe next to the known, concrete, and undeniable universe of direct experience. No 'spiritual realm' postulated by the world's religious traditions is as abstract or metaphysical as the 'external' reality of materialism, for the latter is, by definition, devoid of phenomenal properties or qualities of experience. One is forced to wonder whether this can really be the simplest, most parsimonious and most reasonable metaphysical explanation for our observations.

Can we trust the 'hallucination'?

Let us assume, for the sake of argument, that this materialist view is correct, so that we can explore more of its implications. The first thing to ask yourself is whether there is any reason to believe that the 'copy' of the world inside your head, and which you are experiencing right now, is perfect. Assuming that Darwin's theory of evolution is correct in its more essential aspects, we have to ask ourselves whether evolution would have favored a brain that created a *complete* internal 'copy' of the world, capturing in it *all* aspects of relevance for our understanding of the fundamental mechanisms underlying nature. Furthermore, we have to ask ourselves whether evolution would have favored a brain that, whatever part of the world it *did* capture in its internal 'copy,' copied it *without significant distortions* that could throw us completely off track as far as putting together an accurate worldview. The answer to both questions is *no*.[26]

Evolution favors *physical survival*, not *per se* the accuracy or completeness of internal representations. It is reasonable to think that *some* matching between our brain-generated 'copy' of the world and the world itself is favorable for survival of the physical body: if a tiger is approaching you, it *is* useful to see something like the actual tiger, and not some other non-modulated, dream-like hallucination. But most people, scientists included, far overestimate the survival usefulness of accurate, complete internal representations. My own research on artificial neural networks shows that, very often, it is useful precisely to *distort* certain parts, and *cut out* other parts, of the external stimuli when creating an internal representation of the world in an artificial nervous system.[27] Complete information is often confusing, drowning out the small parts that really matter. Undistorted information is often hard to act upon in a timely manner, due to the subtlety of its nuances. Therefore, these artificial nervous systems perform much more efficiently – and would stand a much better chance of survival if they had to compete in an ecosystem – when their own internal 'copy' of the world is largely *incomplete* and *distorted*. As such, this is what evolution would have favored and there is no strong reason to believe that the 'copy' of the world you and I supposedly live in comes even close to what is *really* going on. Thus, the implication of materialism is that we're intrinsically limited to watching an edited and biased version of the film we're trying to make sense of. Yet, we derive materialism *entirely* from that very film!

Even the scientific instruments that broaden the scope of our sensory perception – like microscopes that allow us to see beyond the smallest features our eyes can discern, or infrared and ultraviolet light sensors that can detect frequency ranges beyond the colors we can see – are fundamentally limited to our narrow and distorted window into reality: they are constructed with materials and methods that are themselves constrained to the edited 'copy' of the world in our brains. *As such, all Western science and philosophy, ancient and modern, from Greek atomism to quantum mechanics, from Democritus and Aristotle to Bohr and Popper, must have been and still be fundamentally limited to the partial and distorted 'copy' of the world in our brains that materialism implies.*

As such, materialism is somewhat self-defeating. After all, the materialist worldview is the result of an internal model of reality whose unreliability is an inescapable implication of that very model. In other words, *if materialism is right, then materialism cannot be trusted.* If materialism is correct, then we may all be locked in a small room trying to explain the entire universe outside by looking through a peephole on the door; availing ourselves only of the limited and distorted images that come through it.

Where do we stand?

Materialism is peddled in our culture as the most intuitive and self-evident worldview. After all, the world *does* look like it is outside ourselves. Things *do* feel solid. However, as we have seen, the intuitiveness of materialism is based largely on a *misapprehension* of what materialism really entails. When one carefully looks at the implications of the materialist metaphysics, it doesn't look intuitive at all. It denies the reality of immediate experience and postulates it to be a 'hallucination' taking place entirely within our heads. It denies that we can ever directly access the 'outside' world. It states that the stars we see in the night sky are all inside our skulls. It completely fails to explain the most compelling and present aspect of existence: consciousness. And it defeats itself by casting doubt upon its own reliability.

Yet, before we can throw out materialism, *we need a coherent alternative* to explain empirical reality. Many of the alternative worldviews circulating through the fringes of the culture today are outrageous, malformed, and cannot be taken seriously at all. Others are fundamentally limited or self-contradictory. Indeed, because of the dominance of materialism, few capable philosophers or intelligent commentators have spent the time and energy required to help construct a coherent and respectable alternative; in any case, a number well under the necessary critical mass. Attempting to do so can end careers and bring professional ridicule upon oneself. It is not a level playing field

24

when it comes to combating materialism. Therefore, it is no surprise that materialism still enjoys the perception of being the only viable game in town. The current shortage of coherent and complete alternatives does not come, in my view, from any particular difficulty in generating one, but from the lack of serious-enough attempts at doing so.

Though I have an extensive academic and professional background in the fields of computer engineering, artificial intelligence, semiconductors technology and high-energy physics, I currently have no professional links with academia. My professional status and source of income are not endangered by the points of view I am now making public with this book. Therefore, unlike most academics, professional scientists, or professional philosophers, I enjoy unrivaled freedom in expressing my views. It is in this context that I thought, perhaps arrogantly, that I could make a contribution towards constructing a credible, saner and more reasonable metaphysical alternative to materialism; an alternative that could, hopefully, help transform the mainstream paradigm under which we live our lives.

In the next chapters, I will attempt to do just that. I don't claim this book to be the final word on a new and complete worldview and corresponding metaphysics. Whatever it is, it is certainly not complete. The articulations you will find in it aim at providing a platform – a *way of thinking* – which others can perhaps build upon in the longer-term project of constructing a robust philosophical system to replace materialism with. This is my hope for the present work.

Chapter 2

Tackling the Mind-Body Problem

The key assumption of materialism is the idea that there is nothing to the mind – to the world of subjective inner *experience* – that cannot be explained by the physical brain and the electro-chemical processes unfolding in it. Materialists express this assumption in two main ways: some state that subjective experience simply *is* electrochemical processes in the brain, the notion that consciousness is somehow *more* than matter being just an illusion. Proponents of this view include materialist philosopher and militant atheist Daniel Dennett.[28] The second way the assumption is expressed by materialists is the notion that, somehow, consciousness is indeed *more* than just physical processes, but that there is a one-to-one correspondence between physical processes and consciousness whereby conscious experience is entirely caused, and fully determined, by those physical processes. This seems to be the view taken, for instance, by eminent neuroscientist Christof Koch.[29]

There is a subtle philosophical distinction between these two materialist views. However, for all practical purposes, they are identical: both entail that the brain causes, and fully determines the qualities of, all conscious experience and that consciousness ends upon physical death. Therefore, for the purposes of this book, we will ignore the fine and abstract philosophical distinction between these views. For a materialist, everything happens as if conscious experience simply *were* electrochemical processes in the brain.

The question of the relationship between conscious experience and brain is called *the mind-body problem*. The materialist answer to this question, as summarized above, is so central to the core worldview of our culture that it is the obvious starting point for our journey towards a more balanced and lucid ontology. Therefore, in this chapter we will delve into the details of the materialist view regarding how the mind relates to the brain, analyze it critically and offer a coherent alternative that explains *more* of the data than materialism.

In this and the next couple of chapters, I will use the terms 'mind,' 'consciousness,' and 'awareness' rather interchangeably. *Whenever I use one of these terms, I will be referring to subjective experience or the potential for it.* I'll also use expressions like 'the flow of mind' or 'the contents of mind' to highlight the varied and dynamic nature of subjective experience. Only from Chapter 4 onwards will we be in a position to begin establishing clear differentiations between these terms and expressions. In Chapter 6 we will define them precisely.

A very brief introduction to neuroscience

Before continuing our discussion we need a little more background on how the brain works. Although neuroscience is a complex discipline, its fundamentals are surprisingly simple. After you read the following few paragraphs you will have a fairly good overview of what happens inside your head.[30] It's simpler than you might suppose and anybody can understand it with little effort, irrespective of background. Moreover, these simple fundamentals will be more than sufficient for you to understand the rest of this chapter. All I ask of you is focused attention for the remainder of this short section.

Here we go. The brain is composed of two main types of cells: *neurons* and *glial cells*. Neurons do the actual work of processing information, while glial cells perform support functions like insulation, structural and metabolic support, etc. For the purposes of this book, we can ignore the glial cells and focus solely on neurons.

Each neuron is composed of three main parts: the neuron's *body*, the *dendrites* and the *axon*. See Figure 1. The neuron's body

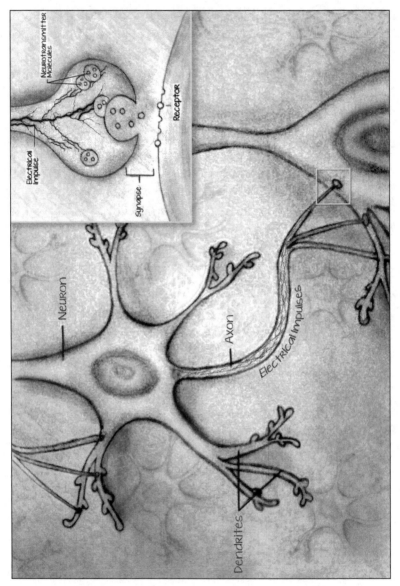

Figure 1. Neurons, synapses and neural networks.

is the main part of the cell, responsible for coordinating all of the neuron's activities. The dendrites are extensions of the neuron's body that contain many branches. The axon is a long, thin, cable-like projection that extends far from the neuron's body so to connect it to other neurons. The tip of the axon typically branches out into several *terminals*.

The brain is basically a giant network of interconnected neurons. Roughly speaking, the axon of a given neuron connects, through its multiple branching terminals, to dendrites of many other neurons. See Figure 1 again. The point where an axon terminal meets a dendrite is called a *synapse*. The terminal and the dendrite don't actually touch: a tiny gap remains in between them, which is called a *synaptic cleft*.

Here is how the whole thing operates: the body of a neuron generates an electric charge. The axon of the neuron carries this electric charge all the way to its terminals. If and when the electric charge grows strong enough to cross a certain threshold, it triggers the release of certain chemicals at the terminals, which are called *neurotransmitters*. When this happens, the neuron is said to have *fired*. The neurotransmitters released then drift across the synaptic cleft and stimulate the dendrites of the neuron on the other side of the cleft by fitting into chemical receptors. This is also illustrated in Figure 1. The corresponding stimulus can be an *excitatory* one – causing the other neuron to *increase* its own electric charge – or an *inhibitory* one – causing the other neuron to *reduce* its electric charge – depending on the neurotransmitter released.

Whether a given neuron fires or not – that is, whether it releases neurotransmitters or not – is thus determined by how many *other* neurons connected to its dendrites are firing or not, and by what type of neurotransmitters – inhibitory or excitatory – they release when they do fire.[31] A neuron only fires when it has been stimulated with enough *excitatory* neurotransmitters released by other neurons and provided that it has not been too inhibited by *inhibitory* neurotransmitters. The entire process has electric aspects – namely, the buildup of electric charge – and chemical aspects – namely, the release of neurotransmitters. We thus say that the brain operates on the basis of *electrochemical* processes.

A *neural network* is basically a set of neurons connected together, through synapses, according to some network topology. There can be huge chains of interconnected neurons in the brain: neurons connected to other neurons, which in turn are connected to other neurons, and so on. These networks can also contain *closed cycles*, whereby a neuron at the end of a chain connects back to a neuron at the beginning of the chain. The brain can be seen as a superset of many neural networks.

Brain *activity* is associated with the *firings* of neurons in a neural network. Though there are many neurons in a network, typically only a subset of them is actually firing when observed. Neuroscientists can scan a living brain and see which subset of a neural network is actually active. We call each one of these active subsets a *neural process*. As we will see below, conscious experience correlates with certain neural processes in the brain, which are then called the *neural correlates of consciousness*.[32] Naturally, neural processes can be *excitatory* or *inhibitory*, depending on whether the neurotransmitters they release respectively *increase* or *decrease* the electric charge of connected neurons.

That's it. Not too difficult, was it? All terms I will use in what follows have been explained above. If you later find a term whose meaning you no longer remember, you can always return to this section and refresh your memory.

The correlations between mind states and brain states

There is an undeniable correlation between brain states and subjective experience. Anyone who has ever been intoxicated with alcohol will be able to attest to marked changes in cognition accompanying the changes in brain chemistry. In addition, alterations of consciousness accompanying physical trauma to the brain, as well as the use of anesthetics and psychiatric drugs, are also examples of the tight link between mind and brain that many of us are personally familiar with. Laboratory studies have provided evidence that this correlation is even more specific than one could infer from direct experience: as mentioned in the previous section, particular conscious experiences have been linked to specific neural processes in the brain.[33] Experiments with Transcranial Magnetic Stimulation (TMS)[34] – whereby neuroscientists run magnetic fields through specific regions of the brain, interfering with the ability of neurons to fire normally – have also demonstrated that deactivation of specific brain regions correlates tightly to specific changes in subjective experience. Therefore, any theoretical hypothesis purporting to explain the ontological status of mind must be able to explain why and how subjective experience seems, ordinarily, so correlated with brain processes.

Yet, that mind states are correlated with brain states does not necessarily imply that brain states *cause* mind states. Assuming so is a known fallacy in science and philosophy called the *'cum hoc ergo propter hoc'* fallacy. For instance, the presence of large numbers of firefighters *correlates* with large fires, but firefighters do not *cause* fires. Similarly, the voices one hears coming out of an analog radio receiver correlate very tightly with the electromagnetic oscillations in the radio's circuitry, but that does not mean that the radio circuitry *synthesizes* the voices. Indeed, many logical possibilities remain open to explain the ordinarily observed correlations between subjective experience and brain activity, not only the materialist assumption that the brain causes the mind.

The mind-body problem according to materialism

By postulating that subjective experiences *are* neural processes, the reigning materialist paradigm tentatively explains the ordinary correlations between mind states and brain states rather simply. Yet, this paradigm is currently articulated in only a vague and promissory manner, in that neuroscience does not specify precisely or unambiguously what measurable parameters of neural processes map onto what qualities of subjective experience.

This is an important point, so let me belabor this a bit. If every conscious experience is nothing but a neural process, then there are two points-of-view from which to observe the *same* information flow associated with any experience: the perspective from the *inside* – that is, the experience itself – and the perspective from the *outside* – that is, what a neuroscientist sees when measuring the activity of a person's brain while the person is having the experience. *If materialism is correct, there always has to be a strict one-to-one correspondence between parameters measured from the outside and the qualities of what is experienced form the inside.* After all, subjective experience supposedly *is* what is measured from the outside. For instance, if I see the color red, there have to be measurable parameters of the corresponding neural process in my brain that are always associated with the color red. After all, my experience of seeing red supposedly *is* the neural process. Similarly, if I feel sad, there have to be measurable parameters of the corresponding neural process in my brain that are always associated with the feeling of sadness. After all, my experience of being sad supposedly *is* the neural process. You get the picture.

As I mentioned above, neuroscience today is very far from being able to provide a consistent one-to-one mapping between the qualities of a subjective experience and measurable parameters of the corresponding neural process. It is possible to argue that this merely reflects our currently limited progress in finding this mapping and that it will be found in the future as more research is done and new techniques are developed for measuring the finer parameters of brain activity. As a vague and promissory argument, this is unfalsifiable. But we should keep two things in mind: first, *decades of research and very high invest-ments have already been made in the pursuit of this mapping,* so it's not like we've just started. Second, *much of what we have found thus far seems to contradict the notion that there is any such consistent one-to-*

one mapping. Empirical observations reveal an inconsistent and even contradictory relationship between subjective experience and measurable parameters of neural processes. For instance, as neuroscientist Giulio Tononi mentions in the *Elsevier Encyclopedia of Neuroscience,* the firing of the same cortical neurons correlates with consciousness some times, but not other times.[35] Naturally, Tononi goes on to propose a sketch of an explanation for this contradiction, under a materialist framework.[36] We will analyze the merits of his attempt in the next section. For now, though, bear with me.

Partly to deal with these contradictions, many neuroscientists speak of *specificity*: certain types of experience, regardless of their complexity or intensity, correlate with the activation of particular subsets of neurons, regardless of the amount of neurons or neural firings involved.[37] Clearly, specificity breaks the one-to-one mapping between the qualities of subjective experience and the parameters of neural processes, for it does away with any kind of proportionality between the two. This is a delicate and often-contentious point, so let me expand on it a bit.

It is true that experience is not *globally* proportional to brain activation because, as we have seen, some neural processes are *inhibitory*, not excitatory. Depending on circumstances, the more certain *inhibitory* processes are active, the less basis there is for conscious experience. It is indeed known in neuroscience that consciousness is often correlated with interplay between excitatory and inhibitory processes. But that does *not* mean that one cannot expect *local* proportionality between an experience and *the particular subset* of neural activity that *is* the experience, whether there is inhibition going on around it or not. *Obviously, the experience and that particular subset of neural activity should be proportional because, according to materialism, they are the same thing!* And this is what specificity seems to throw out the window: if any subjective experience, regardless of complexity or intensity, can *be* any neural process, regardless of the number of neurons or firings involved, it becomes very difficult to see how the qualities of the experience can, in some way, be proportional to parameters of the neural process. And if it isn't proportional, then clearly it cannot *be* the neural process!

Materialists often take the notion of specificity to extremes, especially when trying to explain cases of Near-Death Experiences wherein the subject has no detectable brain activity. They basically suggest that specificity allows for a handful of neurons, whose activity is too faint to be measurable, to hypothetically explain lifetimes of complex and coherent experiences. Resuscitation specialist Dr. Sam Parnia's candid rebuttal of this suggestion seems to frame it best: 'When you die, there's no blood flow going into your brain. If it goes below a certain level, you can't have electric activity. *It takes a lot of imagination to think there's somehow a hidden area of your brain that comes into action when everything else isn't working.*'[38] But even if we grant that there is hidden neural activity somewhere, the materialist position immediately raises the question of why we are born with such large brains if only a handful of neurons were sufficient to confabulate unfathomable dreams. After all, as a species, we pay a high price for our large brains in terms of metabolism and in terms of having to be born basically premature, since a more developed head cannot pass through a woman's birth canal. Moreover, under ordinary conditions, it has been scientifically demonstrated that we generate *measurable* neocortical activity even when we dream of the mere clenching of a hand![39] It is, thus, incoherent to postulate that undetectable neural firings – the extreme of specificity – are sufficient to explain complex experiences.

Either way, specificity does not spare materialists of the obligation to show a one-to-one, *proportional* mapping between the qualities of an experience and measurable parameters of the particular neural process that supposedly *is* the experience. That neuroscience seems unable to find this mapping shows that, unlike what is often claimed in the mainstream media, we are *not* making scientific progress in demonstrating that the brain generates the mind. As if to compound this state of contradiction, there isn't even consensus that experience correlates with neural firings at all: some neuroscientists postulate, for instance, that mental states originate from unobservable quantum-level processes taking place within microtubules – microscopic structures in the neurons – regardless of whether neurotransmitters are being released or not.[40]

Today we find ourselves in a peculiar situation wherein, of all things, *ignorance* is often used to defend materialism: since nobody can specify unambiguously what physiological process supposedly *is* consciousness, neuroscientists can *always* postulate a different hypothetical mapping that conceivably explains any *particular* experience. All that is required is some – *any* – level of activity *anywhere* in the brain, which is not too difficult to find or reasonably assume. The problem, of course, is that one cannot postulate a *different* materialist theory of consciousness for each different situation and still claim that the evidence supports materialism.

The reason such surprising ambiguity is tolerated was already hinted at in Chapter 1: when it comes to consciousness, there is no way – *not even in principle* – to logically deduce the properties of subjective experience from the properties of matter.[41] In other words, there is no way to logically deduce the qualities of conscious perception, cognition, or feeling from the mass, momentum, spin, position, or charge of the subatomic particles making up the brain. Such complete lack of intuition makes it impossible to judge whether a particular mapping between a brain process and a conscious experience is at all *reasonable*. Therefore, *any* proposed mapping looks, at first, just as good (or as bad) as any other, a fact easily misused in support of materialism. In an astonishing acknowledgment of how arbitrary the materialist explanations of consciousness can be, militant skeptic Michael Shermer, of all people, admitted that 'the neuroscience surrounding consciousness' is 'nonfalsifiable.'[42] In all fairness, many neuroscientists readily admit that our current understanding of the brain is very limited. As such, it is entirely legitimate that they remain open to many different alternatives for explaining conscious experience on the basis of material processes. But one cannot make this admission and then turn around and proclaim that neuroscience's progress has been corroborating materialism. To illustrate this further, let us briefly look at what Dr. Christof Koch, one of the world's leading neuroscientists in the field of consciousness research, considers the best materialist theory of consciousness available today:[43] Giulio Tononi's Information Integration Theory.[44]

The materialist theory of consciousness

Tononi's theory states that conscious experience is a result of how much information is integrated by a purely material brain process. The theory takes as input what Tononi calls 'complexes': closed-cycle neural processes in the brain, each entailing a given anatomic organization. The amount of information integrated by a complex, represented by the variable Φ (pronounced 'phi,' as in 'Phi Beta Kappa'), is then calculated for each complex based on its anatomic organization. The idea is that, when Φ crosses a certain threshold, the complex *somehow* becomes conscious. The specific value of this threshold is determined through empirical calibration. When the calibration is reliable, researchers can then predict which neural processes are conscious simply by looking at the corresponding Φ value.[45]

The problem here is this: to claim that a neural process suddenly becomes conscious when it integrates enough information is rather an appeal to magic than to cause-and-effect. What determines this magical threshold for Φ? Where is consciousness coming from? Why does *sufficient* information integration lead to the extraordinary and discontinuous phenomenon of otherwise unconscious neurons suddenly lighting up with consciousness? Now the neurons are unconscious; there comes a little more information; puff! Now they are conscious. Wait... What?!

Tononi's theory provides merely a *heuristic* indicator for the presence of consciousness, an *ad hoc* rule-of-thumb. Φ is like the needle of a speedometer and *it explains consciousness no more than a speedometer explains how a car moves:* when the needle of the speedometer moves up, one knows that the car is moving. But that needle movement provides no insight into the fact that there is a combustion engine freeing up energy stored in the molecular bonds of hydrocarbons, thereby making such energy available for turning a crankshaft connected to an axle, which causes the car's wheels to turn, which in turn grip the irregularities of the road and, through Newton's third law of motion, cause the car to move. The latter would be a causal explanation, but Tononi's theory entails nothing analogous to it. It just gives you the speedometer.

Let us look at an example from the field of biology to make this contrast clearer: the Krebs cycle of cellular respiration[46] is a full causal explanation for how energy is made available to an organism's cells. We know the inputs of the process: molecules of sugars and fats. We understand the oxidization reactions that progressively free up the energy stored in the molecular bonds of these sugar and fat molecules. We know in what form this energy becomes available to the cells: ATP. We know where all of this takes place: in the cells' mitochondria. And we know how the cells put the ATP to use. In other words, we have a complete causal chain that allows us to deduce the properties of the observed phenomenon – that is, the ability of cells to perform work – from the properties of the processes correlated with it – that is, oxidization reactions.

Tononi's theory does not offer us any such causal chain in the case of consciousness. It does not allow us to deduce, not even in principle, the properties of the observed phenomenon – namely, subjective experience – from the properties of the processes correlated with it – namely, neural physiology. It only offers a heuristic indicator without any explanatory model. *Nearly all relevant questions remain unanswered by Φ just like all relevant questions about how the car moves remain unanswered by the speedometer.*

Since Tononi's theory is claimed, *by materialists*, to be the best materialism has to offer, it is fair to conclude that, contrary to the impression often given by mainstream media, materialism currently does not offer an explanatory framework for tackling the mind-body problem. Does that mean that Tononi's work is valueless? Most definitely not. Metaphysics aside, Φ has practical applications. For instance, it can potentially help us determine whether patients in seemingly vegetative states are actually conscious, as in total locked-in syndrome. There is tremendous human value in that. Moreover, the *empirical* observation that neural processes that correlate with conscious experience tend to be complex, *closed cycles of information flow* is also intriguing. However, as we shall see in Chapter 5, this observation in fact substantiates a *non-materialist* solution to the mind-body problem, not a materialist one. The irony here is sweet, but let's not get ahead of ourselves.

An alternative hypothesis

I hope to have established that the notion that consciousness is merely brain activity not only lacks explicit and specific elaboration, it cannot strictly be said to be supported by empirical observations. Therefore, it is legitimate and appropriate to seek and offer alternative explanatory models.

All scientific models need, ultimately, to postulate so-called *ontological primitives*: irreducible aspects of nature that can't themselves be explained but must, instead, be accepted simply to exist. It is on the basis of these ontological primitives that a scientific model attempts to construct explanations for the rest of nature. Today, for instance, the fundamental subatomic particles described in the 'Standard Model' of particle physics are taken to be the irreducible building blocks of nature, on the basis of which everything else is supposedly explainable in principle.[47] Materialism attempts to reduce conscious experience to physical entities like these particles. As such, it assumes consciousness to be derivative, not fundamental.

However, recent and powerful physical evidence indicates strongly that no physical entity or phenomenon can be explained separately from, or independently of, its subjective apprehension in consciousness. This evidence has been published in the prestigious science journal *Nature* in 2007.[48] If this is true, the logical consequence is that consciousness cannot be reduced to matter – *for it appears that it is needed for matter to exist in the first place* – but must itself be fundamental. From a philosophical perspective, this notion is entirely coherent and reasonable, for conscious experience is all we can be certain to exist. Entities outside consciousness are, as far as we can ever know, merely abstractions of mind. *Taking consciousness to be an ontological primitive also circumvents the 'explanatory gap' and the 'hard problem of consciousness,' since both only arise from the attempt to reduce consciousness to matter.*

Therefore, in the hypothesis elaborated upon below, conscious experience is taken to be fundamental and irreducible. But watch out: I am *not* taking consciousness to be just another fundamental property *of* matter, like mass or charge, as panpsychism entails, but an ontological primitive in and by itself, *independent of matter.* Moreover, in the discussion below, for ease of argument, I will more-or-less implicitly presuppose a *dualist* metaphor, which takes non-material consciousness and material brains to be different kinds of 'stuff.' *This is just a metaphor.* The worldview that will slowly unfold through the rest of this book is *not* a dualist one. In Chapter 4, I will transpose all the conclusions of the present chapter onto a non-dualist framework. You will then understand how and why dualism is the most appropriate metaphor at this early stage of our analysis.

So here we go: if consciousness is primary and irreducible, it cannot be the case that the brain *generates* it. How can we then explain the empirical observation that, ordinarily, mind states correlate well with brain states? The hypothesis I submit is that *the function of the brain is to localize consciousness, pinning it to the space-time reference point implied by the physical body.* In doing so, the brain *modulates* conscious perception in accordance with the perspective of the body. When not subject to this localization and modulation mechanism, mind is unbound: it entails consciousness of all there is across space, time, and perhaps beyond. Therefore, by localizing mind, the brain also 'filters out' of consciousness anything that is not correlated with the body's perspective.

According to this *'filter hypothesis'* of mind-brain interaction, no subjective experience is ever generated by the brain, but merely *selected* by it according to the perspective of the body in space-time, as Bergson so cogently argued over a hundred years ago.[49] This selection process is akin to a *'filtering out'* of conscious experience: like a radio receiver selecting, from among the variety of stations present concurrently in the broadcast signal, that which one wants to listen to, all other stations being filtered out and never reaching the consciousness of the listener. The brain activation patterns that ordinarily correlate with conscious experience reflect the filtering process at work: they are analogous to the circuit oscillations in the radio's tuner, which correlate tightly with the sounds the radio emits. The presence of such circuit oscillations obviously does not mean that the radio is *generating* the broadcast signal itself, but merely *selecting* a subset of information from a preexisting signal. Analogously, brain activation patterns, under this hypothesis, do *not* imply that the brain is generating the correlated conscious experience, but merely selecting it from a broader set.

Therefore, the ordinarily observed correlations between brain and mind states are a direct and necessary consequence of the selective filtering of subjective experience: when the filtering mechanism is interfered with – physically, as in a blow to the head, or chemically, as during anesthesia or alcohol intoxication – the filtering process that modulates our conscious experience is perturbed, so that corresponding perturbations of experience follow. Such perturbations are analogous to the confusing and incoherent sounds one hears when messing randomly with the radio's tuning knob. In conclusion, the hypothesis offered here remains consistent with all observed correlations between subjective experience and measurable brain states.

The predictions of the filter hypothesis

An alternative hypothesis for addressing the mind-body problem is only useful insofar as it makes predictions that *differ* from the predictions of the mainstream materialist worldview. Below, I will elaborate on the two most important points where the filter hypothesis discussed above departs from materialism in its predictions.

First, the filter hypothesis implies that consciousness, in its unfiltered state, is unbound. As such, consciousness must be fundamentally unitary and non-individualized, for separateness and individualization entail boundaries. The emergence of multiple, separate and different conscious perspectives, or egos, is a consequence of the filtering and localization process: different egos, entailing different perspectives on space-time, retain awareness of different subsets of all potential subjective experiences, the rest being filtered out. It is the differences across subsets that give each ego its idiosyncratic vantage point, personal history, and sense of personal identity.

The subjective experiences that are filtered out become the so-called 'unconscious' mind of the respective ego. Since each ego allows in only an infinitesimally small part of all potential experiences – given the unfathomable variety of conscious perspectives that exist in potentiality – the 'unconscious' minds of different egos will differ only minimally, the vast majority of the 'unconscious' being identical across egos. As such, the filter hypothesis, unlike materialism, predicts the existence of a *collective unconscious;* a shared repository of potential experiences that far transcends mere genetic predispositions of a species. It is conceivable that, either through natural fluctuations or intentional interference with the filtering mechanisms that modulate our individual experiences, parts of this 'collective unconscious' can occasionally penetrate awareness.

Secondly, and most importantly, the filter hypothesis predicts that one can have experiences that do *not* correlate with one's brain states. Since here the brain is seen merely as a mechanism for filtering out experiences, it is conceivable that, when this mechanism is interfered with so as to be partially or temporarily deactivated, one's subjective experience could delocalize, expand beyond the body in time and space, and perhaps even beyond time and space as such. In other words, the filter hypothesis predicts that transpersonal, non-local experiences can conceivably happen when particular brain processes are partially or temporarily *deactivated*. This possibility, of course, is excluded by the materialist worldview.

The key element of this second prediction of the filter hypothesis is that non-local, transpersonal experiences are predicted to correlate precisely with certain *reductions* of excitatory brain activity. This is counterintuitive from a materialist perspective, since the latter entails that experience *is* brain activity.

Empirical evidence for the filter hypothesis
Empirical evidence for the existence of a 'collective unconscious' was, in the modern era, first compiled by Swiss psychiatrist Carl

Jung.[50] Based on his clinical experience with countless patients, as well as self-experimentation,[51] Jung found that mental contents from the 'collective unconscious' can penetrate awareness through dreams, visions, and other non-ordinary states.

One of the most striking pieces of evidence collected by Jung was the description that one of his psychotic patients gave of his 'hallucinations.' Jung noticed that his patient was looking intently at the sun, through a window, curiously wagging his head as he looked. Jung asked him what he was seeing. The patient replied that he was looking at the sun's penis, which moved to and fro as he – the patient – wagged his head. According to the patient, the wind came from the sun's penis.[52]

After this event, a book was published by philologist Albrecht Dieterich with the first translation of a Mithraic ritual found in a papyrus from ancient Greece. The translation contained the description of *a sun-god from whom a tube hung down, the source of the ministering wind*. It went on to say that *the tube veered west or east, depending on the direction of the wind*. The similarities with the schizophrenic visions of Jung's patient, who could not have known of the Mithraic ritual at the time, are uncanny.[53]

This and countless other examples motivated Jung to postulate that there is a part of mind – shared by all human beings, and perhaps by all *conscious* beings – which is extremely rich in images and narratives. Ordinarily, these collective images and narratives are 'filtered out' of ordinary awareness. However, under certain conditions, they can penetrate awareness. His schizophrenic patient appeared to have gained access – because of a brain *malfunction* – to the same images that populated the minds and reality of certain ancient Greeks.

Diligent students of Jung's work have no doubt that his characterization of the 'collective unconscious' far transcends the scope of mere genetic predispositions. After all, it is prepos-terous to think that the image of a tube hanging down from the sun and blowing wind is somehow encoded in the genes. The observations of Jung have been confirmed and extended by many other modern psychiatrists and psychologists. Indeed, under the umbrella of the field of Transpersonal Psychology,[54] an enormous body of empirical evidence has been accumulated for the existence of an 'unconscious' segment of the mind that spans across individuals. All this evidence is consistent with the filter hypothesis discussed here and contradicts the predictions of materialism.

Moving now to the second key prediction of the filter hypothesis, there is indeed a broad pattern of empirical evidence associating non-local, transpersonal experiences with procedures that *reduce* brain activity:

1. Fainting caused by asphyxiation or other restrictions of blood flow to the brain is known to sometimes induce intense transpersonal experiences and states of non-locality. The highly dangerous 'chocking game,' played mainly by teenagers worldwide, is an attempt to induce such experiences through partial strangulation, often at the risk of death.[55] Erotic asphyxiation is a similar game played in combination with sexual intercourse. The effect has been described as 'a lucid, semi-hallucinogenic state [which,] combined with orgasm, [is said to be] no less powerful than cocaine.'[56]

2. Pilots undergoing G-force induced Loss Of Consciousness (G-LOC) – where blood is forced out of the brain, significantly reducing its activity – report experiences similar to notoriously non-local and transpersonal Near-Death Experiences (NDEs).[57]

3. The technique of Holotropic Breathwork, as well as more traditional Yogic breathing practices, use a form of hyper-ventilation to achieve a similar effect: they increase blood alkalinity levels, thereby constricting blood vessels in the

brain and causing hypoxia and dissociation.[58] This, in turn, reportedly leads to significant transpersonal, non-local experiences.[59] Even straightforward hyperventilation, done informally without specific techniques, can lead to surprisingly intense non-local experiences. For instance, an anonymous male reported the following: 'One of us stood against a tree and breathed deeply for a while and then took a very deep breath. Another pushed down hard on his ribcage or actually just at the place where the ribs end. This rendered the subject immediately unconscious ... When I tried it, I didn't think it would work, but then suddenly I was in a meadow which glowed in yellow and red, everything was extremely beautiful and funny. This seemed to last for ages. I must say that I have never felt such bliss ever again.'[60]

4. Psychedelic substances have been known to induce highly complex, intense, non-local, transpersonal experiences.[61] It had always been assumed that they did so by exciting the parts of the brain correlated with such experiences. Yet, *a recent study has shown that psychedelics actually do the opposite*. The study reported that 'profound changes in consciousness were observed after [the administration of the psychedelic], but surprisingly, only decreases in cerebral blood flow ... were seen.'[62] Indeed, the researchers 'observed no increases in cerebral blood flow in any region.'[63] Even more striking, they reported that 'the magnitude of this decrease [in brain activity] predicted the intensity of the subjective effects.'[64] In other words, the intensity of the experience was *inversely* proportional to the activation of the brain, precisely as predicted by the filter hypothesis.

5. The use of Transcranial Magnetic Stimulation (TMS) can inhibit activity in highly localized areas of the brain by impairing the associated electromagnetic fields. In a

study, when the neural activity in the angular gyrus of a patient with epilepsy was inhibited in this way, Out of Body Experiences (OBEs) were reportedly induced.[65]

6. If the trend above is consistent, we should be able to extrapolate it further: brain damage, through deactivating certain parts of the brain, should also induce non-local, transpersonal experiences *under the right circumstances.* And indeed, this has been reported. Two prominent examples are the case of brain anatomist Dr. Jill Bolte Taylor, who underwent a profound transpersonal experience as a consequence of a stroke,[66] and a systematic study carried out in Italy.[67] In the Italian study, patients were evaluated before and after brain surgery for the removal of tumors. Statistically significant increases in feelings of self-transcendence were reported after the surgery.

7. There are many cases reported in the literature of so-called 'acquired savant syndrome.' In these cases an accident or disease leading to brain injury gives rise to extraordinary, genius-level intellectual or artistic skills.[68] For instance, Dr. Anthony Cicoria, an orthopedic surgeon, became an accomplished composer and piano player after having been struck in the head by lightning.[69] Tommy McHugh, a builder, became an accomplished and compulsive painter after brain damaged suffered as a consequence of a burst aneurism.[70] Orlando Serrell, after being struck on the head during a baseball game, developed the ability to make calendar calculations: one can give him any date since his accident (in 1979, when Serrell was only ten years old) and he can tell almost immediately on which day of the week it fell.[71] Like these examples, there are countless others of genius-level skills arising after meningitis, bullet wounds to the head and even with the progression of dementia![72] Moreover, as Dr.

Darold Treffert observed, 'the special skills [of these savants] are always accompanied by prodigious memory,'[73] as though they had been set free from the space-time locality constraints that ordinarily inhibit recall. The mainstream explanation is that these were latent, 'hidden' skills already developed by the brain and unlocked as a consequence of trauma. One must wonder, however, how the brain could have developed such extraordinary skills without any training. And if these skills – like prodigious memory or aptitude for calculations, which are highly advantageous to survival – are latent in us all without any training, what evolutionary advantage could there be for the brain to suppress them in the first place?

8. 'Psychography' is a form of writing that supposedly entails access, by a medium in a trance state, to a non-local, transcendent source of information. I reserve judgment on the popular interpretation of this transcendent source as a discarnate human personality. Be it as it may, a study of Brazilian mediums revealed that, during the practice of psychography, experienced mediums display marked reduction of brain activity in key brain regions – like the frontal lobes and the hippocampus – when compared to regular, non-trance writing.[74] All written material was then scored for complexity. Surprisingly, the material written under trance states scored consistently higher than material produced without trance. As an observant journalist remarked, more complex writing 'typically would require more activity in the frontal and temporal lobes – but that's precisely the opposite of what was observed. To put this another way, the low level of activity in the experienced mediums' frontal lobes should have resulted in vague, unfocused, obtuse garble. Instead, it resulted in

more complex writing samples than they were able to produce while not entranced.'[75]

9. Near-Death Experiences (NDEs) are the ultimate example of non-local, transpersonal experiences associated with not only reduced, but *practically absent* brain activity. They reportedly entail the experience of places and events across time and space, access to parallel realities, communication with entities, insights about the nature of existence and the purpose of life, and a host of other unfathomable phenomenality.[76] These experiences can be highly structured, coherent, palpable, and carry a strong sense of hyper-reality. Since not everyone is a Jules Verne or a Philip K. Dick, it's reasonable to suppose that most *fully-functional* brains would be challenged to imagine such complex and vivid scenarios, let alone one highly compromised or without the benefit of any blood flow. Yet, evidence for the reality of NDEs continues to be collected under scientific protocols and has been mounting.[77]

10. There are many other traditional examples of practices that supposedly give one access to transcendent insights and information through a deterioration or reduction of brain function. For instance, ancient Greeks used to descend into dark caves seeking the stillness and sensory deprivation that supposedly allowed them to tap into their ancestors' knowledge.[78] Isolation tanks aim to achieve similar goals in the same way.[79] Traditional initiatory rituals in pre-literate cultures sought to reveal the true nature of reality through physical ordeals.[80] It is very reasonable to assume that such ordeals – like long sessions in sweat lodges, exposure to the elements, extreme exertion, and even poisoning – physically compromise brain function.

The pattern here is not only clear, but striking. The most complex, coherent, intense, non-local, and transpersonal experiences people report are associated precisely with *reductions*, or even *elimination*, of brain activity. This is consistent with the filter hypothesis discussed here and contradicts the materialist worldview.

What is most ironic is that materialists often mention the phenomena listed above as if they were evidence *for* materialism! For instance, they construe the similarities between NDEs and the subjective effects of G-LOC to be evidence that these experiences are generated by the brain.[81] The *assumption* here is that, because G-LOC and strangulation are induced by physical means, the corresponding subjective effect must *also* be produced by physical means – that is, the brain. Similarly, the experiments of Dr. Michael Persinger seem to show that subjective experiences of a spiritual and transpersonal nature can be induced by a procedure somewhat analogous to TMS.[82] Many self-proclaimed 'skeptics' jumped to construe this as evidence that the brain generates the mind and that transpersonal experiences are illusions.[83] The assumption, once again, is that no valid transpersonal experience can be triggered by purely physical means like electromagnetic fields flowing through the brain.

Well, such an assumption is, in my view, the product of shallow thinking at best and of prejudice at worst. Just *why* can't a true transpersonal experience be triggered by physical intervention in the brain, given the obvious fact that mind and brain are related in some way? What is in dispute is the *nature* of this relationship, not its existence. If the nature of the relationship is such that the brain modulates and localizes consciousness, without causing it, it is not only reasonable but also *expectable* that physical interference with the brain should change one's subjective state. Not only that, partial de-activation of certain brain processes through physical means – be them psychoactive drugs, magnetic fields, hyper-ventilation, asphyxiation, ordeals, sensory deprivation, etc. – should allow consciousness to partially de-localize and expand, which is perfectly consistent with the types of transpersonal experience listed above. *There is nothing extraordinary about the possibility of inducing valid transpersonal experiences through physical means, just as there is nothing extraordinary about the possibility that consciousness is fundamental and irreducible.* Assuming otherwise is either a throwback to archaic prejudices that modern thinking should be able to overcome, or reflects a concerning lack of theoretical imagination.

In both science and philosophy one must extract conclusions not from local and partial pieces of the data, but from a careful consideration of the data *as a whole*. One must look for *broad patterns,* because it is from these broad patterns that reliable conclusions can be extracted. While particular reports of transpersonal experiences could possibly be explained away, the *broad pattern* that associates peak transpersonal experiences with *reductions* of brain activity clearly points to a robust and consistent phenomenon. And it is a phenomenon that cannot be explained under a materialist metaphysics.

The materialist objection

In the previous section I listed a number of types of transpersonal experience triggered by reductions of overall brain activity. Materialists usually try to explain these experiences in the following way: since there are both *excitatory* and *inhibitory* processes active in the brain at any given moment, it is possible that the reductions in brain activity are associated with the *inhibitory* processes much more than the *excitatory* processes. If that is the case, then the corresponding *reduction in inhibition* could actually lead to an *increase in the number or intensity of neural processes that correlate with consciousness*. It is this increase that could explain the transpersonal experiences. In a nutshell, the idea is that a *reduction in neural inhibition causes new or stronger neural correlates of experience to arise*, which correspond to the hallucinations.

This is an extremely poor explanation and you don't need to be a neuroscientist to see why it doesn't work. In most of the types of transpersonal experience listed in the previous section there is *a generalized reduction in blood flow and oxygen supply to the brain as a whole.* For instance, strangulation reduces blood flow to the entire head. Hyperventilation constricts blood vessels throughout the brain. G-LOC is caused by a reduction of blood supply to the entire upper body. A patient undergoing cardiac arrest and having an NDE has no blood flow anywhere in his body. Therefore, to put it mildly, it is *very difficult* to see how a generalized reduction of blood and oxygen supply to the brain could *selectively* and *preferentially* affect *inhibitory* processes, while still allowing for enough metabolic energy to be available for an *increase* in the neural correlates of consciousness! Such a contrived explanation evokes the absurd image of an army of microscopic 'Maxwell's demons' positioned at every capillary intersection and directing, like mini traffic cops, whatever blood and oxygen supply there still is to new neural correlates of experience, while diverting it away from existing inhibitory processes.

In the particular case of the psychedelic study mentioned in the previous section[84] the reductions in brain activity were indeed more localized, which has to do with the effect of the drug in different parts of the brain. However, the researchers measured *no increase* in activity *anywhere* in the brain. This way, one *still* cannot explain the transpersonal visions of the subjects as an increase in the neural correlates of experience due to reduced inhibition.

Materialism fails to explain many of the transpersonal phenomena listed in the previous section even on a case-by-case basis, let alone when they are taken together as a *broad pattern*.

Wrap-up

The broad pattern that associates peak transpersonal, non-local experiences with *reductions* in brain activity contradicts the tentative, promissory materialist solution to the mind-body problem. Instead, it substantiates the notion that the brain is a kind of filter, or localization mechanism, of consciousness. This filter hypothesis explains how traditional techniques for the attainment of transpersonal insight work: by reducing the activity of certain brain regions, they partially or temporarily take the filtering mechanism offline, allowing consciousness to de-clench and expand beyond the space-time position of the body. While countless reports of mystical, spiritual, and transcendent experiences throughout the millennia cannot be explained by materialism – and, therefore, must somehow be dismissed – the filter hypothesis explains these reports quite naturally. Not only that, the filter hypothesis can explain Near-Death Experiences, the visions of psychedelic trances, the more complex subjective effects of hypoxia and G-LOC and a number of other *repeatable* observations that materialism must arbitrarily dismiss.

In Chapter 4 we will resume the line of thinking started here and expand on it. We will also transpose the conclusions above onto a non-dualist framework. Before we can get to that, however, we need more philosophical foundations for our discussion. This will be the subject of the next chapter.

Chapter 3

Mind as the Medium of Reality

What is mind? The most natural and obvious answer to this ancient question is simply this: mind is the medium of everything you have ever known, seen or felt; everything that has ever meant anything to you. Whatever has never fallen within the embrace of your mind might as well have never existed as far as you are concerned. Your entire life and universe – your parents and the people you love, your first day at school, your first kiss, every time you were sick, the obnoxious boss at work, your dreams and aspirations, your successes, your disappointments, your worldview, etc. – are and have always been phenomena of your mind, existing within its boundaries. As Carl Jung put it, one's psyche is the sole carrier of reality that one can ever know.[85]

Granted that contemporary materialist thought about the nature of reality, as we have seen in Chapter 1, entails that the world is 'out there' and that the contents of your mind are a reconstruction – architected and hosted by your brain – of that external reality. But even if that were true, the implication is still that you live your entire life locked within this brain-constructed hallucination. A world outside and independent of mind is a non-provable abstraction, regardless of how good the theoretical reasons to believe in it may be. Therefore, even if it were true that the world is some external realm of abstract energy fields, and even if it were true that your mind is merely a product of brain activity, your mind would *still* be the sole carrier of reality you *can* know. All materialist ideas about nature and reality are products of mind and exist solely within mind. All the things that are believed to exist outside and independently of mind – your body and brain included – are themselves, as far as we can ever know for sure, images in, and abstractions of, mind. It is impossible to know anything outside mind, for anything that is touched by the act of knowing is inevitably and instantaneously 'dragged into' the sphere of mind.

Is the existence of a world outside mind really intuitive?

The part of the materialist worldview that entails that objects exist outside, and independently, of mind is called *realism*.[86] To Western ears, realism is a very intuitive metaphysics: objects possess an undeniable concreteness and continuity that suggests their autonomous existence outside ourselves. But realism is not the only metaphysics that has been proposed by philosophers over the ages. There is another alternative called *idealism*: the notion that all reality is a phenomenon of, and in, mind.[87] To idealists, there is only the medium of mind and its contents.[88] Everything you see, hear, feel, think, or otherwise cognize right now exists, to an idealist, only insofar as it unfolds in mind. There is no abstract external world outside mind. We can summarize it thus:

Realism: Reality exists outside and independent of mind;

Idealism: Reality consists exclusively of mind and its contents.

Notice that materialism entails realism but goes beyond it: it postulates not only that matter exists outside mind, but that mind itself is generated by matter. For the remainder of this section I will, thus, discuss *materialism*, for it is the more specific term.

The intuitive appeal of materialism seems undeniable. Just look at the world around you right now: tables, chairs, walls, windows, computers, books, solid floor, etc.; they all seem to clearly exist separately from your perception of them. If you were to leave the room and everything in it right now, it would all still remain there, wouldn't it? That seems clear as crystal.

One of the greatest philosophers of the modern period was George Berkeley, Bishop of Cloyne. Berkeley is famous for his cogent defense of idealism.[89] English poet Samuel Johnson is said to have argued against Berkeley's position simply by kicking a large stone and exclaiming: 'I refute it *thus!*'[90] Johnson was clearly appealing to the *felt* concreteness and solidity of the rock to demonstrate that it could not exist only in mind. To this day, many people think that Johnson's argument was sound, a state of affairs that reflects a general misapprehension of what *materialism* actually entails.

As a matter of fact, materialism somewhat *contradicts* Johnson's intuition. According to materialism, the rock Johnson *perceived* existed only inside his head, as discussed at length in Chapter 1. Johnson's entire experience of the rock was supposedly a kind of hallucination produced by the firings of neurons in his brain; a hallucinated 'copy' that more-or-less accurately imitated a 'real rock' in an abstract 'real world' outside his mind. That he *felt* the solidity of the rock while kicking it informs him, according to materialism, mostly of the inner dynamics of his own brain. The 'outside' world itself is devoid of any of the qualities of feeling or perception.

The notion that the rock Johnson felt was not the real thing but a hallucination is, as I will argue shortly, unnecessary and contrived. Not only does it fly in the face of our everyday intuition of reality, it sort of inverts the logical direction of inference: it tries to reconstruct the *known* – that is, what we perceive – from the fundamentally *un*known – namely, an abstract universe outside mind. In building a reasonable worldview, we must start from the data that is right under our noses: experience itself. Postulating an entire 'shadow' universe outside experience is only justifiable if we cannot make sense of reality without it. However, as I hope to show, we very well *can*. As such, the abstract 'shadow' world of materialism does nothing but complicate and inflate our models of reality by adding unnecessary, unprovable elements.

Suppose, thus, that we drop such an inflationary notion and reject a 'shadow' world outside mind. What we are then left with is a conception of reality that reflects precisely what reality seems to be: all that which we *experience*. Notice how this completely validates Johnson's intuition: *the rock he felt was indeed the real rock, not a hallucination of his brain!* And yet, *that is precisely the reason why Berkeley was right in his idealism.* When you avoid creating an unnecessary and unprovable 'shadow' of the world of experience, the only world you are left with *is* the world of experience, *the world of mind.*

According to materialism, the tables, chairs, walls, windows, computers, books, floor, etc., which you are experiencing right now are not really the real things, but merely hallucinated copies inside your head. The real world is some abstract realm of inter-acting electromagnetic fields that you cannot even visualize. According to idealism, on the other hand, the tables, chairs, walls, windows, computers, books, floor, etc., are all the real deal. You are not creating mental copies of anything, but having direct access to what is truly real. If the book or electronic reader in your hands right now feels real, it's because it *is* real, not the brain-constructed copy that materialists would have you believe.

The key implications of idealism

It is easier to build my case for idealism if you have, since early on, a good understanding of what its implications are. The most important implication is this: if idealism is correct, then *mind is not within the brain, because it is the brain that is within mind.* If you recall our discussion in Chapter 2, this inversion of the relationship between brain and mind sounds promising as a potential explanation for transpersonal experiences, an idea we will explore in more details in Chapter 4.

According to idealism, all of reality – the entire universe – exists in mind, although *not all in your egoic mind alone* (this is a crucial point that we will discuss in depth shortly). Mind is not generated by configurations of matter and energy. Instead, configurations of matter and energy arise from the dynamics of mind. They only exist insofar as they are *experienced*. Mind is the ground of the real.

Notice that, when I say that everything exists *in mind,* I am *not* implying that everything exists *in someone's head.* My hypothesis is that *your head is in mind, not mind in your head.* Mind is not bound or circumscribed by any physical structure, because all physical structures arise in mind. Like any other object you perceive, your own body is a product of mind in much the same way that a dreamed-up body in a nightly dream is a product of your dreaming mind.

The materialist assumption that your mind is somehow within your body is inculcated by Western education since very early on. It's very hard to suspend it, even temporarily. Yet, a temporary suspension of this assumption is precisely what I ask of you, so you can interpret my argument correctly, even if ultimately you don't agree with it. All you have ever known or experienced about your body has been, after all, perceptions and ideas in your mind. There is nothing to what you call your body that is not, or has not been, a content of your mind: perceived images on a mirror, inner sensations, smells, descriptions you heard from others, concepts and theories learned in school, etc. Even if you looked down right now and observed your body 'directly,' that would still be just a visual perception in your mind. Even if you dropped the book or electronic reader you have in your hands right now and palpated your torso, head, and legs, those would all still be just subjective sensations in your mind. Ponder about this for a moment and then ask yourself: what do you have more empirical reason to believe in: that your mind is in your body, or that your body is in your mind?

In Chapter 4 I will be proposing that the body is a mental artifact that grounds a localized point-of-view within mind in much the same way that a dreamed-up body grounds a certain localized perspective within a nightly dream. Yet, it's the dream that is in you, not you in the dream. But let's not jump ahead...

One mind

Western education and culture take for granted that mind is personal and discontinuous across people – that is, that your mind is entirely your own and fundamentally separate from everybody else's minds. Yet, if idealism is true and all reality is indeed in mind, then the simplest hypothesis is that there is but one mind; one irreducible medium in which the dance of existence unfolds. Otherwise, one would have to postulate that mind has arisen irreducibly countless times in nature, once for every conscious being. This is, of course, a tremendously inflationary postulate. So we will stick to the most parsimonious alternative: there is but one irreducible medium of mind, the sole ontological primitive of all reality.

My hypothesis is that mind is a broad and continuous medium unlimited in either space or time; a canvas where the entire play of existence unfolds, including space and time themselves. Your egoic mind – that limited awareness you identify yourself with – is, in this context, merely a segment of the broad, universal canvas of mind. Your impression that your mind is separate from all the rest is, as I will argue later, the result of a 'filtering' process induced by a specific, localized topological feature of the canvas of mind. We will go into details and specifics of all this; all I ask of you right now is a critical but open mind, and some patience.

Empirical evidence for idealism

In Chapter 2 I referred to a paper published in *Nature* magazine, in 2007,[91] which suggests strongly that no physical reality can exist without being perceived subjectively in mind. As I argued then, the implication is that mind cannot be reduced to matter, for the paper suggests that matter cannot exist without mind being there in the first place. I concluded then that mind is an *ontological primitive*: a fundamental, irreducible aspect of nature which itself cannot be explained in terms of anything else. In this chapter, we are making the case for idealism, which entails that *everything else* in nature can be explained and described in terms of mind, the sole ontological primitive.

The 2007 *Nature* paper refutes most realist theories of nature, but with a couple of potential exceptions. The technical discussion in the paper is quite esoteric, but the key point is what physicists call 'non-contextuality.' Don't let the big word put you off: non-contextuality is very simple. It basically means that the properties of a physical entity do not depend on the process of observation. For instance, if a certain theory of nature entails that tables and chairs have the properties they have – that is, a certain size, weight, color, texture, etc. – whether they are observed or not, then the theory is non-contextual. According to non-contextual theories, when you observe a table you simply *find out* what the properties of the table are, but you do not *change* those properties by the mere act of observing the table. To put it simply: non-contextuality entails that nature is what it is, regardless of what you know about it. Observation simply gives you knowledge of what nature already was at the instant immediately prior to observation. Clearly, *non-contextuality is almost synonymous with realism*. Think about it: if reality exists outside, and independently, of mind, how could the mere act of observing a physical entity with your mind change what the physical entity *is*?

All right. Now, at the risk of some over-simplification, we can say this: the *Nature* paper refutes all realist theories of nature *except a couple that abandon non-contextuality*. In other words, the *Nature* paper implies either that (a) some form of idealism is correct, or that (b) realism is correct but *contextual*, instead of *non*-contextual. Option (a) is the case I am making. Option (b), as argued above, sounds contradictory, so let us look at it in more detail to see what it means and how seriously we can take it.

To reconcile contextuality – that is, the notion that the act of observation physically changes what is observed – with realism, one has to imagine the human body as an objective measurement device that interacts, *instantaneously and at a distance*, with the objective world around itself, *changing that world instantly as it perceives it*. Everything you see becomes *physically* the result of your own perceptual processes at work. Before you looked, the world supposedly existed in state A; at the instant you looked, however, the world physically changed into state B. So you never actually see the world as it was (state A), but solely as it *became* because you looked at it (state B).

This way, the empirical results in the *Nature* paper show us that the price of preserving the notion that the world exists objectively, outside mind, is to give our eyes the magical power of physically changing that world at a mere glance! Superman looks puny in comparison. Moreover, notice that this is just a much more contrived way to arrive at *the same conclusion* of idealism: namely, that *reality is the result of mind in action*.

Let us summarize what you *must* accept if, in view of the empirical results in the *Nature* paper, you still want to reject idealism:

1. You must accept that, when you observe the world around you, you *physically change* that world by the mere act of observation;

2. You must accept that this happens *instantaneously, regardless of the distance* between you and what you observe; and

3. You must accept that there exists a world independent of your observation (state A), *even though you fundamentally can never see it, neither directly nor indirectly*, for you can only see what the world *became* because you looked at it (state B).

Do you see how tortuous this is? One is hard-pressed to think of something more fantastic. Effectively, state A is merely a theoretical abstraction, forever outside the realm of experience or direct empirical verification. To integrate this unobservable state into a theory that matches with experimental results requires complicated mathematical acrobatics. As Thomas Kuhn eloquently argued, once the scientific community settles on a certain paradigm of thought, most of scientific activity turns into the solving of puzzles to refine and reinforce the paradigm.[92] As part-and-parcel of the current paradigm, the contrived mathematical exercises aimed at producing a viable formulation of realism are just imaginary puzzles. One should not confuse imaginary puzzles with reality.

I submit to you a much simpler alternative: *there is no state A.* If there were, we could, *by definition*, never see it anyway. State A is just a mental abstraction of smart human beings engaged in fun puzzle-solving. And neither do we have the magical power to change the universe 'out there' merely by the act of glancing at it. Yes, nature is contextual, but contextuality does not require superhero powers: it is simply another way to say that reality is the unfolding of mind; that is, the unfolding of the observer in the process of observation.

Is there empirical support for realism?

The 2007 *Nature* paper[93] contains strong empirical support for idealism. To rescue a precarious form of realism – and, therefore, materialism – from its results requires a surprising departure from intuition and reason. As if this weren't enough, the question of empirical support can also be reversed: is there any direct empirical evidence for realism?

There cannot be. Since knowledge exists only in mind, everything touched by the fingertip of knowledge, no matter how slightly and subtly, is instantaneously 'brought into' the domain of mind. Fundamentally, we can never *know* anything supposedly outside mind. Idealism is, thus, the default metaphysics unless there are substantive reasons to think otherwise. And, as I intend to show in this book, there aren't.

Realism, on the other hand, is an *unprovable* abstraction. Moreover, from an epistemic viewpoint, it is also a *useless* abstraction, as I will argue in Chapter 6. If there ever was a perfect candidate to be sliced clean out of existence by Occam's razor,[94] it ought to be the notion that an entire unprovable universe exists outside mind.

The logical case for idealism

In addition to empirical evidence in its favor, idealism also has a *logical* advantage when compared to materialism. As a matter of fact, I believe that *idealism is a much more skeptical metaphysics than materialism.* In this section, I'd like to expand on this.

Materialism requires the following four statements about reality to be true:

1. Your conscious perceptions exist;
2. The conscious perceptions of other living entities, different from your own, also exist;
3. There are things that exist independently of, and outside, conscious perception;
4. Things that exist independently of, and outside, conscious perception generate conscious perception.

Notice that the statements are ordered according to how many new assumptions they require. Indeed, statement 1 is very close to the famous *cogito ergo sum,* 'I think, therefore I am.' If you can be sure of anything at all, it is that your conscious perceptions exist. So statement 1 is the one absolute certainty you can ever have.

Statement 2 requires a small leap of faith: it states that there are other conscious entities, like other people or animals. You can never be *absolutely* sure that anything or anybody else is conscious. For all you know, everybody else could be unconscious zombies faking consciousness in a very convincing manner through their external behavior, but operating entirely 'in the dark' as far as their inner lives.[95] Yet, the leap of faith here is small, since it merely postulates other *instances* of a category – namely, conscious perceptions – that you already know to exist.

Statement 3, on the other hand, requires a much more significant leap of faith, since it postulates an entirely new *category* – namely, things outside conscious perception – for which you can never have any direct evidence. Indeed, everything you can ever know comes into consciousness the moment you know it, so the belief that there are things outside consciousness is an abstraction beyond knowledge.

Statement 4 is even worse. It postulates that things you can never know to exist are actually responsible for the only thing you can be absolutely sure to exist: your own consciousness. *It postulates that abstractions generate what is concrete.* This is quite an extraordinary statement in that it completely inverts the natural direction of inference: normally, one infers the unknown from the known, not the known from the unknown!

Idealism requires only statements 1 and 2 to hold. In other words, it acknowledges the most certain and then requires merely a small leap of faith. The reigning materialist worldview, on the other hand, requires all four statements above to hold; a gargantuan leap of faith. Clearly, idealism is the more skeptical, cautious metaphysics. The only reason we've come to believe in statements 3 and 4, as discussed earlier, is that they provide an explanation for the fact that we all seem to share a common world. If you and I, sitting at the beach, describe the same environment, we conclude that there must be an environment outside and independent of each of our minds – namely, the beach – which we are both contemplating simultaneously. Otherwise, how could our conscious perceptions be so similar? But, as it will become clear in Chapters 4 to 6, there are elegant and reasonable formulations of idealism that can perfectly explain our shared experience of a common world without requiring the enormous leaps of faith entailed by statements 3 and 4 above.

A sober, sane view of reality should be extremely skeptical of statements 3 and 4. For too long have we replaced reality with our mad systems of abstraction. We have become lost in a dense fog of unreal suppositions, taken for granted without critical thought. It is time we woke up to what is truly real: to our *immediate experience of reality*. It is time we realized that the models of physics inform us not about a reality 'out there,' but about ourselves; about how our deeper mind – our collective, shared, non-egoic mind – flows according to certain patterns and regularities.

Idealism is not solipsism

Let us look more carefully at a point that was already briefly mentioned before: the erroneous notion that idealism somehow entails what is called 'solipsism' in philosophy. Solipsism is the notion that all that exists are my own conscious experiences. In other words, reality is purely *my* private dream. There are no other conscious entities, like other conscious people. They are merely figments of my own imagination. If I were a solipsist, I wouldn't believe that you, dear reader, have inner life at all. I would believe simply that your external appearance and behavior, as far as I can perceive them, are imagined by my own mind.

Now, notice that solipsism entails the acknowledgement of statement 1 of the previous section and the rejection of statements 2, 3, and 4. *Therefore, it is not idealism.* Idealism grants reality to statement 2. 'Why?' I hear you ask. After all, if we are already following this road of radical skepticism anyway, why grant reality to statement 2? *Because believing in statement 2 is the simplest explanation for observations.* As discussed earlier, I can explain much of my own external behavior to myself by the fact that I am conscious, and so can you. It is your conscious feelings that explain your facial expressions, your impulsive reactions, your dislike of certain people and your love for others, etc. And you undoubtedly observe very similar external behaviors in others: their facial expressions, impulsive reactions, likes and dislikes, etc. To explain these behaviors of others while assuming that others are *not* conscious – that is, by assuming solipsism – would require an entirely different explanation for largely the same phenomena that you observe in yourself. In other words, very similar observations would require very different explanations. Clearly, this isn't the simplest alternative. It is simpler and more elegant to infer that others are *also* conscious and manifest their external behavior for the exact same reasons that you manifest yours, particularly given the fact that others have physical bodies entirely analogous to yours.

You could argue that other people's behavior is so analogous to your own because you *project* your conscious life onto them, in the same way that the characters of your nightly dreams all have human-like reactions while being merely projections of your mind. This way, other people would still be characters of your private solipsist dream, behaving like you do simply because your 'subconscious' mind is projecting your own patterns of behavior onto them. This sounds reasonable, doesn't it? There is, however, a hole in this argument. Indeed, more than likely you have observed many types of behavior in other people that you could not yet explain based on your own experiences, because at the time you made those observations you had not yet had the experiences that would explain such behaviors. For instance, as a young child, I could already observe the peculiar behavior of adults in love without ever having had that feeling myself. I just couldn't figure out why people would act like fools in those situations. Later in life, as I experienced romantic love myself, I could immediately match that new personal experience to prior observations of the 'foolish' behavior of others and explain them retroactively by granting consciousness to those other people. As a young child, *I couldn't have projected onto others an experience I had not yet had.* Therefore, once again, it is simplest and most reasonable to accept statement 2 of the previous section. Idealism is very reasonable and skeptic, but it differs from solipsism in that the latter seems to be *un*reasonably skeptic.

Idealism is not panpsychism

Idealism entails that all reality is *in mind.* But that does not imply that rocks, tables, and chairs have their own form of consciousness. One should not confuse the claim that all of reality is *in consciousness* with the idea that everything *is conscious.* Idealism does not entail that rocks and chairs *experience* things subjectively the way you and I do.

When I say that everything is *in* mind I am saying that things exist only insofar as they play themselves out in the mind of a conscious observer. For instance, when you dream at night, everything in your dream exists only insofar as it is in your mind. The stuff in your dreams clearly does not have an independent existence outside your mind. But that does not mean that every person or animal in your dreams has a conscious point-of-view of its own. They do not necessarily have a subjective inner life separate from yours.

Idealism entails that, like a dream, reality exists only insofar as it is in mind, *but not that everything in it is conscious and has an inner life of its own.* For instance, while acknowledging that other living entities are conscious – that is, while granting validity to statement 2 discussed earlier – I do not subscribe to the notion that rocks, windmills, home thermostats, or computers are conscious in and of themselves, having their own individual, subjective points-of-view. Technically speaking, my formulation of idealism does not entail *panpsychism*, the idea – as we've seen in Chapter 1 – that inanimate objects have some form of individual, subjective inner life.

Other common misconceptions about Idealism

While debating my ideas on idealism before I started writing this book, I was confronted with a number of criticisms. While many of them were valid and will be tackled in later chapters, others merely reflected misunderstandings of idealism. Let us discuss a couple of these latter ones here to get potential misunderstandings out of the way before we get to more substance.

Idealism proposes that all reality is in mind and, as such, one can say metaphorically that everything is 'made of' the *substrate* of mind. Many people then conclude that this implies the existence of some kind of literal 'mind stuff.' Several even asked me whether there was any empirical evidence for the existence of this 'mind stuff' that everything is supposedly made of. Well, there is no such stuff. Idealism does not entail that the substrate of mind is the stuff of existence, insofar as we define 'stuff' as some objective substance or material that supposedly exists independently of, and outside, subjective perception. Instead, what idealism is saying is precisely that *there is no stuff*. There is *only* subjective perception. The word 'stuff' is just a way to describe certain modalities and regularities of perception. When one asks about the 'stuff' of mind one is 'subconsciously' falling back into realist assumptions; into thinking that reality is 'out there,' even mind itself!

According to idealism, all stuff – all materials, objects, etc. – exist *only insofar* as they are subjectively apprehended in mind. The *substrate* of mind itself is not stuff: *it is the subject, not an object.* It is the medium from which perceptions arise, but is itself not perceivable for exactly the same reason that the eye that sees cannot see itself without a mirror; or – as Alan Watts put it – that you can't bite your own teeth.[96] As such, the substrate of mind cannot be measured, detected, or analyzed like some kind of stuff, *because it is that which measures, detects, and analyzes* in the first place. The substrate of mind is not a material, but that which imagines all materials. Do you see what I am trying to say? If not, no worries: this will become a lot clearer and more explicit in Chapter 6.

Our language is itself constructed around dualities like subject/object, verb/noun, past/future, etc. Therefore, it is impossible to talk about mind without objectifying it in some way. I ask for your alertness from this point on: whenever I seem to objectify mind, as in referring to it as a 'medium' or a 'substrate', I will be speaking *metaphorically*, because of the inherent limitations of language. The substrate of mind is not an object, nor a material. It is the forever-elusive subject wherein all 'objects' arise as imagined figures.

Another common misunderstanding of idealism is reflected on this question: if everything is in mind, why can't we influence reality at will, just like we can influence our own thoughts and fantasies at will? The misunderstanding here – a very forgivable one – is to equate mind at large with that particular, limited, small part of mind that we call the ego. The ego can even be *defined* as the part of mind that we ordinarily identify with and feel we can control. But there is nothing in my formulation of idealism restricting mind to the ego; on the contrary.

Whatever you ordinarily think of as your own mind should be looked upon, in the context of my hypothesis, as a very small segment of the broader medium of mind. How this small segment shapes itself to create the egoic illusion of separateness is something we will tackle in Chapters 5 and 6. For now, consider this example: you probably accept that other people also are conscious. Therefore, you must accept that their entire inner lives take place in other segments of mind that are external to your ego and which you have no control over. Now, imagine that there are even more segments of the medium of mind that transcend what we would associate with any biological, embodied entity within space-time. Those segments, too, are not excluded from my formulation of idealism. Mind itself is unfathomably larger than any one of our individual egos. Therefore, that the broader medium of mind can operate in a way that feels external to, and outside the sphere of influence of, your ego should come as no surprise at all to you. To say that everything is in mind does not imply that everything falls within the scope and whims of your or my egoic will.

Moreover, to say that all reality unfolds in mind does not deny that reality – as empirically observed – unfolds according to certain stable patterns and regularities that we've come to call the 'laws of nature.' In my hypothesis, the laws of nature represent the patterns and regularities according to which certain contents of mind preferentially flow, carrying a certain momentum as they so do. Indeed, my formulation of idealism is entirely compatible with the notion that, given certain regularities, the contents of mind may flow with so much momentum that attempting to change the course of their flow would be akin to trying to stop a speeding train with your bare hands and feet. This reconciles idealism with the known stability and robustness of the laws of nature. Let us look at this in more details now.

Idealism and the laws of physics

As discussed earlier, idealism entails that the world is what you consciously perceive: it's the book or electronic reader in your hands; it's the room around you, with all its colors, textures, and depth; it's the sounds and smells in the air; it's the feeling you have of being in your own skin right now. In contrast, the reigning materialist worldview in our culture is rather abstract: it postulates that, behind the 'copy' of the world you're experiencing right now, there is the 'real' world, which is *not* what you are experiencing. The dynamics of objects and living entities in that 'real' world supposedly unfold according to certain regularities and patterns – the laws of physics – that exist outside mind. As it unfolds, it leaves an imprint on your sense organs – like footprints – which your brain then uses to perform a reconstruction of the world inside your head. That reconstruction is, supposedly, what you are experiencing right now.

A big part of the motivation for our culture's current embrace of materialism is the observed regularities according to which reality seems to unfold: it is hard for most people to imagine that it is the unfolding of contents of mind itself – that otherwise voluble and rather unstable medium we associate with the ego – that obeys what we call the 'laws of physics.' Moreover, the world 'outside' *feels* very separate from our egoic minds. We don't seem to have any direct mental influence on the world and often feel entirely at the mercy of impersonal, external forces.

As we discussed above, this impression arises solely because we ordinarily identify ourselves with only a very small part of our minds: our personal egoic awareness. Yet, each one of us has direct experience of the broader aspects of mind: when we dream at night, it is undeniably our minds that construct and project the entire universe of our dreams. Nonetheless, that dreamed-up universe feels pretty much autonomous and outside our conscious control. Indeed, if we identified with those aspects of our minds that produce dreams we would never feel anxiety during our nightmares, for we would know at once that we were making the whole thing up ourselves. Moreover, if we had control of those dream-producing aspects of our minds we would never have nightmares to begin with. Similarly, neuroses and psychoses – such as some obsessions, phobias, and schizophrenic visions – all seem to arise from a part of mind that we do not at all identify with; a part of mind that feels entirely alien, external to the ego. It is, thus, not so difficult to imagine that it is *also* a part of mind that we do not identify with, and do not seem to have control over, that projects the so-called 'external world.' And then, it is also not so difficult to conceive that the contents of this part of mind unfold according to stable patterns and regularities.

Imagine mind as the screen of a movie theater. Images on the screen represent the entire set of your subjective experiences. Materialism states that those images have an external source and are captured by 'cameras' – our sense organs – used to record the movie you are watching. Under idealism, on the other hand, only the movie theater exists: all images you see are generated in the theatre itself, like a computer animation rendered in real-time, and have no external source (we will discuss the role of our sense organs under idealism in Chapter 4). We can empirically identify certain patterns and regularities in the unfolding of these images. *The so-called 'laws of physics' are simply a model of these observed patterns and regularities according to which the 'pixels' of the images seem to change.* In other words, the 'laws' reflect the observed regularities of the behavior of the 'pixels' in the 'computer-generated' images, as opposed to representing rules governing how events in an abstract external world unfold.

This is easier to grok if we take completely abstract images as examples and study how they unfold. See Figure 2. The sequence

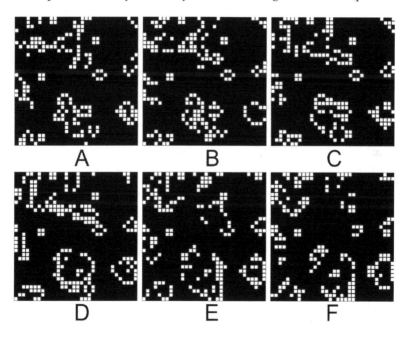

Figure 2. The unfolding of an imagined universe according to stable patterns and regularities.

of abstract images in the figure clearly does not represent anything in an outside world. They are not 'copies' of anything, but realities in their own right. The advantage of using such abstract images is that they help by-pass all of your cultural programming, since you won't be able to find any recognizable pattern in them that your mind already assumes to represent an external object.

If you take some time to carefully study the image sequence in Figure 2, at some point you will likely be able to identify patterns or regularities according to which chunks of pixels seem to move and change from one frame to the next. For instance, there are three clearly identifiable chunks of pixels along the right edge of each frame, which seem to preserve some coherence from one frame to the next. Other somewhat coherent chunks can be seen throughout each frame. The coherence of such chunks of pixels across frames seems to reflect certain regularities and patterns in the unfolding of the images. *Yet, we would never attribute such regularities and patterns to some abstract world separate from the images in Figure 2.* Clearly, whatever regularities there are, are regularities *of the images themselves.* The images aren't an isomorphic copy of something else, but a self-contained phenomenon.

Now, transpose this thinking to your visual perception of the world around you right now: look around yourself; try to imagine that you were just born a moment ago and you don't know what chairs, tables, walls, windows, books, or computers are. What do you see? You see just pixels. The chunks and regularities you then observe are simply the patterns according to which these pixels seem to organize themselves and change over time. It wouldn't even occur to you to abstract from these patterns a world outside mind where certain laws govern the unfolding of events. You would just think: 'Oh, this is how these images evolve.' *That* is idealism, the most intuitive – even self-evident – worldview from the point-of-view of anyone not yet exposed to the madness of Western culture.

The chunks of pixels in Figure 2 are analogous to macroscopic objects like tables and chairs. Instead of thinking of tables and chairs as objects of an abstract world outside your mind, try to think of them as particular, coherent groups of pixels in the images unfolding *in the medium of your mind*, just as in Figure 2. You may want to take a few seconds to carry out this thought exercise before reading on.

Do you see the subtle flip in perspective that I am attempting to instigate in you?

We tend to tile the entire world around us with an intricate web of *concepts* derived from language. We live inside a self-woven conceptual cocoon that insulates us from raw reality. Studies have shown, for instance, that people whose languages categorize colors differently from our Western languages actually *see* colors very differently too.[97] The conceptual tiling we place onto reality is often so dense that we lose sight of the raw perceptual 'pixels' hidden underneath: we only see wooden tables and chairs, not pixels of various brownish shades coming together in astoundingly rich and fluid combinations.

At the very moment we tile raw pixels with concepts, we automatically project onto reality the entire set of attributes that our culture associates with those concepts: tables and chairs are supposed to be objects of a world *outside mind,* so every time we look around we see objects *outside mind,* as opposed to the raw pixels of the tapestry of mind. Do you see what I mean? We no longer see reality as it is, but as our education and cultural milieu inculcated into us. I invite you to try and briefly remove the conceptual tiling that blocks your view of reality, so you can see the raw chunks of perceptual pixels in the medium of mind. If you can see reality that way, freed from conceptual projections, even if just for a short moment, you may surprise yourself with how natural idealism will feel to you. If you are able to see the 'pixels' of perceptual experience in the same way that you see the pixels of Figure 2, you will have removed part of the veil of culture.

Scientists try to go deeper in their own way. They are not satisfied with identifying the rough patterns that seem to govern the behavior of macroscopic objects like tables and chairs. Instead, they use microscopes and particle smashers to look deep into the heart of matter, to try and identify the more fundamental, underlying regularities of nature on the basis of which one could potentially construct explanations for the behavior of *all* objects and entities. In Figure 2, this would be analogous to looking past the rough chunks of pixels and trying to find the patterns that govern how *individual pixels* change from one frame to the next. If you do that carefully, you will find out that, in Figure 2:

1. A pixel that is white in a given frame stays white in the next frame if, and only if, it has two or three white neighbors;
2. A pixel that is black in a given frame becomes white in the next frame if, and only if, it has exactly three white neighbors.

Have a look again at Figure 2 and try to prove to yourself that the two simple rules above fully determine the evolution of the images from one frame to the next. The behavior of chunks of pixels is an emergent epiphenomenon derived directly from these simple rules. This is analogous to how macroscopic objects, such as tables and chairs, are supposedly an emergent epiphenomenon of the laws that govern the behavior of microscopic subatomic particles.

The point I am trying to make is this: Figure 2 provides a clean analogy for our reductionist scientific models, including the emergence of macroscopic entities and phenomena from microscopic laws. Yet, *the images in Figure 2 are not a 'copy', or a 'representation,' of any other reality. They are a self-contained phenomenon in their own right.* The two rules underlying the evolution of the frames in Figure 2 govern how *the image pixels themselves* behave, not the dynamics of an 'outside world' supposedly represented by those pixels. Similarly, idealism entails that the observed patterns and regularities of nature, which we've come to call the 'laws of physics,' simply govern how some of the 'pixels' of the tapestry of mind unfold. They have nothing to do with any abstract 'shadow' universe outside mind.

Idealism in a nutshell

We have seen that all reality we can ever know is a flow of subjective perceptions, thoughts, feelings and ideas in mind. We postulate an abstract world outside mind merely to explain to ourselves the patterns and regularities of experience – that is, the so-called 'laws of nature' – and the consistencies of these experiences across observers. For instance, if another person were sitting next to you right now and were asked to describe where she is, she would describe a room very similar to the one you are experiencing. We explain these commonalities of experience by saying that there is a common external world – a room, in this case – that you and the other person both occupy simultaneously, and which modulates both of your experiences of it. But there are other ways to explain both the regularities and the commonalities of experience across observers without postulating an entire 'shadow' universe outside mind. *These alternative models are based on the idea that the flow of the contents of mind obeys certain patterns and regularities:* the 'laws of mind.' In the coming chapters I will elaborate on one such model through a series of metaphors, which will culminate in Chapter 6.

If my idealist formulation is correct, then all reality is in mind, including your body and brain. I acknowledge that such an idea may sound farfetched at first. After all, you and I have both grown up in a cultural milieu where the very opposite notion has been inculcated into us from early childhood. We grew up to believe that mind is a product of the brain, not the other way around. Yet, I ask that you try and suspend your natural disbelief and give my case a fair hearing. *There is nothing illogical, inconsistent, incoherent, or absurd about the idea that the medium of reality is mind itself.* You are just not used to it. In fact, it is the most natural and intuitive idea. In the remainder of this book we will systematically investigate how all salient aspects of reality can be neatly explained under this hypothesis, without defying any empirical observation of nature. Even the mathematical formalisms behind the cutting edge of theoretical physics can be seamlessly ported onto an idealist framework, as we shall see.

Chapter 4

The Brain as a Knot of Mind

In the previous chapter we discussed the notion that all of reality is a phenomenon of, and in, mind. Instead of postulating an abstract, objective world outside mind – which unfolds according to the laws of physics and modulates our conscious perceptions via electromagnetic signals captured by our sense organs – we discussed the hypothesis that it is the flow of the contents of mind that obeys certain patterns and regularities. No abstract universe outside mind is needed: reality can be explained by observing and modeling the behavior of mind directly. Concrete ideas about how to do it will be hinted upon later in this chapter and discussed at length in Chapter 6. For now, though, we must face a more immediate and fundamental problem: the nature and role of the brain and sense organs in the context of our idealist hypothesis.

Mind filtering mind

Indeed, we have concluded in Chapter 2 that the brain is a kind of filter of mind: it selects and localizes the flow of certain contents of mind, which would otherwise be unbound and non-local. The problem, of course, is the following: if the brain itself exists in mind, how can it filter that which gives it its very existence? A water filter is not made of water. A coffee filter is not made of coffee. How can a mind filter be itself 'made of' mind? It sounds like a self-referential contradiction. Yet, unless this apparent contradiction is resolved, idealism cannot be reconciled with the filter hypothesis.

The first step in resolving this apparent conflict is to emphasize that the word 'filter' is used metaphorically. Strictly speaking, what is meant here is that *the brain is the image of a process by means of which mind limits and localizes the flow of its own contents.* Consider this for a moment: if there is a self-localization process taking place in mind that is in some – likely partial – way still perceptible from the perspective of the ego, then this process will necessarily appear to the ego according to some form. In other words, there will necessarily be an *image* according to which the ego perceives this process, in much the same way that the process of combustion is perceived by the ego as flames; or that the process of sudden electric discharge in the atmosphere is perceived as lightning; or that the process of blood coagulation is perceived as clots; etc. What I am thus claiming is that *the brain is the image of a process of localization of mental contents.* This is what the brain *is*, primarily. Any other qualities or properties we attach to the concept 'brain' reflect simply our culture's current (mis)understanding of that *image.* Moreover, unless and until we have good reasons to believe otherwise, we must assume that this image is a *partial* one. It does not necessarily capture all relevant information about the process it depicts, just like clots don't capture in their form and color all relevant information about the process of coagulation.

To expect mind to manifest in space-time *without* a brain is like expecting regular combustion without flames or coagulation without clots. Instead of magically generating mind, the brain simply *is* the partial image of mind in the process of self-local-izing. This is why observations of brain states seem to correlate so well with ordinary mind states: brain states are simply part of that *image of the process* of consciousness localization. The corre-lation breaks when consciousness partially or temporarily de-localizes.

It is thus not at all surprising, in the context of the worldview we are constructing, to find an 'object' – an image – in the empirical world that seems to play the role of filtering the contents of mind, even though this process is itself in mind. Everything we concluded in Chapter 2 is entirely consistent with the formulation of idealism that we have just laid out in Chapter 3. In Chapter 2 we simply used a dualist metaphor, for ease of communication, to describe a process that we will now transpose onto an idealist framework without any loss or contradiction.

Since the very structure of our language, as a product of our culture, is massively influenced by realist assumptions, we do not have an explicit and unambiguous terminology to articulate our discussion. Therefore, we will need to continue to rely on analogies and metaphors. In the remainder of this chapter, as well as throughout the next two chapters, I will use several different metaphors to convey and explore the key ideas of this book. These metaphors will, at first sight, appear different from, and even contradictory with, one another as far as the imagery they evoke. *But they are entirely consistent with one another when one groks the core ideas and intuitions they seek to convey.* As is the case with any metaphor, the particular images they use are merely *vehicles* to carry an essential, underlying *meaning* or *intuition*. I will try to help you separate underlying meaning from mere vehicle as we make our way. Indeed, my use of *various* and *different* metaphors is entirely intentional: the essential meaning of the metaphors can be distilled and separated from the background noise of images by comparing what they all have *in common*, as opposed to how they *differ. Their true message lies precisely in their subtle commonalities,* while their superficial differences should be considered mere metaphorical noise; disposable vehicles to carry ideas. It will be helpful for you to try and keep this in mind from this point on.

The whirlpool metaphor

Think of mind as a stream. Water can flow along the stream through its entire length; that is, water is not localized in the stream, but traverses it unhindered. Now imagine a small whirlpool in the stream: it has a visible and identifiable existence; one can locate a whirlpool and roughly delineate its boundaries; one can point at it and say 'Here is a whirlpool!' There seems to be no question about how clear and concrete the whirlpool is as an identifiable object. Moreover, the whirlpool limits the flow of water: the water molecules trapped in it can no longer traverse the entire stream freely, but instead become locked in place, swirling around a specific and well-defined location. *The whirlpool localizes the flow of water in the stream.* See Figure 3. Moreover, the water molecules that do *not* get trapped in it are, so to speak, *'filtered out' of the whirlpool,* since they are kept away from it by the whirlpool's very dynamics. Indeed, anyone observing a whirlpool will notice that, at its outer edges, it seems to 'push away' whatever part of the flow it doesn't capture within itself.

Yet, *there is nothing to the whirlpool but water itself.* The whirlpool is just a specific *pattern* of water movement that reflects, first, a localization of that water within the stream and, second, a 'filtering out' of other water molecules. When I talk of the brain as an image in mind, which reflects a localization of

Figure 3. A whirlpool in a stream is a metaphor for a brain in the medium of mind.

contents of mind, I mean something very analogous to the whirlpool in the stream. *There is nothing to the brain but mind, yet it is a concrete and identifiable image of the localization of mind,* just like a whirlpool is a concrete and identifiable image of the localization of water in the stream. You can point at the brain and say 'Here is a brain!' Moreover, just like the whirlpool can be said to 'filter out' the water molecules that do not get trapped in it, we can say that the brain 'filters out' the aspects of reality – that is, experiences – that do not fall within its own boundaries.

As such, to say that the brain *generates* mind is as absurd as to say that a whirlpool generates water! To say that the brain is the *cause* of consciousness is as absurd as to say that lightning is the cause of atmospheric electric discharge. Lightning is merely how atmospheric electric discharge *looks,* not the cause of it. Do you see what I mean? The brain is a partial *image* of the process of consciousness localization, *as viewed from a second-person perspective,* in exactly the same way that flames are a partial image of the process of combustion, as viewed from the outside. In the same way that the patterns and colors of flames correlate well with the inner-workings of the process of combustion, measured brain activity correlates well with the first-person view of consciousness – that is, direct experience.

Notice that understanding the brain as a partial *image* of the process of consciousness localization eliminates the 'hard problem of consciousness' entirely: the correlations between brain states and mind states are explained by understanding the former to be merely a partial image of the latter as perceived from a second-person perspective. There is no attempt to reduce mind to objective brain activity 'outside mind,' so there is no 'hard problem' at all. The brain and its processes, *as images in mind,* are of exactly the same nature as any other subjective experience. There is no need to magically derive experience from something outside experience because there is no need to postulate anything outside experience to begin with. *The brain is an experience, an image in mind of a certain process of mind.*

In the whirlpool metaphor the *medium* of mind is represented by water. The *contents* of mind – that is, particular subjective experiences – are represented by *the particular movements* of water molecules as they flow. The flow of each water molecule in the stream represents a coherent subjective experience in time, whether the molecule is trapped in the whirlpool or not. For simplicity, we will assume that all water molecules in the stream are moving and, as such, represent experiences. The metaphor leaves the possibility open, however, for there to be parts of the medium of mind where there is *no* experience: think, for instance, of a puddle where water is entirely at rest. In this case, there is still the *medium* of mind, but it comprises no *contents*. As such, the *medium* of mind – water itself – always entails the *potential* for subjective experience. If water is at rest, there is only the potential. If water begins to move, there is actual experience. The *qualities* of the experience are represented by the particular *pattern* of this movement, such as trajectory, speed, oscillations, etc. Notice also that *there is nothing to the contents of mind but the medium of mind itself:* it's all just water. Ultimately, the only thing that exists is the medium of mind – or, to make it simpler, *mind.* Particular experiences – that is, particular contents of mind – are just *mind in movement.*

The whirlpool represents a partial localization of the flow of experiences in the stream. This localization demarcates a centralized, local perspective: the very center of the whirlpool, the vantage point from which each one of us witnesses our personal subset of the contents of mind. This is, after all, how we ordinarily experience reality: from a particular vantage point in the middle of the vortex of experiences swirling around us. Ordinarily, we are only aware of the flow of water molecules captured in our respective whirlpool, not the broader stream outside.

Indeed, by its very structure and dynamics, the whirlpool of mind 'filters out' of itself most subjective experiences unfolding in nature. In the metaphor, these experiences are represented by the flow of the water molecules that do *not* get trapped in the vortex of the whirlpool, but instead remain free to flow across the entire length of the stream. In the terminology of analytical psychology, this would correspond to our 'collective unconscious,'[98] an unfathomably large part of the contents of mind, shared by all humans, which ordinarily doesn't penetrate egoic awareness.

We will leave it to Chapter 5 to explain how and why the experiences represented by the water molecules *not* captured in the whirlpool, *although still in mind,* become somehow 'unconscious' from the point-of-view of the ego.

The mind-body problem revisited

In Chapter 2 we've seen that subjective experience can be influenced, sometimes dramatically, by physical interference with the brain. Examples of this are alcohol intoxication, psychiatric drugs, brain trauma as a consequence of injury or illness, etc. All these things clearly alter one's cognition, state of mind, and how one generally experiences reality. At the extreme, subjective experience can be permanently altered by brain injury or illness leading to physical death. So how can we account for this in the context of the whirlpool metaphor?

Notice that a whirlpool is a fragile process that can be easily disrupted through external physical intervention. If the flow of water upstream is disrupted, causing it to become turbulent and irregular, the patterns of flow within a whirlpool downstream will be noticeably affected. If the brain is a whirlpool of mind, the patterns of whose flow determine the qualities of subjective experience, then physical interference with the brain *should indeed* alter subjective experience insofar as it changes such patterns; that is, insofar as it messes with the whirlpool. External interference with normal brain function is akin to a turbulent flow upstream.

A whirlpool is, to a degree, a self-sustaining process: it is its own existence that creates some of the conditions necessary for it to continue to exist; for instance, by creating pressure gradients in the water flow surrounding it. So if the stream becomes too turbulent, the whirlpool may be disrupted to the point of no longer being able to maintain itself. It then dissipates and doesn't reform even after the flow has stabilized again. Transposing this to the case of the brain, it is entirely expectable that too severe a physical intervention would lead to irreversible damage: the 'whirlpool' that is the living brain is disrupted to the point of not being able to maintain itself.

Even permanent changes to the brain that are caused by external physical intervention, but do not lead to death, can be easily placed in the context of the whirlpool metaphor. Take, for instance, the case of people who had their *corpus callosum* – the structure that connects the two hemispheres of the brain – physically severed by surgery. These individuals are reported to have two separate centers of consciousness, as if they had become two different individuals.[99] In the context of the metaphor, this could be understood as a delicate (as any surgery is!) disturbance of the upstream flow that succeeded in gently splitting one downstream whirlpool into two smaller, neighboring ones.

Another thing to consider is this: when I say that the brain is like a whirlpool in the stream of mind, I am implying a correspondence – a mapping – between the qualities of subjective experience and the patterns of flow within this whirlpool. If an active brain is merely a partial image of these patterns of flow, the implication may sound entirely analogous to the materialist position that experience must map one-to-one onto measurable parameters of brain processes. Yet, in Chapter 2, I argued precisely that this mapping, while being superficially there in the form of high-level neural correlates of consciousness, breaks down when we look more carefully into the details and circumstances. Therefore, one may think that my argument in Chapter 2 defeats the whirlpool metaphor just as much as it defeats materialism. This is not so for at least two reasons.

The first reason is the following: materialism inverts the situation by taking the *image* of the phenomenon – that is, the brain – to be primary, to be the *source* of the phenomenon, instead of one of its *results*. The peculiar consequence of this inversion is that, for materialists, there cannot be anything to the phenomenon of experience other than what can be seen in its image. In other words, the mapping between experiences and neural processes has to be *complete* and *unambiguous*, for neural processes aren't seen as mere images, but as the very source of experience. This is what I sought to defeat in Chapter 2. Notice that the materialist position here is analogous to saying that there cannot be anything to combustion other than what is visible in the accompanying flames; or that there cannot be anything to atmospheric electric discharge other than what is visible in lightning. It is as though materialists interpreted lightning as the source of electric discharge, as opposed to how electric discharge looks. Do you see the peculiar inversion of reasoning here? The brain is not the source of localized experience; it is how localized experience looks from a second-person perspective.

The whirlpool metaphor entails that the brain is a *partial image* of the process of consciousness localization, not the *sole cause* of conscious experience. Unlike a cause, an image does *not* need to be complete or unambiguous, in the sense that it doesn't need to capture in itself every aspect of the process it reflects. For instance, when we look at another person we see an *image* that reflects the other person's life processes. But we cannot see every aspect of these processes: what is going on under her skin, the molecular details of her metabolism, or even what the backside of the person looks like if the person is facing us. So, while the image *correlates* fairly well with the life processes it reflects –

after all, we *can* see if the person is severely ill, or upset, or starving, or jubilant, or tanned, etc. – it is not *complete* in capturing every aspect of such life processes. There are high-level correlations, but not a fully accessible one-to-one mapping.

It is true that, according to idealism, everything in nature must be in mind. So there is a sense in which all qualities of any subjective experience must be available in the broader medium of mind. And indeed they are, at least in the mind of the person who has the experience! But idealism does *not* require that all the details of a person's experiences be *also* available from a second-person perspective – that is, as an image perceivable by another person, by another 'whirlpool' of mind. As a matter of fact, the whirlpool metaphor entails that what we perceive in ordinary awareness is a 'filtered down' version of the images available in the broader medium of mind. It is no wonder, then, that the brain we can see and study, *as a 'filtered down' image in awareness*, is but a *partial* image of the process of consciousness localization. Therefore, it is entirely reasonable to expect to find high-level *correlations* between this incomplete image, on the one hand, and the qualities of subjective experience, on the other hand. These correlations have been found empirically and, as we have seen in Chapter 2, materialists often use them as evidence that the mind is nothing but the brain. But, unlike materialism, the whirlpool metaphor does *not* require a strict and complete one-to-one correspondence in all cases, for it accepts this image to be incomplete. As it turns out, evidence indicates precisely that.

The discussion above makes clear that an implication of the whirlpool metaphor, because of its filtering aspect, is that the world we perceive in ordinary awareness isn't necessarily causally closed; that is, that we may be fundamentally unable to explain everything in nature in terms of the stuff we ordinarily perceive. Indeed, as I argued in Chapter 6 of my earlier book *Rationalist Spirituality*, science today is nowhere near showing that the material world is causally closed. Moreover, as argued in

Chapter 1, we have no reason to believe that the perceptual and cognitive apparatuses of our physical bodies would have evolved to capture *all* of reality. It is perfectly conceivable that there are entire universes unavailable to ordinary awareness – comprising the flow of experiences that never get caught in the whirlpool – but which, nonetheless, can have subtle causal influence on the world we ordinarily see. If this is so, one can speculate that this influence expresses itself through the more delicate and subtle aspects of our physical reality, like molecular-level metabolism and brain function.

Does the acknowledgment that we do not ordinarily perceive all relevant aspects of reality mean that the whirlpool formulation casts doubt on itself? Does it mean that it is just as self-defeating as materialism? No. For making fewer assumptions about reality, the whirlpool formulation is more robust than materialism. Moreover, *materialism relies almost entirely on perception and very little on introspection.* Therefore, if one cannot trust the perceptual data, one cannot trust materialism. The whirlpool formulation, on the other hand, relies equally on perception *and* introspection. It assesses perceptual data more critically and within a broader context. It takes into account not only what is perceived, but also the *perceiver* and the *process of perception* as a holistic and integrated system. It asks: How does what I see relate to who I am? Who am I in the context of what I see? What does it mean to 'see'? How does 'seeing' relate to who I am? How does 'seeing' relate to what I see? What conclusions can I safely extract on the basis of this interplay? And so on. This will be further substantiated and become clearer over the next sections and chapters.

The second reason why my argument in Chapter 2 does not defeat the whirlpool metaphor is this: it is true that the metaphor, like materialism, entails a strong correlation between the qualities of experience and parameters of neural processes, *but only under ordinary – that is, highly localized – states of consciousness.* In other words, when the consciousness of a subject is well-localized and the brain is operating regularly, the whirlpool metaphor does require some correspondence between mind states and brain states – albeit, as argued above, not as much or as strictly as materialism. However, unlike materialism, the whirlpool metaphor predicts that this correspondence breaks upon a partial or temporary de-localization of consciousness caused by reduction of brain function. After all, if brain function is the image of consciousness *localization,* then a *reduction* of brain function must, of course, be the image of a *de*-localization of consciousness! As such, the examples of transpersonal experiences mentioned in Chapter 2 can be explained as a disturbance and partial dissolution of the whirlpool, leading to a partial release of the center of consciousness into the broader stream of mind. Death, in this context, would be a complete and irreversible version of this release.

The knot metaphor

Let us try another analogy to deepen our intuition of this. Think of the brain as a 'knot' that mind ties on itself. Indeed, a whirlpool is a kind of single-loop knot that water ties on itself and, thereby, restricts its own movement along a simple circular trajectory. A single-loop knot is the simplest there is. Perhaps one could imagine the nervous system of a roundworm (*C. elegans*), with its 302 neurons, as a single-loop knot of mind that is extremely restrictive to consciousness. The flow of mind in such a loop is trapped into one of the simplest trajectories possible. As nervous systems become more complex, the constraints of the filter relax; more loops are added to the knot; complex tangles emerge. Although the flow of mind is still restricted to the localization system, it now has more room to take on more complex trajectories.

Extrapolating this line of thinking, the broadest nervous system would be one the size of the universe itself, so the trajectories entailed by the countless loops of its unfathomably complex 'knot' would be co-extensive with the degrees of freedom of all existence. But this amounts to saying that such ultimate nervous system would *be* the universe, in the same way that a whirlpool the size of the stream would *be* the stream (a circular one). This brings us neatly back to our conclusion in Chapter 2: the broadest nervous system – as far as the freedom, breadth, and depth of consciousness in it – is *no* nervous system at all, in the same way that a whirlpool that *is* the stream basically does not exist as anything other than the stream itself. The ultimate breadth of mind is achieved when its flow is not limited by the brain that captures and 'filters' it down. Does it mean that there is no point to life as human beings with filtered awareness? There certainly is, and it's extraordinarily significant. But let's leave this angle for the next chapters.

Like the image of a whirlpool in water, a process by means of which mind limits and localizes its own flow should also produce an *image* in mind. It is thus entirely unsurprising that there is such a thing as a brain. If you contemplate it with some poetic license, you will see that the very structure of the brain evokes the idea of complex knots that somehow capture the flow of mind in a closed tangle. As a matter of fact, we can go one level deeper in this analysis than mere appearances and poetic interpretations: since we know something about the neural correlates of consciousness, we can do some sanity checks to see if this notion of the brain as a kind of self-limiting knot in the fabric of mind is consistent with empirical observations. In the next chapter we will do precisely that. For now, bear with me a little longer.

Going beyond the brain

The brain is an integral part of a larger and interdependent system we call a body. Without the rest of the body the brain could not perform its function. Therefore, it is not only the brain that is a partial image of the whirlpool of mind, *but the whole body.* The entire body is integral to the localization mechanism of the contents of mind; the 'filter of mind' that we talked about in Chapter 2.

But wait. We cannot stop here. The body is inextricably connected to its environment. It draws food, water, air, and sunlight from it. It releases waste products into it. We cannot look upon the body as an independent, self-contained system.

Do you see where I am going with this? Everything – the entire universe – is just the flow of the contents of mind. The body – *as part of the universe and, thus, also a content of mind* – is not separate from mind at large in the same way that a whirlpool is not separate from the stream. Indeed, the whirlpool is just a local *pattern* in the flow. You can't take a body out of the broader medium of mind for exactly the same reason that you can't lift a whirlpool out of the stream!

The water that flows around the whirlpool, without being captured in it, forms currents and pressure gradients without which the whirlpool would dissolve. Despite not being part of the whirlpool, these currents are absolutely necessary for its existence in the same way that the environment is absolutely necessary for the existence of the body. *The whirlpool grows from the broader flow of water just as the body grows from the broader medium of mind.* Reality *is* mind.

Universes and neural processes

Let us now review and illustrate, with a thought experiment, some key elements of what has already been discussed. Imagine a neuroscientist looking at a computer screen wirelessly connected to a brain scanner. The screen displays the neural processes associated with the inner life of a volunteer;[100] that is, the *neural correlates of consciousness* we spoke of in Chapter 2. These neural processes are the images of certain internal dynamics – currents and undulations – of the volunteer's whirlpool of mind as it swirls.

Imagine also that wearable scanner technology is used, which allows the volunteer to wear the brain scanner 24 hours a day, throughout his entire life. This way, the neuroscientist can see *all* neural processes that *ever* unfold inside the volunteer's head; all the relevant internal dynamics of the volunteer's whirlpool. What the neuroscientist sees corresponds, thus, to the subjective universe of the volunteer.

Yet, it is obvious that neural processes displayed on a computer screen cannot *be* the universe the volunteer lives in. After all, while the volunteer and the neuroscientist share the same universe, there is much more to the neuroscientist's reality than neural processes on a computer screen! Clearly, thus, there must be more to the universe the volunteer lives in than what is captured by the brain scanner he wears.

Materialism and the idealist formulation I am putting forward here deal with this question in completely different ways. Let us look at it.

Materialism claims that the electrochemical processes in the volunteer's brain are merely a *partial copy* – an incomplete internal representation – of the real universe the volunteer lives in. This real universe lies outside the volunteer's mind and is much broader than the neural processes displayed in the neuro-scientist's computer screen. It is this real universe outside mind that is shared by both the volunteer and the neuroscientist.

But since we are operating under idealism, we cannot use the same argument. Under idealism, the world of your ordinary awareness is not a copy of some abstract universe outside mind; *it is the actual world*. To us, in this book, there is no reality other than what is experienced in some part of the broad medium of mind, and what is experienced *is* the actual reality. Yet, clearly, neural processes on a computer screen cannot possibly be the whole story about the volunteer's universe.

The key here is to notice that, under idealism, there is merely a *correspondence* between the neural processes and the volunteer's inner life. Let's clarify this with another thought experiment.

Universes and images

Imagine that you are talking to a friend on the other side of the Earth via internet video link. Your friend sees a two-dimensional, relatively low resolution image of you on her computer screen. She knows that the image *corresponds* to you and may even think of the image as *being* you. *But the image is not you by any stretch of the imagination.* After all, you are on the other side of the planet! Clear, isn't it?

Now transpose this idea to our thought experiment above. The neural processes the neuroscientist sees are just images that *correspond partially* to the subjective world of the volunteer. But they are *not* that subjective world, in the same way that the low-resolution image on your friend's computer screen is not you. *The neural processes are just the way the volunteer's world looks from the vantage point of the neuroscientist.* Just as most of the information, nuance, and concreteness of *you* is lost in the image displayed on your friend's computer screen, most of the information, nuance, and concreteness of the volunteer's subjective universe is lost in the image we call neural processes.

A neural process is an image, but the image is not the phenomenon it represents. The image is just how the phenomenon appears when observed from a second-person vantage point. The world of the volunteer *appears* to the neuroscientist as chains of neural firings because the localization process of the volunteer's consciousness must appear to others in some form, just as combustion must appear as flames or coagulation as clots. But those chains of neural firings are *not* the volunteer's world, in the same way that a clot *isn't* the process of coagulation. The chains of neural firings are just a partial image of the volunteer's world that retains certain correspondences with it.

Multiple communicating whirlpools

The neuroscientist and the volunteer are two different people partaking in space-time. Each has his own 'field' of awareness. Therefore, according to the whirlpool metaphor, *each must correspond to a different whirlpool in the broader stream of mind*. See Figure 4. The same applies to every living human being: each corresponds to a different whirlpool. Now, every whirlpool represents the subjective world of its respective human being. Ordinarily, the neuroscientist is only aware of contents of mind trapped in his own whirlpool. Similarly, the volunteer is, ordinarily, only aware of contents of mind trapped in his respective whirlpool.

Yet, the neuroscientist can see the volunteer's neural processes. Therefore, contents of mind consisting of *images* of the volunteer's subjective world must be trapped in the neuroscientist's whirlpool. Not only that: the neuroscientist could also see the volunteer himself, in person, shake his hand and talk to him. Therefore, contents of mind corresponding to images of the volunteer's entire body and actions must also be trapped in the

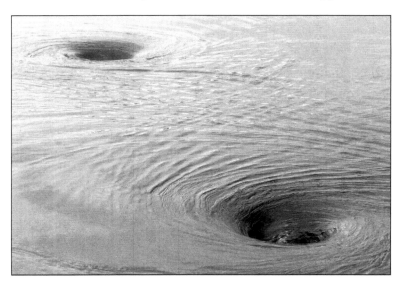

Figure 4. Multiple 'communicating' whirlpools in a stream.

93

neuroscientist's whirlpool. Clearly, *there is some form of communi-cation – information transfer – across whirlpools of mind.*

In the context of our metaphor, one simple way to visualize how this communication takes place is as follows: imagine that one steadily pours some color dye in the middle of a first whirlpool in the stream, thereby forming a dyed streamline. The dyed streamline swirls around a few times and acquires an undulation determined by the patterns of flow inside the first whirlpool. Eventually it escapes the first whirlpool, *carrying the undulation with it.* This now undulating dyed streamline eventually reaches a second whirlpool where it again gets trapped. But now, as it gets trapped, its undulations influence the internal dynamics of the second whirlpool. This way, *information about the dynamics inside the first whirlpool has been carried into the second whirlpool.* What happens in the second whirlpool is now partially determined by what happened in the first whirlpool. This is a way to think about how people can see each other, communicate with each other, and peek into each other's brains to see their neural processes: *undulations released in the broader medium of mind carry information across whirlpools* – that is, across people. With a bit of imagination, you can see the two whirlpools in Figure 4 'communicating' through undulating streamlines going across them.

In current scientific language these undulations are called photons (light), or air vibrations (sounds), or particular scent molecules (odors), etc. Ultimately, they are all disturbances of an electromagnetic field picked up by our sense organs. The difference is that materialism sees these photons, air vibrations, and scent molecules as objective entities existing outside, and independent of, mind. According to the whirlpool metaphor, on the other hand, they are just *undulations – disturbances – of the medium of mind itself,* capable of carrying information across different whirlpools in the stream. Mathematically, things could be modeled in exactly the same way as they are in materialism:

according to Maxwell's equations of electromagnetism, for instance. But the ontological *interpretation* of this modeling is radically different between idealism and materialism.

According to the whirlpool metaphor, the stimuli from the 'outside' world that you receive through your sense organs – in the form of sights, sounds, odors, etc. – are undulations propagating through the broader stream of mind that penetrate the whirlpool of your personal awareness and, thus, influence its internal dynamics. One can discern these 'external' undulations in the broader stream in Figure 4, as they penetrate multiple whirlpools. *Your sense organs are partial images of the particular entry-points of your whirlpool through which these undulations can come in.* What you see aren't photons from a world outside mind, but undulations of the broader stream of mind that you trap, and which then swirl around the knot of your inner life.

Your very presence and actions, as a knot of consciousness, in the broader medium of mind cause disturbances in it in the same way that you cause ripples on water if you step on a puddle. Just as ripples propagate out from their point of origin, the disturbances caused by your presence and actions in the medium of mind also propagate far and wide. Other people perceive you through these disturbances – these *undulations* – that spread out from your location and, eventually, reach and get captured by other whirlpools. The undulations you release carry information about you in the same manner that the dyed streamline leaving the first whirlpool carries information about it. But they *aren't* you, in the same way that the dyed streamline leaving the first whirlpool *isn't* the first whirlpool.

This way, unlike what materialism entails, a neural process *isn't* the subjective experience it correlates with, but merely a *partial image of it* released as undulations into the broader stream of mind. There is a certain *correspondence* between the two, in the sense that there is also a correspondence between the tracks left behind by an animal and the animal's gait. But the tracks aren't the gait, in the same way that the neural processes the neuroscientist sees *aren't* the experiences of the volunteer. When materialists like Daniel Dennett[101] say that a person's experiences *are* the chains of neural firings in her brain *they are mistaking the tracks for the gait; the imprinted image for the phenomenon.*

Is an 'external' region of mind equivalent to an external world?

According to the whirlpool metaphor, what we normally think of as the 'external world' is global undulations propagating through the broader stream of mind, which penetrate our respective whirlpools through the entry-points we call our sense organs. See Figure 4 again. Trees, stars, other people, your dog, all are dynamic mental processes that cause disturbances in the broader medium of mind – in the form of those global undulations – in the same way that a moving boat leaves a wake behind. To anticipate a topic that will be explored more in depth in Chapter 6, the reason we seem to share the same world is that these undulations, like waves spreading in multiple directions, penetrate multiple whirlpools concurrently, injecting the same – or similar – information into each one of them. As such, the undulations are stimuli that come from a part of the medium of mind that is *external* to that which we think of as ourselves. You may then ask: isn't it exactly what materialism says? Doesn't this confirm the existence of an external universe that we apprehend through the stimuli captured by our sense organs?

The answer is a categorical 'no.' Bear with me now, because this is a crucial point. I am not disputing the general intuition that there exists a world outside our *personal awareness*; a world we don't identify with and do not seem to have any control over. This is obvious to even casual observation, so it would be silly to deny it. *But I do deny that such world exists outside mind.* The whirlpool metaphor shows that there are global stimuli – originating from regions of the medium of mind external to our respective whirlpools – that penetrate our ordinary awareness in the form of undulations. But that does not require the existence of an abstract world devoid of qualities, fundamentally outside and independent of mind itself. Do you see the crucial difference?

Let us belabor this point a bit because it is important. Think of it in terms of a regular dream: in a dream you have a dreamed-up 'avatar' – a character – that you identify yourself with, but you also see a seemingly external world with trees, buildings, and even other people. You do not identify with that 'external' world of your dreams. In fact, during the dream, you think you *inhabit* it just like you think you inhabit the 'real' world. Yet, clearly, the dreamed-up world is generated by your mind. It's not outside your mind. It's just that it is generated by a part of your mind that you do not identify with or have control over during the dream. Summarizing: there is a part of your mind that you identify with as an avatar in your dream and another, seemingly separate part of your mind that generates the 'outside world' of the dream, in which your avatar lives. So far so good, right?

Now, *clearly there is a form of communication between these two parts of your dreaming mind.* After all, your dreamed-up avatar *experiences and interacts with* the seemingly external world of the dream. Therefore, in every ordinary dream there are two regions of mind *communicating* with each other: one you think of as yourself, while the other feels external to you. The point of the whirlpool metaphor is to illustrate that *the same thing can be happening right now,* in your waking reality, as you read this. Waking reality is itself a dream generated by mind. Like in every dream, there is a part of the stream of mind that you identify with and feel you can control – the whirlpool – and there is another part of mind that you don't think of as yourself – the broader stream *around* the whirlpool – but which communicates with you through undulations eventually caught within your whirlpool. The structures of the whirlpool that are configured to capture these incoming undulations *appear to us* as skin, eyes, ears, noses, and tongues. Our sense organs are *the image in consciousness* of structures of the whirlpool that are open to the broader stream of mind, thereby allowing undulations in. Just like most water molecules in the stream never get caught within the whirlpool, most undulations of the broader medium of mind never get caught by our sense organs.

So yes, the whirlpool metaphor entails that there are 'external' regions of the medium of mind, in the sense that there are regions that you do not identify yourself with. *But it does not entail that there is an abstract 'shadow' universe outside mind, for the same reason that the 'external' world of your dreams does not entail anything happening outside your dreaming mind.* If you think that this is a minor difference with respect to materialism, think again! The implications are dramatically different.

For instance, if reality is a kind of shared dream, *then it is your body that is in the dream, not the dream in the body.* Therefore, there is absolutely no reason to think that your consciousness will end when your body dissolves into an entropic soup; at least no more reason than you have to believe that you physically die when your avatar in a dream dies within the dream. When your avatar dies in a dream the real you just wakes up in another state of mind. But if your consciousness were indeed just an epiphenomenon of matter in a universe fundamentally outside mind, as materialism would have you believe, then it would be all over when you died. Moreover, my formulation of idealism can explain the phenomenon of de-localized consciousness discussed at length in Chapter 2, while materialism cannot. Also, as we shall see later, my formulation of idealism can explain psychic phenomena, while materialism cannot. There is, thus, an enormous practical difference between materialism and what I am trying to get across with these metaphors, a difference that is exceedingly relevant to one's worldview.

I am *not* suggesting that the reason to believe in my case is that it provides reassurance about life after death or cool psychic phenomena. That would be intellectually dishonest. The reasons to believe in what this book puts forward are: that it makes good sense; that it is well substantiated by empirical evidence; that it is consistent with all observations and, in fact, explains more of them than the materialist alternative; and, finally, that it is also the most parsimonious metaphysical model. I just said what I said above in order to make clear to you that, while the whirlpool metaphor acknowledges that there is a region of the medium of mind that *feels* external to each one of us – just like regular dreams demonstrate – that is not the same as materialism by any stretch of the imagination.

Culture has it precisely the wrong way around

Notice that the whirlpool and knot metaphors imply something very close to our ordinary, everyday sense of reality: the world we see is the *actual* world, not some kind of hallucinated copy. And the 'world outside' is *indeed* outside the part of mind that we identify ourselves with. Yet, when people hear about the basic definitions of materialism and idealism, their first impulse is to reverse the implications: to think of idealism as entailing that reality is inside our heads, while believing materialism to say that the world we experience is outside ourselves. *Well, it's exactly the other way around!* It is materialism that states that the world we experience is entirely within our heads, stars and all. And it is idealism that states that it is our heads that are inside the world we experience. Do you see the inversion? How it came to pass that our culture – even, and perhaps most notably, the intellectual elite – could reverse the logic of the situation so dramatically baffles me.

Ironically, the intuitive appeal of materialism is based on a kind of perverse intellectual game of steal-and-switch: our culture mistakenly attributes to materialism the intuitiveness of idealism, while attributing to idealism the absurdity of materialism. Go figure.

Give this some thought

Despite my claim that idealism is the only metaphysics consistent
with our most innate intuitions about reality, one should not
underestimate how deeply ingrained in our thinking materialism
has become. Therefore, I invite you to think about the metaphors
discussed in this chapter over the coming days. You will need to
allow them to sink in, so you can take them for their *essence*, not
their superficial appearance. After all, neither do human bodies
look like whirlpools, nor do whirlpools have eyes, ears, or noses!
It takes some time to find the right way to match the
metaphorical images with the forms of everyday experience, so to
grok what the metaphors are really trying to convey. It's a matter
of nurturing a certain *way of thinking* about everything you
perceive and feel, in light of the ideas developed in this chapter.
The difficulty lies in escaping the way of thinking that education
and culture have already imposed on you and which you've had
a lifetime to get used to and take for granted.

A new metaphysics does not require a new physics

One final comment is needed at this point. As I mentioned above,
this chapter is about developing a new *way of thinking* about
reality, an exercise that we will continue in the next chapters. As
such, this book is not meant to offer new science, but new ways
of *interpreting* science from an ontological perspective. After all,
science itself – as discussed in Chapter 1 – is ontologically neutral
and does not entail any particular interpretation of its models.
The modeling of Maxwell's equations applies equally well to
electromagnetic fields in a world outside mind or to 'undulations' of the stream of mind.

Neither is new science necessary, for the worldview laid out in
this book does not contradict current scientific models. It only
contradicts what many scientists, and the intellectual elite in

general, *make of these models* as far as building their worldviews. One should, therefore, not expect me to offer an alternative physics here. The ideas carried in this book do not, in any way, invalidate our existing observations and models of the patterns and regularities of nature. They do not contradict physical theory but, instead, offer an interpretative framework in terms of which physical theory can be looked upon. Under this framework, the patterns and regularities captured by the models of physics are the patterns and regularities of the tapestry of mind itself, as it flows and swirls.

Chapter 5

A Mercurial Metaphor

As mentioned in the preceding chapter, the whirlpool metaphor, as currently laid out, has a weakness: if all reality is a set of experiences flowing in the stream of *one* mind, *why do the localized points-of-view corresponding to each whirlpool 'forget' everything outside their respective whirlpools?* After all, it is all going on within the same mind! Indeed, a whirlpool-like localization mechanism is only sufficient to explain *differences in the way we experience,* on the one hand, the contents of mind that penetrate the whirlpool through the sense organs and, on the other hand, those that do *not.* But it is not sufficient to explain our *lack of experience* of the latter. Therefore, to validate the argument thus far, we need to extend the metaphor a bit. Before getting to that, however, I want to try and make sure that you are convinced that there is indeed a problem here that needs resolving.

Potential differences between the way we experience contents of mind flowing respectively inside and outside the whirlpool are due to the respective differences in trajectories of flow, which represent the qualities of experience. These differences suffice to explain the emergence of local perspectives on reality, correlated with particular locations in space and time, and the illusion of personal identity. But they do not suffice to explain our inability to experience, *in some way that transcends our sense organs,* what's going on *outside* our respective whirlpools. Since all experiences are *in one and the same mind,* the whirlpool metaphor entails that we should all, in principle, have a form of *extrasensory perception* – qualitatively different from perception through the sense organs – of *all* experiences flowing in the broader stream. The metaphor implies that *we should all, in principle, have complete, non-local clairvoyance of everything going on across time, space, and beyond, while still preserving a strong sense of individual identity and having local perception through our sense organs.* Yet, it is an incontestable fact that we do not ordinarily have total clairvoyance through extrasensory perception, this being what remains to be explained.

Here is an analogy to help clarify the problem yet further: we are all aware of *both* the central, localized focus of our vision *and* of our broader, non-local peripheral vision *at the same time.* You can verify this yourself right now: fix your gaze on an object relatively near you, like your hand extended in front of your face. You will be able to see both your hand – in focus – *and* the wall or objects behind your hand – out of focus – *concurrently.* The center of your gaze is analogous to the perspective from the center of the whirlpool, while your peripheral vision is analogous to the extrasensory perception of the non-localized experiences flowing in the broader stream of mind. Why have we lost the latter? A localization of certain contents of mind brings them into a kind of 'focus,' but does not explain our amnesia of all the rest. *Why have we, as localized points-of-view of mind, become blind to our 'peripheral vision' of everything outside the whirlpool?* Why have we become 'unconscious' of so much of what is going on in mind?

Answering all these questions is the focus of the present chapter. The previous chapter explained the relationship between ourselves and what we ordinarily perceive as the *'exterior'* world. In this chapter, on the other hand, the challenge is to explain the different qualities and levels of what we ordinarily perceive as the *'interior'* world: our subjective inner lives, including what analytical psychology calls the 'ego,' the 'personal unconscious,' and the 'collective unconscious.'

To avoid confusion, I will stick to the following terminological convention from now on: I will consistently use the term 'mind' in the broad idealist sense, meaning the unified medium of all existence. Whenever I want to refer specifically to the segment of mind corresponding to an individual, human or animal, I will use the traditional term 'psyche' instead. Naturally, mind includes psyche, but not the other way around. Also, as you probably already noticed, I consistently write the term 'unconscious' between quotes. The reason for this will become clear in what follows.

Consciousness and the 'unconscious'

We intuitively associate our psyches with the contents of consciousness. Whatever I am not conscious of – we tend to think – is not within the scope of my psyche. Consciousness seems to be the *sine qua non* of the psyche, even a synonym for it. Yet, since the late 19th century, depth psychology has been talking about an 'unconscious' part of the psyche.[102] Modern consensus on the issue entails that, in fact, the majority of our psyches are indeed 'unconscious.'[103]

If something is in the psyche but is not in consciousness, where exactly is it? Materialist neuroscience offers an explanation: 'unconscious' processes are neural processes that, for whatever reason, do not become conscious, but still exist as material phenomena in the brain. As such, the psyche is defined as the collection of electrochemical processes taking place in the nervous system, only a subset of which, somehow, magically becomes conscious. Ignoring the need for a magical step for a moment, this view seems logical: we all know experientially that many neural processes seem to fall outside our awareness, like those that keep our hearts beating, control our breathing when we are not thinking of it, regulate digestion, etc. However, for this explanation to work, a neural process would need to exist fundamentally *outside* mind and then somehow *cause* mind. As we've seen in the previous chapters, this is unreasonable.

How do we, then, explain the 'unconscious' in our idealist formulation? How can an individual's psyche – merely a localized point-of-view of the broad medium of mind – become seemingly disconnected from other experiences unfolding in the very mind it is a part of?

It cannot. And here is what I will argue below: *there is actually no real unconscious.* As we've seen in Chapter 3, many materialists absurdly suggest that consciousness is a kind of illusion, a suggestion that immediately contradicts itself by negating the very consciousness where the purported illusion should exist in the first place. Well, I submit to you that *it is the unconscious that is an illusion,* albeit an extraordinarily powerful one. Notice that, unlike the materialist suggestion, my position raises no contradictions: it is consciousness that is having the illusion of the 'unconscious.' I will argue that our intuition that consciousness is the *sine qua non* of mind is actually correct: there is nothing in mind that is not in consciousness, even though consciousness may delude itself about what it actually comprises. If I am right, then there is a sense in which you, I, and everyone else in the world are all conscious of everything unfolding in the theater of existence right now, as you read these words. *We are all conscious, at all times, of absolutely everything that exists in time, space, and beyond.*

At first, this will sound absurd to you. But the perceived absurdity lies more in the ambiguities and lack of precision of ordinary language than in actuality. Once we carefully deconstruct my assertion above, contemplate what it means, and define some new language to talk about it more precisely, you will see that it is not absurd at all, not even unreasonable. Indeed, you may come to think of it as something very natural, which you can relate easily to your personal experiences in everyday life.

Egoic awareness is self-reflective

Let us carry out a little exercise in introspection right now. Consider your awareness of the book or electronic reader in your hands right now: in addition to perceiving the book itself, *you also consciously know that you are perceiving it.* Clearly, not only are you aware of the book, you are also aware that you are aware of it. And you can repeat this exercise recursively: aren't you *also* aware that you are aware that you are aware of the book? Surely you are. I think you can already guess where I am going with this: you are aware that you are aware ... that you are aware of whatever you are aware of. Each level of awareness becomes a seeming *object* of awareness one level higher, in a potentially infinite recursion of self-referential awareness.

The ability to turn conscious apprehension itself into an object of conscious apprehension is what fundamentally characterizes our ordinary state of consciousness. In fact, my claim is that this is what defines what psychology calls the 'ego': the ego is the part of our psyches that is recursively and self-referentially aware. Douglas Hofstadter explored this relationship between self-referential recursion and the ego in his book *I am a Strange Loop.*[104] Though Hofstadter did it from a materialist perspective, his observations are helpful for the argument I am trying to make here. Indeed, I believe a transposition of his argument onto an idealist framework would solve his argument's main contradictions and difficulties, including the 'hard problem of consciousness' that it falls prey to.

There is a very intuitive way to visualize this process of recursive, self-referential awareness: two mirrors facing each other. Each mirror reflects the image of the other, including its own image reflected on the other. See Figure 5. Each reflection can be seen as a step in the recursion of awareness, wherein an image becomes itself part of another image at a higher level, and that image part of another image at a yet higher level, and so forth. *Each image is both awareness at its own level and an object of awareness at a higher level.* I submit to you that egoic consciousness is analogous to these two mutually-facing mirrors: our ordinary awareness is *recursively self-reflective.*

Figure 5. Amplification through recursive self-reflection.

What the 'unconscious' really is

Because of this, any content of mind that falls within the field of self-reflectiveness of the ego becomes hugely *amplified*. Like the image in Figure 5, any experience that falls within the scope of the ego is recursively reflected on the mirrors of awareness until it creates an unfathomably intense mental imprint. I submit to you that most things you are ordinarily aware of, like the book or electronic reader in your hands right now, are amplified like that. You don't notice it simply because you have become accustomed to these levels of mental amplification to the point of taking them to be the norm. Think of it as the case of a teenager who listens to loud music so often that a reasonable volume level on the TV challenges his ability to hear. His notion of what constitutes normal volume has changed.

Now, if this is so, what happens to the experiences flowing in the broader medium of mind that do *not* fall within the scope of the ego? They do not get amplified at all. *Therefore, from the point-of-view of the ego, they become practically imperceptible!* This, in my view, is how we've come to speak of an 'unconscious' segment of the psyche. There is no unconscious; there are only regions of the medium of mind whose experiences, for not falling within the field of egoic self-reflectiveness, become *obfuscated* by whatever *does* fall within the scope of the ego.

Here is another analogy to help you develop an intuition for this. When you look up at a clear sky, at noon, you only see blue. You can't see the stars that, at night, would be unmistakably there. *Yet, the stars are all still there* and their light is still reaching your eyes, just like it would at night. You can't see them because they become *obfuscated* by the much stronger glare of the sun refracting on the atmosphere. The photons coming from distant stars are still there, interspersed throughout the many more photons emanating from atmospheric refraction. My view is that the 'unconscious' experiences flowing along the broader stream of mind are all still there in consciousness, at all times, *interspersed throughout the amplified contents of egoic awareness,* just like the photons from distant stars at noon. The contents of the 'unconscious' fit, so to speak, in the tiny gaps left *in between* the unfathomably stronger contents of self-reflective awareness. They are, in a way, just under our noses at all times.

As such, there is really no unconscious. But the result, in practice, is almost identical: the 'glare' of the contents of mind that fall within the field of self-reflective awareness obfuscates everything else, making it all practically invisible, just like the stars at noon. The experiences in the 'unconscious' aren't weak; they are regular undulations of mind. It's just that they fade in comparison to self-reflective amplification, almost disappearing in the interstices of the flow of egoic experiences.

Notice that this explanation eliminates any *absolute* difference between the conscious and 'unconscious' segments of mind. It all becomes a matter of *relative* amplification. Indeed, this is crucial: as we've seen in Chapter 2, explaining how consciousness can arise from something truly unconscious is an insoluble problem. It requires a magical step. In the framework of materialism, this problem expresses itself as the 'hard problem of consciousness.'[105] Even under idealism, if we were to acknowledge the existence of both conscious and unconscious segments of mind, an analogous problem would remain: by what magical step could an unconscious mental content suddenly become conscious? The question, however, disappears under the notion that the 'unconscious' is, in fact, conscious. It *appears* unconscious merely because of a *relative* difference in amplification with respect to other mental contents.

It is not so difficult to gain some direct intuition that this notion is indeed true. We have all had experiences that we know have been conscious, but yet felt unconscious. For instance: have you ever driven home from work one evening, mulling over your problems, just to suddenly find yourself at home having no idea how you got there? Obviously you were conscious of your driving, otherwise you wouldn't have made it home. But you were not fully *self-reflectively* aware of it. Instead, you were self-reflectively aware of your problems, which obfuscated the experience of driving and made it *seem* unconscious. Here is another example: for the past several minutes you have been 'unconscious' of your breathing. But at the very moment you read this, your breathing – the air flowing in and out, the movements of your diaphragm, the inflation of your lungs, etc. – rushes into your field of self-reflective awareness. Were you truly unconscious of your breathing a moment ago? Or were you merely unaware *that* you were conscious of your breathing?

These two examples illustrate but a very slight level of obfuscation of mental contents. The driving and the breathing were already on the edge of self-reflective awareness anyway, so we eventually figure it all out, as you just did regarding your breathing. However, extrapolating this line of thinking, it's easy to see that, if obfuscation were to become sufficiently stronger, we would never figure it out. Indeed, maybe this is precisely what's going on right now with respect to your 'unconscious'!

An ocean of quicksilver

How do we accommodate these new insights into our whirlpool metaphor? As we have seen in the previous chapter, the whirlpool metaphor allows us to explain the formation of localized points-of-view in the medium of mind as vortices in the flow of experience. This, in turn, explains the emergence of the illusion of individuality. But we now need to extend the metaphor to incorporate our insights from the previous section and explain, finally, why these localized points-of-view become seemingly amnesic of everything that doesn't fall within their respective vortices.

We will take a hint from the idea of mutually-facing mirrors and *postulate that mind, as a medium, is inherently reflective.* This postulate is well-grounded on introspection, as discussed above. To incorporate the inherent reflectivity of mind in our metaphor, we will replace water with quicksilver – that is, mercury. Mercury, although a liquid, is reflective like a mirror. See figure 6. Instead of a stream of water, we will think of the medium of mind as an ocean of mercury. Analogously to what we did before, we will model *experiences* as undulations – ripples – in this ocean of mercury. The particular patterns these ripples assume will represent the qualities of particular subjective experiences in the medium of mind. See Figure 7. Again, just like before, if the ocean of mercury is entirely at rest – that is, no ripples – then there is only the *potential* for experience.

Whirlpools can still form in the ocean of mercury. Most correspond to conscious entities that have not entirely lost connection with their 'unconscious' minds. One could speculate, for instance, about the extent to which social insects – like bees, termites, and ants – can still access a broader region of mind than that entailed by their individual whirlpools. After all, it is not quite clear how ant colonies, for instance, comprising millions of separate individuals, can behave as though they were coordinated by a kind of global ant 'overmind' spanning across individuals.[106] There is no question that individual ants have their own localized points-of-view and perspectives on reality. There is also no question that they are equipped with sense organs to allow certain undulations of the broader medium of mind into their respective whirlpools. But, in addition to that,

Figure 6. Mirror-like liquid mercury.

Figure 7. Ripples on an ocean of mercury.

one could speculate that they can access – through extrasensory means – a broader mental framework of which they are just a part. All these speculations can be cleanly accommodated by the regular whirlpool metaphor, as discussed in the previous chapter.

But now we need to incorporate *self-reflective* awareness, of the kind we experience as humans, in the metaphor. So here we go: notice that, although a whirlpool begins as a more-or-less flat circular pattern of water motion (see Figure 3 again), when this motion gathers sufficient momentum the center of the whirlpool sinks into itself like a hollow, spinning cone. See Figure 8.

Because we are now postulating that the medium of mind is inherently reflective – the whirlpool now forming in an ocean of liquid mercury, instead of water – *the internal surfaces of this cone will face each other and behave just like the mutually-facing mirrors of Figure 5:* they will reflect the part of the ocean of mercury directly across. There is a strong sense in which the formation of this hollow cone is entailed by the natural evolution of a whirlpool as it gathers momentum.

As mentioned above, experiences are ripples on the surface of the mercury, movements of the medium of mind. When a hollow cone is formed, these ripples can still propagate through the internal surfaces of the cone. As they propagate, their images are *reflected* on the opposite side of the cone. Moreover, the very reflections are also reflected back on the other side, and so on, just like the two mutually-facing mirrors of Figure 5.

Assume that the *reflection* of ripples is *also* registered by mind as an *experience*, not only the ripples themselves. So what you get on the inside of the hollow cone is a – potentially infinite – recursion of reflected ripples analogous to the recursion of reflected awareness of the ego. *A hollow, spinning cone at the center of a whirlpool in the ocean of mercury is, thus, a way of thinking about our self-reflective egoic awareness.* The faster the spinning motion, the more the cone sinks in; the more it sinks in, the more vertical its internal surfaces become; and the more vertical these surfaces become, the more optimally they face each other like mirrors, increasing self-reflective amplification. Egoic awareness is, as such, entailed by the natural evolution of the process of mind localization, increasing as it gathers momentum.

The ripples propagating through the interior surfaces of the cone are the original, primary experiences of reality, as seen from the perspective of the ego. As such, your primary conscious perception of the book or electronic reader in your hands right now – as well as of the room you're in, the other objects you see, etc. – are ripples traveling along the inside of the spinning cone

Figure 8. A whirlpool cone representing egoic awareness.

of mind that you call your ego. Your awareness that you are consciously perceiving the book is an image of those ripples reflected on another internal surface of the cone. Your awareness of your awareness that you are consciously perceiving the book is a reflection of the reflection of the primary ripples on an opposite surface, and so on. I guess you get the picture.

Notice that there is a clear but hard-to-pin-down difference between our primary conscious perception of something and the awareness *of* that conscious perception. For instance, your awareness that you are consciously perceiving the floor under your feet right now is not quite the same as the primary conscious perception of the floor the way, say, a cat would experience it. Yet, there is a clear *correspondence of form* between the two. After all, it feels very different to be aware of consciously perceiving the book in your hands, as opposed to being aware of consciously perceiving the floor. All this is captured in the spinning mercury cone metaphor: the primary conscious perception is an actual ripple on an internal surface of the cone. The awareness *of* this conscious perception is no longer a ripple, but a *reflected image* of the ripple on the opposite surface. Yet, there is an obvious correspondence of form between a ripple and its reflection, and both are registered by mind as mutually-reinforcing experiences.

To summarize, the idea behind the spinning mercury cone metaphor is that mind should be thought of as a medium inherently capable of reflecting itself like a mirror. Experiences happen when mind *moves*, as in the movement of ripples. The role of science is to find and model the patterns and regularities of the behavior of such ripples. When the ripples propagating in the medium of mind self-localize, as in when they form a flat whirlpool, an individual point-of-view emerges in mind, but connection with the broader medium is preserved. This could represent, for instance, the psyches of social insects like ants. Self-reflectiveness arises when the medium of mind arranges itself, according to some topological configuration, so that different segments of its surface face each other. Then, both ripples *and their reflections* are registered as experiences and egoic awareness arises. This is represented by the whirlpool gathering so much spinning momentum that its center sinks into itself, forming a hollow cone. The cone localizes the flow of the ripples just like the periphery of the whirlpool does, but *also* creates mutually-facing reflective surfaces. According to this metaphor, our egos correspond to these reflective spinning cones in the medium of mind.

Empirical support for the mutually-facing mirrors metaphor

If these ideas are correct, then the neural correlates of egoic experience are *the partial image*, as viewed from a second-person perspective, of a self-reflective configuration of the flow of mind. It is, thus, fair to expect a review of neuroscientific data to yield correspondences between the metaphor of mutually-facing mirrors – according to which conscious experiences bounce back-and-forth between two reflective mental surfaces – and empirical observations. And, as a matter of fact, there are indeed plenty of correspondences.

In a paper published in *Science* magazine, in May 2011,[107] neuroscientists in Belgium reported on an innovative experiment to identify the neural processes that correlate with conscious experience. It was already known that the frontoparietal cortex is an area of the brain associated with consciousness. But it turns out that it is not sufficient for a neural process to simply take place in the frontoparietal cortex for it to be conscious. Something else is needed. The Belgian scientists realized through their experiment that, unless there was a kind of *back-and-forth flow of information between the frontoparietal cortex and lower-level sensory areas,* the neural process wouldn't become conscious. The study involved both healthy controls and patients in a vegetative state. The researchers wrote that 'the only significant difference between patients in a vegetative state and controls was an impairment of backward connectivity from frontal to temporal cortices.'[108] Thus, *egoic consciousness seems to be associated with a back-and-forth flow of information between different brain areas, analo-*

gously to how images bounce back-and-forth between two mutually-facing mirrors. In vegetative patients, this back-and-forth flow was somehow broken, which correlated with a loss of egoic consciousness.

Let us look in more details at the association I am suggesting between brain processes involving a back-and-forth flow of information and the spinning cone metaphor. If you look upon a hollow mercury cone as two half-cones facing each other, like two mutually-facing mirrors, what you get is a recursive back-and-forth flow of reflections – that is, of information – between the two. Moreover, the respective surfaces aren't completely flat because of the ripples propagating on them, so each reflection is distorted – that is, modulated – by such ripples. Therefore, *information from one half of the mercury cone is recursively modulated and reflected back by the other half of the cone.* Analogously, as we've seen, in the neural correlates of egoic awareness there is a recursive back-and-forth flow of information between two brain regions. The information received by a first brain region is modulated by the neural activity taking place in it and then sent to a second brain region. The neural activity taking place in the second brain region, in turn, further modulates the information received and sends the result back to the first brain region; and so on. Therefore, *information produced by a neural process is recursively modulated and reflected back by another neural process.* This is the similarity of form – the isomorphism – that the empirical results reported in the Belgian study have with the mercury cone metaphor. The metaphor is a *way of visualizing and interpreting* the results of the study.

But the Belgian study isn't alone. A similar article in the *Scientific American Mind* magazine of November 2011 seems to confirm its results. The article reports on a Dutch-French study, summarizing the results as follows: 'Activity in a certain [brain] region is not sufficient to generate consciousness … instead … *different regions must exchange information* before consciousness can arise.'[109] Again, the suggestion is that egoic consciousness is associated with a recursive, back-and-forth flow of information in the brain, analogous to mutually-facing mirrors.

Even the influential study of Giulio Tononi,[110] which we looked at briefly in Chapter 2, provides indication that the neural correlates of egoic consciousness indeed have this recursive, self-reflective structure: closed-cycle neural processes seem necessary, according to Tononi, to integrate enough information to produce sufficiently high values of Φ. And a closed-cycle neural process is analogous to mutually-facing mirrors in the sense that information can flow recursively, back-and-forth, *only within a closed cycle.*

Notice that my earlier criticism of Tononi's theory was that it does not offer a causal framework to explain consciousness on the basis of matter, which it indeed doesn't. But, as it turns out, *Tononi's work does provide suggestive empirical support for the hypothesis that I am putting forward.* The empirical observations underlying Tononi's work are evocative of the notion of egoic consciousness as a recursive, self-amplifying process. After all, under the idealist formulation we are using, 'information' is just another word for 'contents of mind' or 'ripples.' Therefore, a closed cycle of information flow is analogous to a recursive, back-and-forth flow of ripple reflections. Ripple reflections on mutually-facing mirrors are a *way of seeing and interpreting* closed-cycle information flow.

I will speculate further, for this is rich territory. Tononi's Φ variable, representing the amount of information integrated by a neural process, is directly proportional to how many ripples are trapped in a whirlpool's spinning cone and to how well the internal surfaces of the cone face each other – that is, how vertical they are. As such, neural processes become 'conscious' when Φ crosses a certain threshold because, at that threshold, *enough amplification of enough mental contents is achieved for our hard-of-hearing teenager to register an impression in the ego.* Whatever is not registered in the ego is still experienced, but cannot be recalled *from* the ego, just like you could not recall your commute back home. *What Tononi is measuring is not consciousness, but a specific form of it: self-reflective awareness.* When Φ crosses its empirically-measured threshold, what is happening is not the magical appearance of consciousness out of dead matter, but a transition of consciousness from the so-called 'unconscious' level – that is, the level of non-amplified mental contents – to the self-reflective level. As such, I see Tononi's empirical observations and the body of knowledge regarding neural correlates of (egoic) consciousness as being consistent with, and even suggestive of, the ontological interpretation I am presenting.

Spinning cones and the 'external' world

According to the cone metaphor, all the objects and phenomena of what we ordinarily call the 'external' world are, *insofar as you experience them,* merely ripples propagating *within* the spinning cone of mind that you call your ego. Everything you ordinarily see, hear, smell, taste, or feel through your skin is just these trapped ripples. Recursive self-reflection amplifies these ripples enormously, obfuscating everything going on *outside* the cone, just like the sun's glare at noon obfuscates distant stars.

The cone metaphor can still neatly explain the consistency of reality across individuals; that is, the fact that we all seem to share the same 'external' world: each whirlpool forms in the broader medium of mind and, as such, has contact points with it along its rim. Metaphorically speaking, these contact points correspond to our sense organs: skin, eyes, nose, ears, and tongue. An alternative way to say the same thing is to state that the rim of a whirlpool is a *way of seeing* our sense organs. Ripples propagating in that broader mercury ocean can, thus, penetrate the whirlpool through its contact points and get trapped within its internal, circular flow. Some of these trapped ripples will make their way to the center of the whirlpool and fall within its spinning cone. These correspond to the perceptions that we are ordinarily conscious of, like the letters on this page as you read them right now. Other ripples trapped in the whirlpool will remain circulating in its periphery and never make it to the center. These correspond to subliminal perceptions that, because they do not become amplified, remain under the threshold of egoic awareness, like the feeling of air passing through your nose until just before you read this.

Now, imagine that there is a source of disturbances somewhere in this common medium, which generates ripples with certain patterns. The patterns of these ripples represent *information*. The ripples then propagate broadly, *carrying the same information across large areas of the medium*. Eventually, they reach the rims of different whirlpools in the broader mercury ocean, *injecting roughly the same information into each of them,* except perhaps for some idiosyncratic differences related to the position of each whirlpool and the particular configuration of its rim. It is this common information that eventually makes its way to the spinning cone at the center of each whirlpool, enters the field of self-reflective awareness and then gives rise to the perception of a shared environment. This is how each one of us perceives roughly the same 'outside' world – that is, the same *incoming information stream* penetrating our sense organs – apart from certain idiosyncrasies related to our particular positions in space-time and the particular way our perceptual apparatuses filter reality.

Like before, it is important that you keep in mind that we are talking about *metaphors* here. The *actual* images of reality aren't the rims of mercury whirlpools, but people, skin, eyes, noses, etc. The actual image of the universe is not an ocean of mercury, but the sky, planets, stars, etc. What I am suggesting is *not* that you try and replace these actual images with metaphorical ones, *but that you try to think of the actual images in terms of what the metaphors suggest.* Try to think of a human body as a whirlpool in the common medium of mind that we perceive as the universe, maintaining contact points with it in the form of skin, eyes, ears, nose, and tongue. Try to think of the body as the outer image of a process whereby contents of mind become localized. Try to think of certain closed-cycle neural processes in the brain as a system of mutually-facing mirrors, which amplifies whatever ripples penetrate it. Try to think of this amplification as obfuscating everything else in the universe, thereby making it very hard for you to perceive any content of mind that doesn't find its way to the spinning cone at the center of your whirlpool. People, stars, trees, dogs, and cats: all are *dynamic processes of mind* that release undulations in their wake, these undulations eventually penetrating another particular process of mind that you happen to call yourself. There's nothing outside mind. Mind is not in you; you are in mind. When that vortex-like process of mind that you call your physical body eventually dissipates, the subject of your inner life – that which, ultimately, is the only *you* that there has ever been – will still exist because it is the only thing that exists. It will go nowhere because it has nowhere to go. But it will perceive reality in a different, less localized, and probably less self-reflective way. That's no magic or spiritual 'woo woo.' That's just how nature is, as far as reason and observation allow us to infer.

Recognizing the obfuscated ripples of mind

As seen by neuroscience and psychology today, the 'unconscious' mind is supposedly an alien mental space outside the boundaries of your sense of identity. You can perceive *the effects* of the 'unconscious' – you can even communicate with it through lucid dreams, vision quests, and active imagination[111] – but you cannot recognize it as part of your consciousness. Yet, if my hypothesis is correct, the 'unconscious' is indeed an integral part of your conscious self; just a part that your ego ordinarily obfuscates beyond recognition. So is there any way you could validate my hypothesis based on your own experiences, beyond the rather superficial examples of driving and breathing discussed earlier? I think there is.

If the mainstream view of the 'unconscious' is correct, then, whenever previously 'unconscious' material emerges into egoic awareness *for the very first time,* it should be *always* registered by the ego as entirely new information, like reading the latest headlines. However, if my hypothesis is correct, occasionally something else should happen. *When certain ripples of the broader ocean of mind penetrate our spinning cones of self-reflective awareness for the first time, at least occasionally we should register them as familiar memories, not as new information.* After all, they were in consciousness all along, just obfuscated. Like forgotten dreams suddenly remembered, they should be occasionally recognized as familiar experiences.

Now, how many times have you felt, upon learning new information or arriving at a new insight, *that you had somehow known it all along?* You say to yourself: 'Darn! I don't know *how,* but I have *always* known this!' This is a puzzling and disarming feeling, for we can often ascertain that there was no way we could have known the information before. The recognition that a new insight or piece of information has somehow *always* been known to us is, in my view, a hallmark of the 'unconscious.' And it shows that the 'unconscious' knowledge was, in fact, *in consciousness all along,* even though we weren't *self-reflectively* aware of it. The knowledge was always there, diffused in the interstices of egoic awareness. Then, when an event suddenly triggers its insertion into the field of self-reflection, we suddenly *become aware that we were conscious* of the knowledge all along. I believe this kind of personal experience, which we all share, supports my hypothesis that there is no unconscious, but just contents of mind that are obfuscated by the glare of self-reflective awareness.

There are documented historical examples of sudden incursions of knowledge into the field of self-reflective awareness that relate to the kind of personal experiences I attempted to describe above. For instance, it was only about six centuries ago, during the Renaissance, that Europeans became self-reflectively aware of *three-dimensional perspective*. Some authors refer to this development as the 'discovery' of perspective.[112] Well, obviously every sight-capable human being has been seeing perspective since the dawn of our species, so it couldn't have been discovered in the 15th century. One just needs to look at the world around to see it everywhere. What did happen is that, at that time, European artists first became *aware that they were conscious* of perspective. Three-dimensional perspective wasn't new in consciousness, but new in the field of self-reflection. After it entered this field, it was immediately recognized as something people had *always* known, yet didn't know *that* they knew it.

It is critical for ordinary human thinking that we not only know something, but that *we know that we know it*. After all, how helpful is it to know something if you don't know that you know it? Ponder about this for a moment. *A lack of self-reflective awareness is, for us humans, a practical equivalent to a true lack of consciousness.* That's why psychologists came to speak of an 'unconscious' psyche when, in fact, consciousness is the *sine qua non* of the psyche. That's why many fail to see the distinction between knowledge and *self-reflective* knowledge, ending up stating, for instance, that perspective was 'discovered' in the 15th century as if it had never been in consciousness before. Yet, there is a clear difference between these two modalities of conscious apprehension, as I sought to illustrate above. Indeed, we may all be conscious of whole universes beyond consensus reality, all unfolding right under our noses in the interstices of egoic awareness; universes that we may one day realize, in awe, that we have always known.

A new theory of truth

The very notion of what constitutes truth is called into question under an idealist metaphysics, because there is no world outside mind to determine the validity of perceptions, impressions, or thoughts. So what is truth according to the worldview we're developing here? We couldn't answer this question earlier, but now we are finally equipped to tackle it.

Under materialism, the notion of truth is determined by what is called the 'correspondence theory of truth.'[113] Suppose that, one winter afternoon, you look out the window and see a huge and colorful bird flying across the sky. You may describe this to your neighbor who then calls into question the validity of your statement. He may say, for instance, that in the area where you both live there are no large and colorful birds flying around at this time of the year. Generalizing from this example, one can always call into question whether any one of your perceptions is really true or merely a hallucination created by your psyche. How is the question settled then? Here is how it goes: your perception is considered true if it accurately *corresponds* to an object, event, or phenomenon happening outside mind; and it is considered false if no suitable correspondence can be found. So the bird image in your mind is true if there was indeed a bird flying around outside mind. This, in a nutshell, is the correspondence theory of truth.

Yet, in Chapter 3, we've seen how absurd it is to infer a whole unprovable, 'shadow' universe outside mind. The direct consequence of this conclusion is that the correspondence theory of truth is void.

You may now ask: if idealism is right, what meaning is there in questioning the truth of any statement? After all, the idealist metaphysics entails that the sole, necessary, and sufficient determinant of reality is subjective experience. In other words, *only subjective experience is real* and *all subjective experience is real*. Since a so-called hallucination is unquestionably a subjective experience, we must acknowledge it to be real under idealism. Does that mean that we must do away with all discrimination between fact and fantasy? Must we abandon all hope to differentiate delusion from empirical reality? No, not at all. But we do need to reformulate our basis for this discrimination in a more mature and better-grounded way than the naïve and illusory correspondence theory of truth.

Defining new language can help us break away from ingrained assumptions and habits of thought here. So, instead of talking about *true perceptions* and *false perceptions,* let's talk about *personal reality* and *collective reality.* The idea here is to move away from the need to categorize an experience as true or false since, under idealism, all experiences are true. What we are *actually* interested in is determining to what degree an experience is purely personal and idiosyncratic – like so-called hallucinations – or collective and shared across individuals – like so-called empirical facts. Indeed, when we say that a person's vision was mere hallucination, what we are actually trying to say is that *only that person had the vision;* that anyone else standing next to the person at the moment she had the vision would not have shared the corresponding perceptions.

Under the spinning cone metaphor, the experiences you ordinarily have are ripples moving along the internal surfaces of your cone. Some of those ripples may have originally come from the broader sea of mercury outside your whirlpool, penetrating it through its points of contact – that is, your sense organs. These ripples of the broader ocean correspond, as we have seen earlier, to the 'external world' and inject roughly the same information into many different cones. What you ordinarily call *empirical facts* correspond to ripples within your cone that originated from outside and which embody collective information injected into many other cones as well. Therefore, these ripples represent a *collective reality.*

But it is possible that other ripples moving along the internal surface of your spinning cone of mind were created internally, within your whirlpool itself, through a local excitation of the mercury surface. As such, they do not comprise information shared with other cones, but are entirely idiosyncratic. Moreover, ripples that originally penetrated your whirlpool from the outside may become highly distorted through interference with local, internal excitations. In all these cases, what you get are *personal realities*, which we ordinarily call fantasies, hallucinations, dreams, visions, imagination, etc.

The important thing to notice is that the only criterion of discrimination here is the degree to which an experience is, or can potentially be, consistently shared across cones – that is, across self-reflective points-of-view of mind. There is no point in talking about what is 'true' or what is 'false' in any absolute sense, since there is no external reference system, outside mind, to ground the truth-value of anything. All reality is experience and all experience is real. All that is useful to know is the extent to which an experience is shared in actuality or at least in potentiality. I elaborated more extensively on this point, under different formulations, in my earlier books *Dreamed up Reality* and *Meaning in Absurdity*.

The 'collective unconscious,' the 'personal unconscious,' and memory

Analytical psychology recognizes two different levels in our 'unconscious' psyches: the so-called 'personal unconscious' and the 'collective unconscious.' Much of our discussion above applies directly to the 'collective unconscious': it consists of the ripples of the broader ocean of mind that get obfuscated by self-reflective awareness. Indeed, the ripples propagating in the broader ocean that happen to penetrate the cones explain our shared world. But those that don't are the contents of the 'collective unconscious.'

The question now is whether our metaphors can also accommodate the 'personal unconscious':[114] the repository of mental contents that are personal but not within the field of self-reflective awareness. These mental contents are not shared across individuals – that is, across whirlpools – but belong to a person. They comprise personal experiences that were once in self-reflective awareness but have become forgotten or repressed. Clearly, there is a strong relationship between the 'personal unconscious' and memory. Indeed, the 'personal unconscious' contains all those experiences that we can potentially recall and remember but which, right now, are not in egoic awareness. All of your potential memories – childhood images, past events, repressed feelings, etc. – are 'stored' in your own 'personal unconscious.'

The first step is to understand how the spinning mercury cone metaphor explains our ability to forget and then remember things: whatever ripples were once flowing along the inner surfaces of the cone, but have since escaped it, become obfuscated and, therefore, 'forgotten.' They are still ripples in the ocean of mind and, as such, *they remain in consciousness.* But, since they are no longer self-reflected, they become overwhelmed by the amplified mental contents flowing within the cone. If, as a result of whatever change in the structure or dynamics of the whirlpool, those 'forgotten' ripples re-enter the cone, they are then 'remembered,' for they again become amplified like images in mutually-facing mirrors.

If the structure of mind comprised only a broader surface and spinning cones, there would be no space for a 'personal unconscious': whatever ripples escaped a cone would land straight onto the broader surface that would constitute the 'collective unconscious.' But a spinning cone is only the very center of a whirlpool. Around each cone there is the periphery of its respective whirlpool, which doesn't sink into itself like the cone but still localizes the flow of mind in a circular trajectory. The cone corresponds to our self-reflective awareness, or ego. In turn, *the periphery of the whirlpool, which surrounds the cone, corresponds to our 'personal unconscious.'* The 'personal unconscious' isn't self-reflective, but it is localized. Undulations that were once propagating in the cone, but have since been 'forgotten,' may remain trapped in the periphery of the whirlpool. As they remain in local circulation – instead of drifting away to the broader medium of mind – they can eventually penetrate the cone again, thereby being 'remembered.' This, in a nutshell, is the mechanism of ordinary memory.

As such, forgetting and recalling things are processes whereby contents of mind go in and out of the field of self-reflective awareness, but never really leave consciousness. Even when forgotten, personal mental contents can remain 'nearby,' localized in the surrounding vortex of the flow of mind, potentially re-entering the egoic field if conditions are appropriate. Our effort to recall things may be seen as an attempt to manipulate the configuration of the whirlpool of mind in order to push back into the cone mental contents circulating in the periphery of the whirlpool.

Once again, it is critical that you do not get too focused on the particular metaphorical images I'm using here, but try instead to step back and distill the *way of thinking* they are trying to convey. A living human body-brain system is the *actual* – albeit partial – image of the 'whirlpools' and 'cones' I am discussing. Clearly, a body-brain system, at least at first sight, doesn't look anything like a whirlpool with a cone at its center! The point of the metaphor is to evoke an understanding of how the different segments of the human psyche are formed and operate under idealism. In a first segment, mental contents are amplified through recursive self-reflectiveness, obfuscating whatever else is present in all other segments. The actual image of this process is closed-cycle neural processes where information is transmitted back and forth in the brain. These amplified mental contents may sometimes slip out of this first segment and land onto a second segment of the psyche, where they remain localized, circulating at the edges of egoic awareness, but without self-reflective amplification. Neural processes that do not correlate with ordinary egoic consciousness may be partial images of this local circulation. And, beyond these two personal segments, the human psyche is fundamentally connected with the broader medium of mind, the matrix of all existence.

The trade-off of self-reflectiveness

Self-reflective awareness is an amazing and priceless form of conscious apprehension. It allows us to turn our thoughts into *objects* of thought; that is, *to think about our own thoughts and evaluate them critically*. Without it, we would be incapable of self-evaluation, self-realization and growth as individuals. We would operate according to fixed and unchanging patterns, unable to 'step outside ourselves' and see where our thinking and actions go astray. We would be as unquestioning of our own behavior as instinct-driven animals. Through self-reflective awareness we can also observe our own feelings and passions and then ask ourselves: "Why am I feeling like this? What is it in me that is causing me to suffer? What are the underlying motivations of my gut reactions?" And so on. *It enables self-inquiry.*

As if all this weren't enough, it is self-reflective awareness that enables philosophy: it equips us to ponder about who we are, what our role in life is, and what the meaning of it all might be. Without self-reflective awareness you wouldn't have the inner questions that drove you to read this book. You would have thoughts and feelings, all right, but you would be as much at their mercy as a dog or a cat is at the mercy of its instincts, incapable of 'stepping out of itself' to evaluate, learn from, and potentially change, its own behavior. Instead of being a learning observer of the flow of mind, you would be immersed in it, carried away by it like a rag doll in a tsunami.

Clearly, it is impossible to overestimate the value of self-reflective awareness. Yet, it comes with a price, for it is self-reflective awareness that obfuscates everything that doesn't happen to fall within its field of action. *It is self-reflective awareness that creates the 'unconscious,'* causing us to become amnesic of an entire universe of experiences whose unfathomable breadth is impossible to even estimate. All the richness and uniqueness of those forgotten experiences pass us by. How much awe, excitement and amazement would be within our reach if we could still see the stars at noon?

Jean Gebser saw an aspect of this trade-off in his discussion of the 'discovery' of perspective in the 15th century. He linked such a seminal event to the coalescence of the ego: 'The unperspectival world is related to the anonymous "one" or the tribal "we," the perspectival to the "I" or "Ego."'[115] He then went on to say that perspective 'locates and determines the observer as well as the observed. The positive result is a concretion of man and space; the negative result is the restriction of man to a limited segment where he perceives only one sector of reality. ... Man separates from the whole only that part which his view or thinking can encompass, and forgets those sectors that lie adjacent, beyond, or even behind.'[116]

Self-reflective awareness represents a trade-off of cosmic proportions. While the value we derive from it is our very humanness, we lose so much because of it. Could there be a way to reconcile self-reflective awareness with a restoration of access to the forgotten, 'unconscious' universe of mind? We will later come back to this point. First, though, we will explore yet another extension of the metaphor that will allow us to complete our metaphysical interpretation of reality.

Chapter 6

The Oscillating Membrane Metaphor

One thing we often overlook as we busy ourselves with our everyday activities is the bewildering variety and richness of the different states of mind we can find ourselves in: daydreaming; contemplation; creative flow; drunkenness; erotic enchantment; indifference or apathy; concentration; ecstasy; meditative and other types of trance; mental loops of worry, obsession or anxiety; introverted self-questioning and judgment; extroverted outward projection; etc. There aren't enough word combinations in language to capture all the nuances, subtleties, and general gestalts of our potential states of mind.

In fact, the part of our everyday experiences that is common across people is, upon careful inspection, surprisingly small in comparison to that which is unique to ourselves. Two people sitting in the same movie theater and watching the exact same movie at the same time may have utterly different experiences, practically as though they were watching different movies. This dawned on me when, in the early nineties, I watched Kieslowski's masterpiece *La Double Vie de Veronique*: I was, and remain, convinced that no two people in that theater saw the same movie; not only at an emotional level, but at a perceptual level as well.

Our particular states of mind color and frame the whole of our experiences. We live under the illusion that we all share the exact same world because *our language has evolved to pick out precisely the few aspects of our experiences that are common and shared, while ignoring those that are completely personal and idiosyncratic.* For some reason, we tend to lose self-reflective awareness of whatever we cannot talk about or articulate to ourselves in words. But, if you pay careful attention, you will notice that each one of us seems to live in a largely private environment: some in a reality of bright hues, round forms, excitement, and mystery; others in a gray and bland reality of indifference, hopelessness, and quiet existential despair; yet others in a world of sharp angles, straight lines, strong contrasts, loud noises, order and hierarchy; etc. Our worlds are determined by our unique states of mind.

Any metaphor that seeks to provide images in terms of which one could make sense of mind and reality must have enough degrees of freedom to capture all this rich variety. The whirlpool, knot, and mercury cone metaphors have been very useful thus far, but they do not provide sufficient degrees of freedom in this regard. It is a key goal of this chapter to extend those metaphors so we can capture the bewildering variety of mind states.

Another important goal of this chapter is to provide a framework onto which we can map our current understanding of the laws of physics in a more direct and specific manner. After all, a metaphor for mind and reality should be able to fully capture the patterns and regularities of nature as currently understood by physics.

The basics of vibration

To achieve these goals we will need to make use of the notion of *vibration*. We are all intuitively familiar with vibration: a mobile phone vibrates when ringing; piano and guitar strings vibrate when being played; the ground vibrates during an earthquake. Vibration has to do with a repetitive, oscillatory movement of a somewhat elastic medium, be it a guitar string, a mobile phone or the Earth itself. Before we go on, let us review a few key and easy aspects of the theory of vibrations so we are equipped to easily make sense of what follows.[117] I will also introduce a few terms here that will be used later. You can always come back to this section to review the meaning of these terms if you forget them later on. No terms will be used that have not been explained below.

As any movement, vibration can take place in one, two, three, and theoretically even more dimensions of space. The simplest form of vibration is that which happens in a single dimension, like the oscillations of a guitar string. Imagine a guitar string pinned at both ends: when plucked, it begins to vibrate. Its ends stay in a fixed position because they are pinned in place by the structure of the guitar or the fingers of the player, but the middle of the string bulges up and down because of the elasticity of the material. The top line of Figure 9 shows the two extreme configurations of the string as it bulges up and down: the so-called *envelope* of the string's vibration.

The *frequency* of the vibration is a measure of how fast the

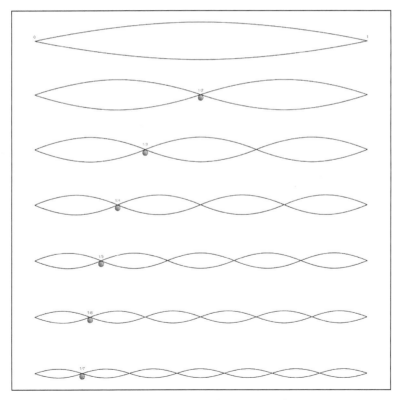

Figure 9. Different modes of vibration of a string.

string moves up and down. The faster the movement is, the higher the frequency. Every string has a set of *natural frequencies* of vibration determined by the elasticity of the string, its length, and the tension applied to it. The natural frequencies correspond to the specific speeds with which the string naturally 'wants' to vibrate. In a guitar, the thicker wound strings have lower natural frequencies, while the thinner plain strings have higher natural frequencies.

The top line of Figure 9 illustrates the *fundamental mode of vibration* of a guitar string, corresponding to its lowest natural frequency. When the string vibrates with a higher natural frequency, the shape of the envelope changes, as illustrated by the other lines of Figure 9. For instance, in the second line from the top, one half of the string bulges up while the other half bulges down, and vice-versa. The point in the middle never moves; not because it's pinned, but because the waves propagating along the string cancel each other out at that point. In the third line from the top, the middle third of the string bulges up while the two side thirds bulge down, and vice-versa. Two points along the length of the string never move. And so on. Each *natural mode of vibration* corresponds to a different envelope and a different natural frequency. Figure 9, thus, illustrates seven different natural modes of vibration of a guitar string. Each corresponding envelope is a graphical illustration of the associated *pattern of vibration*.

All these ideas about vibration can be easily extended to two dimensions, like the vibrations of a drumhead. Instead of different segments of a string bulging up and down according to a one-dimensional pattern, what you get are different regions of a *membrane* bulging up and down according to a two-dimensional pattern. Figure 10 illustrates several natural modes of vibration of a square membrane unpinned at the edges. The images are generated by spreading salt on the black membrane as it vibrates. The salt grains then congregate along the lines where the membrane remains static, without bulging, analogously to the points that never move in the strings of Figure 9. Clearly, incredibly varied, sophisticated and nuanced patterns can be formed by mere vibration.

Figure 10. Different modes of vibration of a membrane.

Like the case of strings, the specific modes of vibration of a membrane – which can be visualized in the patterns of Figure 10 – depend on the *structure* of the membrane, particularly its shape (circular, square, triangular, irregular, etc.). Generally speaking, *the modes of vibration of any object depend on the object's structure.* Moreover, the complexity of the modes of vibration also depends on how much 'wiggle room' the membrane has to vibrate, which is given by boundary conditions like whether its edges are pinned or not. More generally, the 'wiggle room' is a function of how many *degrees of freedom* the membrane has to vibrate.

The square membrane in Figure 10 is, in principle, free to vibrate in all the three dimensions of space that we ordinarily see. Imagine, however, that there were extra, hidden dimensions of space that the membrane could vibrate in. This would give the membrane *more degrees of freedom* to vibrate and, therefore, produce *more complex patterns* of vibration. Such a hypothesis can be mathematically defined and simulated in a very precise manner. Although we can only see a *projection* of the higher-dimensional patterns of vibration onto ordinary three-dimensional space, the projections themselves can already be much richer and more complex than the patterns seen in Figure 10.

Moreover, in a space with more than three dimensions, the membrane itself could have more than just two dimensions. The word 'membrane' refers to a structure that has fewer dimensions than the space it occupies: an ordinary membrane has two dimensions, one less than the ordinary three dimensions of space. But in, say, ten-dimensional space something like a membrane could have three, four, or even more dimensions. That would allow for *yet more complexity and variety* in the resulting patterns of vibration. The reason I am emphasizing these purely theoretical notions will become clear later.

Regardless of how many dimensions the medium has, or how many spatial dimensions it can vibrate in, the basic notions remain always the same: an *elastic medium* vibrates according to certain *natural modes,* each mode corresponding to a *natural frequency* and an *envelope* of vibration. The envelope is a graphical illustration of the *pattern of vibration,* as shown in Figures 9 and 10 for one and two dimensions, respectively. The particular modes of vibration of an elastic medium depend on its *structure*.

The last notion we need to review is that of *resonance*. Luckily, this is a very intuitive notion: imagine yourself pushing a child on a swing. The swing moves repetitively back and forth, which in essence is just a slow *vibration*. To get the swing to go far and high you need to push it at the same pace that it naturally 'wants' to sway at. If you push it too fast or too slow you will disrupt the swing's vibration instead of contributing to its buildup. But, if you push it just right, your own movements will *resonate* with the movements of the swing, amplifying the latter. This, in essence, is resonance.

To put it more formally, *resonance happens when the stimulus applied to a vibrating system has the same frequency as one of the system's natural modes of vibration.* The swing has a natural mode of vibration; that is, a certain pace at which it naturally 'wants' to sway. If you apply a stimulus to it with that same frequency, and at the right time, it will sway increasingly high. You don't even need to apply much force, so long as the pace is right. The energy you apply each time you push contributes *cumulatively* to the movement of the swing. But, if you apply the stimulus at the wrong frequency, the energy application will conflict with the movement of the system.

A dramatic illustration of the power of resonance occurred in 1940, when the first Tacoma Narrows Bridge in Washington State, USA, collapsed because of a mild 42 mph (68 km/h) wind. It turned out that the wind had a frequency that matched almost perfectly the natural mode of vibration of the bridge, so they *resonated*. The energy of the wind began feeding slowly but *cumulatively* into the vibration of the bridge, just like a person gently pushing a swing at the right pace. The bridge then began to sway harder and harder, to the horror of people frantically abandoning their cars and running off the bridge. Eventually, the entire structure came apart and fell into the Tacoma Narrows.

The entire event was caught on tape. Fortunately, nobody perished.

Through resonance, the bridge acquired and amplified the vibration of the wind. This is the key point about resonance that we will need later on: *a system can acquire and amplify the vibration of an external stimulus if they resonate,* much like a piano begins to vibrate when an appropriate tuning fork rings nearby.

The membrane metaphor proper

Now that we have sufficient foundation, let's get straight to extending our metaphor. Take the mercury ocean metaphor as our starting point. *But now, instead of an ocean of liquid mercury, imagine a reflective membrane, like tinfoil.* See Figure 11. This way, the medium of mind is now a thin, mirror-like membrane with some rigidity, but also some elasticity. Naturally, we can no longer visualize experiences as ripples, for the membrane is not a fluid. *Imagine instead that experiences are vibrations of the membrane.*

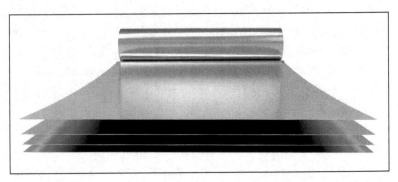

Figure 11. A tinfoil membrane as a metaphor for the medium of mind.

The qualities of experience now correspond to the specific patterns of vibration of the membrane. When you witness the power of an ocean, such an experience is a specific pattern of vibration of the membrane of mind. When you watch in horror as war unfolds around you, such an experience is *another, different* pattern of vibration of the membrane of mind. When you smell coffee, that is yet another pattern of vibration. And so on. As we've seen in Figure 10, the vibrations of a membrane can take on a bewildering variety of highly complex patterns.

Yet, the patterns we *perceive* around us are three-dimensional images that cannot be captured by the vibratory modes of a two-dimensional membrane, regardless of how complex they may be. When you factor in the need for the membrane of mind to model all of human *emotion* and *thought patterns*, which transcend the degrees of freedom of ordinary space, it becomes clear that a two-dimensional structure vibrating in three-dimensional space doesn't suffice in our metaphor.

Therefore, we need to imagine the medium of mind as a membrane with *more* than two dimensions vibrating in *more* than three dimensions of space. Only then can we get enough degrees of freedom to represent all of human experience. Such a membrane would support modes of vibration arbitrarily more complex and nuanced than those shown in Figure 10. Indeed, a sufficiently complex membrane vibrating with enough degrees of freedom can conceivably support patterns equivalent to anything and everything we can perceive or feel: landscapes, oceans, people, art, anger, love, belonging, etc.

If this metaphor is correct, then everything you see, hear, or otherwise perceive around you right now are just compound vibrations of the medium of mind, analogous to the patterns of Figure 10, but much more complex and nuanced. Moreover, whatever you feel or think right now are *also* patterns of vibration of the membrane of mind. When mind vibrates, it does so according to patterns that we register as sight, sound, touch, smell, texture, warmth, anguish, love, fear, orgasm, thought, insight, understanding, etc. All these are just the manifestations of the medium of mind as it *vibrates.*

Naturally, just as before, *there is nothing to reality but the medium of mind itself.* There exists nothing but the membrane. When the membrane is at rest, there is no experience as such, but only the *potential* for experience. After all, the membrane *can* start vibrating. When the membrane does vibrate, then experience arises. But what is a vibration other than the medium that vibrates? There is nothing to a vibrating guitar string but the string itself. As such, experiences – the 'contents' of mind – are nothing but mind itself, manifesting a certain *behavior* in the form of vibrations. The 'contents' of mind aren't separate ontological entities. All there is is the medium of mind itself. So don't let realism creep in unnoticed: this membrane is not something outside mind; it is not 'stuff;' *it is mind itself as witness*. And the witness witnesses its own vibrations. These vibrations are subjective experiences of the kind you are having right now, as you read this.

As such, it is fundamentally impossible for us to investigate, analyze, or measure the membrane of mind directly, for it is the membrane of mind that investigates, analyzes, and measures. All we can investigate are the *vibrations* of the membrane, for those are *experiences*. The membrane is the subject. Its vibrations are the experiences of the subject, which include the illusion of objects.

Figure 12. A wave folding in on itself.

It is impossible for the eye that sees to see itself without a mirror. But, in the case of the membrane of mind, there is no mirror, since the membrane is all there is. Unless... it can fold in on itself, like a wave folds in on itself, to form a hollow loop! See Figure 12. By folding in on itself, the membrane of mind can 'look at itself in the mirror.' The loop thus formed has internal reflective surfaces that face each other and produce the recursive self-reflective effect shown in Figure 5. As such, the hollow loop of the tinfoil membrane is entirely analogous to the hollow mercury cone of the previous chapter.

Yet, two empty mirrors facing each other reflect only emptiness; there is no image to be reflected. Unless, of course, the *vibrations* of mind create *patterns,* as in Figure 10, which *can* be recursively reflected within a loop. The entire mental process that occurred in my psyche as I wrote this book has been an attempt by mind to 'see' and investigate itself through the reflected images in the mirrored membrane loop that my ego is. The entire mental process that is occurring in *your* psyche as you read this right now is also an attempt by mind to 'see' and understand itself through the mirrored membrane loop that your ego is. You and I are examples of a living attempt by the 'eye' of mind to create, out of itself, a mirror upon which it can contemplate itself and answer the ultimate questions: What am I? What is going on? One can only imagine the unbearable 'itch' that these questions create in the deepest realms of the 'unconscious;' an itch that seems to unleash enough mental energy for the membrane of mind to contort itself into a topology – a loop – that promises the vague possibility of answers.

The individual and the world arising from the membrane

We now need to transpose onto this vibrating membrane metaphor our earlier discussion about how egos form and gain access to a shared, collective, apparently external reality. Earlier, we visualized this external reality as global ripples propagating

in the broader ocean of mercury, and which injected similar information into multiple mercury whirlpools. Here the metaphor will
be a bit different but more powerful.

Each individual conscious entity – say, a person or an animal
– can be visualized as a segment of the membrane of mind rising
up, like a *protrusion,* from the broader membrane underneath,
while remaining connected to it. See Figure 13 for a couple of
illustrative examples. Such protrusions are local *structures* – not
necessarily folded in on themselves yet – with their own characteristics and boundary constraints.

Figure 13, A and B. Different protrusions rising in the membrane
of mind.

As we've seen earlier, each of these protrusions will have its own *modes of vibration,* determined by its particular structure and how it is connected to the broader membrane underneath. These modes of vibration entail specific *natural frequencies* and *patterns of vibration,* analogous to those in Figure 10, but much more complex and spanning many more than just two dimensions. As such, some of the patterns of vibration of each protrusion can be individual and unique, as given by the protrusion's particular structure. Since patterns of vibration represent experiences, each protrusion can have its own individual, idiosyncratic experiences. Each protrusion corresponds, thus, to an *individual psyche.*

All protrusions remain connected to the underlying membrane and form integral parts of it, just like your arms remain connected to your body and form integral parts of your body. Therefore, when the underlying membrane vibrates, these broader vibrations affect what happens within each protrusion. As we've seen earlier, if the underlying membrane vibrates with a frequency matching one of the natural modes of vibration of a protrusion, *then the protrusion will resonate with the underlying membrane.* The vibrations of the underlying membrane will feed cumulatively into the vibrations of the protrusion, just like the vibrations of the wind fed cumulatively into the swaying of the original Tacoma Narrows Bridge. To put it in other words, *the resonating protrusion will acquire and amplify the vibrations of the underlying membrane.*

Here is another analogy: during an earthquake a building vibrates along with the movement of the ground. But when the structure of the building *resonates* with the frequency of the earthquake, it acquires and cumulatively amplifies those movements, shaking more violently than the ground itself. It is as though the earthquake were pushing the building, like a swing, at just the right pace. Engineers try to avoid this resonance by *changing the structure* of the building with inertial dampeners, so no cumulative effect takes place. Now, notice that buildings rise from the ground just like individual psyches rise, as protrusions, from the underlying membrane of mind. When the structure of a protrusion is such that it resonates with the vibrations of the underlying membrane, it acquires and cumulatively amplifies these vibrations, just like the resonating building does during an earthquake.

As individual psyches rising from the one medium of mind, we all 'vibrate along' with the medium, whatever pattern of vibration is unfolding there. This is analogous to how every building moves along with the ground during an earthquake, regardless of whether there is resonance or not. But, *in the absence of any resonance,* these vibrations may be practically imperceptible. In other words, because these underlying, non-resonating vibrations are a constant – always in the background of experience, like the sound of cars in a nearby highway – it is entirely expectable that most conscious entities would ignore them in the presence of those vibrations that *do* resonate and, thus, 'jump out' of the background.

Such a notion avoids a problem we had with the previous metaphor: since self-reflective obfuscation was the only mechanism we had to explain why most contents of mind become seemingly unconscious, the implication was that egoless conscious entities, like most animals, should be able to perceive – through extrasensory means – everything in the universe. Observation tells us this doesn't seem to be the case, even though some animals often do display higher non-local sensitivity than humans.[118] Now we can explain this limited perception also in the case of egoless entities: the particular structure of a protrusion of the membrane of mind – say, an animal – determines its modes of vibration and, therefore, which patterns of vibration of the underlying membrane it will resonate with and amplify. *Only the amplified patterns are then registered in ordinary consciousness.* And all of this happens without any self-reflectiveness.

To summarize, we now have *two distinct mechanisms* to explain why conscious entities seem to 'forget' the experiences unfolding in the broader medium of mind. The *first* is when a protrusion of the membrane resonates with certain vibrations taking place underneath, like a building resonating with the ground vibrations of an earthquake. Whatever patterns of vibration do resonate are then amplified, registered in ordinary consciousness, and thereby 'obfuscate' whatever does *not* resonate. This happens independently of whether there is any self-reflective awareness – that is, an ego – or not. The *second*, independent mechanism is when a part of the protrusion folds in on itself, creating the recursive two-mirror effect shown in Figure 5. This amplifies certain patterns of vibration *even further* and corresponds to a *second level* of obfuscation.

As suggested above, an ego forms when *a part* of this protrusion of the membrane of mind folds in on itself, forming a hollow loop. In Figure 13B you can see – if you allow yourself some imagination – the beginning of this folding process on the right-upper corner. In a way, the egoic loop rises from the protrusion in the same way that the protrusion rises from the broader membrane. The particular structure of the loop determines its modes of vibration and, therefore, which vibratory patterns of the underlying protrusion resonate within it. *Patterns that do not resonate do not penetrate the loop.* Let us call the system comprising the raised protrusion and the folded-in loop on top of it the *psychic structure.*

If you feel that the metaphor is now becoming too complex and losing touch with the empirical reality it seeks to explain, please have a little patience and bear with me a little longer. It will soon become abundantly clear how all of this helps us understand the world in and around us.

Since the membrane is reflective like a mirror, the internal, mutually-facing surfaces of the hollow loop create recursive reflections in exactly the same way discussed in the previous chapter. The only difference is that the images reflected now aren't those of ripples, as in Figure 7, but of patterns of vibration, like those in Figure 10. The rest of the rationale of the previous chapter remains valid here: our sense organs are partial images of the points of contact between the psychic structure and the underlying membrane of mind, through which resonance can take place; the very presence of a protrusion alters the vibratory dynamics in its vicinity, leaving a vibratory imprint on the broader membrane of mind and, thereby, allowing others to perceive our presence and actions in the world; patterns of vibration within a particular psychic structure can also 'leak out' into the broader membrane by resonating with the underlying medium, thereby allowing communication to take place between protrusions; etc.

Instead of *ripples*, we must now think of *patterns of vibration*. Since the notion of vibration is more powerful, everything we discussed under the image of ripples maps straightforwardly onto vibrations. After all, all ripples are vibrations, even though not all vibrations are ripples. Therefore, we lose none of the explanatory power of the mercury ocean metaphor while making a transition to the vibrating membrane metaphor. We only gain. To avoid boring you I will, therefore, refrain from repeating all previous discussions under this new metaphorical context.

It is my contention that the psychic structures of *all* human beings resonate with certain particular patterns of vibration of the underlying membrane. We call these particular patterns the 'outside world.' The similarities of psychic structure across us all – corresponding to commonalities of DNA – enable us all to 'tune into' the same subset of the broader patterns of vibration. *Our experiential realities are determined by our psychic structures, so the similarities of our psychic structures allow for a shared experiential reality to emerge across humans.* The physical body – particularly the brain – is but a *partial image* of these psychic structures. Yet, our bodies and brains do not need to be identical to enable us to share a world. As a matter of fact, our shared world is clearly but a small part of the total set of our experiences: our dreams, feelings, thoughts and the projections we place onto reality are all private. Therefore, modest similarities of psychic structure – reflected in modestly similar bodies and brains – could already create the impression of a shared world. After all, even animals seem to share an environment with us.

So let us broaden this discussion and include egoless conscious entities in it. As we've seen, each conscious entity corresponds to a particular protrusion of the membrane of mind. Different species – say, cats and ants – correspond to protrusions with different structures that, therefore, resonate with different modes of the underlying vibrations. While there clearly is a small subset that overlaps and is shared across all species, essentially each species lives in an experiential reality of its own. The small overlapping subset accounts for why there are *cross-correspondences* between the realities of different species sharing apparently the same world. For instance, something intense seems to happen in my cat's reality when, in my reality, I accidently step on her tail. But how much of my reality does my cat *really* share?

From an information-theoretical perspective, cross-correspondences require relatively little information to be shared across species: mere flags or pointers. For instance, when gamers play multiplayer games online, the entire virtual reality of the game is rendered locally, within each gamer's console. Only low-bandwidth flags and pointers are shared via the network to keep the different local renderings in synch. If a programmer so wanted, he could easily program a viable multiplayer game where each player is immersed in a completely different virtual reality, only cross-correspondences being shared so the players would still think they are playing the same game. One player could be shooting and being shot at in a jungle, while another would be throwing and dodging knives in an alley, yet they would still be able to 'kill' each other. The loser would be certain that he was 'killed' by a knife in an alley, while the winner would be certain that he 'killed' his opponent with a bullet in a jungle. The abstract event of a 'hit' or a 'kill' would be a cross-correspondence in this case, but most of the virtual reality experienced by each gamer would be private and idiosyncratic.

Language, as a communication tool, has evolved to capture only these abstract cross-correspondences. As a result, we naïvely reassure ourselves *with words* that we are all living in the same world. But you cannot know for sure what another person truly experiences when she reports, for instance, to be seeing green. She could be seeing an entirely different color, so long as she consistently used the word 'green' for everything that you consider to be green. Even what she calls 'vision' could be, for all you know, a different sense altogether. So long as the cross-correspondences, *as reflected in language,* remained consistent with what you call vision, you'd be none the wiser.[119]

It is impossible for anyone to be sure of the degree of experiential commonality across two people, let alone know how the world of, say, a frog looks and feels. After all, *what you call a 'frog' is just a partial image: a vibratory pattern imprinted onto the broader membrane of mind by another protrusion, which then resonates within your own protrusion.* This way, the reality that counts is the patterns of vibration within each psychic structure: our own, private realities. Relatively little information needs to arrive, through resonance, from the broader membrane of mind in order to create the linguistic illusion of a shared world.

The 'collective unconscious' and the filter hypothesis revisited

Although the entire articulation of the mercury ocean metaphor in the previous chapter can be straightforwardly ported onto the vibrating membrane metaphor, I do want to discuss one particular point more explicitly. Indeed, in the previous chapter we made a map of the psyche in the following way: (a) the contents of the 'collective unconscious' corresponded to ripples of the broader ocean of mind; (b) the 'personal unconscious' corresponded to the periphery of a whirlpool in the ocean; and (c) the ego corresponded to a hollow spinning cone at the center of the whirlpool. In the present chapter the map of the psyche is analogous but slightly different: (a) the contents of the 'collective unconscious' correspond to vibratory patterns of the underlying membrane; (b) the 'personal unconscious' now corresponds to the structured protrusion rising from the membrane, as illustrated in Figure 13; and (c) the ego corresponds to a segment of the protrusion that folds in on itself, forming a hollow loop. The psychic structure comprises items (b) and (c).

Notice that, according to the idealist formulation being laid out, there is a fundamental equivalence between the experiences we associate with the empirical world – landscapes, trees, buildings, other people and animals, etc. – and the contents of the 'collective unconscious': both correspond to broad vibratory patterns of the underlying membrane.[120] *The difference is that the structure of the human ego – the loop – is such that the vibrations we call the 'empirical world' consistently resonate with it, while the vibrations we associate with the 'collective unconscious' do not.* Put in other words, the egoic loop only resonates with, and therefore perceives, a small subset of the underlying vibrations of the broader membrane. We happen to call this small subset the empirical world. The rest is 'filtered out.' If the contents of the 'collective unconscious' also resonated with our egos, we would simply consider them part of the empirical world, just like mountains and buildings.

Notice also that the metaphor of the 'filter,' discussed in Chapter 2, comes to life here in a much stronger way than before. The contents of the 'collective unconscious' are almost literally 'filtered out' by the structure of each egoic loop. Indeed, analog electronic radios tune into a certain station – thereby filtering out the others – precisely by adjusting the *structure* of their circuitry so that it *resonates* only with the vibratory signal corresponding to that chosen station. The circuitry that does this is actually called a 'band-pass *filter*.'

Origami of mind

If this metaphor is correct, it opens up room for a potentially infinite variety of structures as far as the protrusions are concerned. Like origami, the membrane of mind can conceivably protrude and fold in on itself according to a vast, potentially infinite array of shapes. As we have seen, each shape will correspond to a specific set of natural frequencies and patterns of vibration, resonating in different ways with the underlying membrane. A bewildering variety of experiential realities can thus arise. Some of the protrusions will have vast overlapping modes of vibration, thereby sharing large chunks of their realities. Others will have no overlapping modes, their experiential realities remaining totally disjoint.

Perhaps a modern physicist would feel tempted to deploy the metaphors of 'extra dimensions' or 'parallel universes' to describe this situation, but such metaphors are inappropriate here: they entail segments of space outside mind; that is, realism. Here, instead, we're talking about different segments of the medium of mind itself, which operate on disjoint frequency ranges. I am sure you can already imagine how the notions of aliens, spiritual realms, and non-physical entities – if there is validity to them – can be interpreted under this metaphor rather straightforwardly and non-supernaturally. But we will leave speculation on all this for the next chapter.

One last point must be made before we move on to the next section: it is the vast variety of structures of the protrusions in general – and of egoic loops in particular – that accounts for the enormous differences in personality, character, temperament, intellectual capabilities, inclinations and general psychological predispositions across members of a species. *Variations in brain*

Figure 14, A and B. Different loop topologies.

anatomy and function are how these differences ordinarily appear to us, brain anatomy and function being *partial images* of the structures in question. Indeed, not only can the protrusions have countless different shapes, as suggested in Figure 13, but the egoic loops can close in a vast variety of different ways too. For instance, Figure 14 illustrates two different loop topologies: a cone-like and a doughnut-like topology. Notice that both can give rise to the double-mirror effect shown in Figure 5.

Living with a paradox

Before we go any further, we must now address a very difficult element of the entire story. It cannot be postponed any longer.

The main thrust of this book has been the claim that *only experience exists.* Yet, I am postulating a metaphorical 'medium of mind' – visualized in the form of a water stream, or an ocean of mercury, or a tinfoil membrane – from which experience ultimately originates. As such, it is fair to state that the medium of mind itself is *not* an experience. But wait… isn't experience all that exists? A contradiction seems to arise. Let's attempt to elucidate this somewhat.

All we can ever know to exist is experience, so let us stick to our original conclusion: there is only experience, as far as we *can* know. Now, since experience is modeled as the *movement* of the medium of mind, the necessary consequence is that *the medium of mind itself must be empty – a void – in the sense that it fundamentally transcends all experience and knowledge.* Here is a way to think about it: imagine that the only sense you ever had was the sense of hearing. This way, you couldn't see, touch, smell, or taste anything from birth. Now imagine a guitar string. The only way you could possibly register the existence of the guitar string would be if it vibrated, so you could hear the corresponding sound. But if the guitar string weren't vibrating, it would fall fundamentally outside your ability to ever know or experience it, or even to form a conception of it. *The guitar string at rest would become, in an important way, void.* The same idea applies to the medium of mind: its existence can only be registered by itself when it vibrates, and even then *only in the form of vibrations.*

Otherwise, it is void.

Yet, there is a sense in which this void cannot really be nothing, for it entails a *latent potential* to move. Existence arises when this potential *concretizes into actual movement*. We can then say that all that exists is the *movement of the void*. Since the subject of all experiences is the medium of mind itself, it too only becomes actualized in the form of experience: the one universal subject exists only insofar as the experiences it has.

So, on the one hand, it is entirely valid to say that only experience exists, for the medium of mind is merely a *potential,* not an actuality. It concretizes into existence only when it moves and, at that point, *it is nothing but the corresponding experiences.* On the other hand, it is also entirely valid to talk metaphorically about a 'medium of mind,' insofar as this is a reference to a *potential,* not an actuality. In doing so, I am trying to convey a metaphorical image by means of which one can visualize this potential.

Although the elucidation above has probably helped you 'swallow' the paradox, it's probably not really satisfying. In the same way that there is nothing to the vibration of a guitar string other than the string itself, *ultimately there is nothing to experience – and therefore to existence – other than the void that vibrates.* So everything is a void or, as Adyashanti brilliantly put it, 'emptiness dancing.'[121] *Existence is but a disturbance of the void and, thus, fundamentally empty.* At the same time, obviously existence is *not* empty: just look around!

If it serves as consolation, notice that *all worldviews, including materialism, entail analogous paradoxes when it comes to the ultimate origin of everything.* Big Bang theory, for instance, carries this contradiction in another form: how did everything, in the form of a bang, come out of an absolute void? What was there to bang? One is immediately confronted with the contradiction that, while there was *nothing* in the beginning, there had to be at least a *potential,* with certain properties and attributes, which could have led to a bang.[122] Moreover, under modern materialism, it's not only the remote past that carries contradictions: in order to make sense of what happens in nature *today*, Quantum Field Theory needs to postulate that countless subatomic particles are constantly popping into existence out of... nothing.[123] So either something *can* magically come out of nothing or we must embrace the paradox that everything that is anything somehow remains *void*. In that sense, the so-called 'quantum field' of modern physics is analogous to the membrane of mind: both are and never cease to be *empty*, yet somehow *become everything* when excited.[124] Both are somewhat precarious intellectual models – *metaphors* – for something that fundamentally transcends the intellect. We will come back to this shortly.

There's just no way around some form of this paradox under any otherwise coherent metaphysics – materialist, idealist, or otherwise – that is honestly and diligently pursued to its ultimate implications.

Freewill

Now we need to tackle another critical point that has also been left out of the discussion thus far. We're cleaning up the house before taking a major step forward shortly.

In all metaphors described, there is always an element of *movement:* the flow of water, the ripples of mercury and the vibrations of the membrane. But setting something in motion requires *energetic action* of some sort: water flows because of gravitational pull; ripples form because of surface disturbances; vibrations must be initiated and powered in some way. So, in the context of all these metaphors, *what is it that makes mind move?*

Notice that the answer to this question cannot be a phenomenon of experience, since experience is already mind in motion! Whatever the *primary cause* of the movement of mind is, it cannot itself be a movement of mind. Thus, we cannot find the primary cause in physics, biology, psychology, or any area of *knowledge.* The difficulty here is the same one behind the impossibility to describe the medium of mind itself: since all knowledge is a *movement* of the medium of mind, that which sets mind in motion cannot be known directly. *But we can gain intuition about it indirectly, by observing its most immediate effects in experience and then trying to infer their invisible source.*

Our ordinary lives entail unfathomably complex chains of cause and effect: one thing leading to another, which in turn leads to another ... and another, along the outlines of a blooming, unfolding pattern that we call the laws of nature. But at the very root of the chain of causality there seems to be something ineffable, tantalizingly close to experience, yet *just* beyond it: *freewill.*

Whenever you make a decision, like choosing to close your hand into a fist, you have a strong sense that you were free to make the choice. But usually that sense comes only *after* the choice is made – *immediately* after – in the form of the heartfelt certainty that you *could* have made a different choice. The *direct experience of freewill,* however, remains ambiguous: before you make the choice it is not there; and then the very next experience seems to be already that of *having made* the choice. The experience of *making* the choice seems lost in a kind of vanishing in-between limbo, too elusive and slippery to catch at work. It is as though freewill were outside time, only its effects insinuating themselves into time.

Yet, freewill can be so tantalizingly close to experience – perhaps arbitrarily close – that many people are convinced that they *feel* the actual choice *being* made. Personally, despite having paid careful attention, I have never managed to satisfactorily 'catch' this elusive experience in an unambiguous manner. I can't prove it is not there, but I hope to have evoked enough doubt about it that you are open to the possibility that *choice itself is outside experience.* We only really experience the prelude and the immediate aftermath of choice, never the *making* of a choice.

When materialist scientists say that freewill is an illusion, they probably have this elusiveness in mind. While agreeing with them on this particular aspect, I do *not* deny the validity of the subsequent, heartfelt certainty that we *could* have made a different choice. My position here is subtle, so please bear with me to avoid misunderstandings.

Though I am aware that this is the trickiest element of my entire argument – resting, as it does, more on introspection than logic – *I contend that freewill proper is the primary cause of all movements of mind; the freewill of the one subject of all existence. Freewill can never be experienced directly: it is the driving force behind all experience and, thus, never an experience itself.* But we can *infer* its existence from the retroactive *sense of free choice* that we have immediately *after* making a decision. This sense of free choice is, so to speak, the 'echo' of the primary cause reverberating within our psychic structures.

Freewill is the 'mental energy' that sets the membrane of mind in motion. It may, in some ways, be related to the empirical notion of 'psychic energy' in depth psychology.[125] As such, it can play two roles: (a) it can make the membrane vibrate; and (b) it can reconfigure the topography and topology of the membrane, respectively creating protrusions and folded-in loops with various shapes. Notice that vibrations and topographical/topological contortions are fundamentally the same thing: movements of the membrane. The difference between them is merely relative: vibrations are rather fast and repetitive movements, while topographical/topological re-arrangements are rather slow and discrete movements. This way, *fundamentally there is only one process unfolding under the influence of the primary cause: the movement of mind.* We can *interpret* this single process, for ease of visualization, as an amalgamation between vibrations and topographical/topological contortions.

One should *not* look upon the primary cause as another ontological primitive separate from the medium of mind, *but as an intrinsic property of the medium of mind itself.* Its energy is the mental energy inherent to the medium, in the same way that physicists today consider the universe to have a certain inherent amount of physical energy. It simply is so that the medium of mind carries the potential to move. Were it not to be so, there would be no experience. The medium of mind remains the sole ontological primitive of all existence, for it alone concretizes the primary cause.

An implication of what I contend above is that freewill is fundamentally unexplainable, for it is a process that we cannot experience directly. This may sound like a copout. But if the word has any meaning at all, *freewill must not have any explanation, otherwise it wouldn't be free.* An explanation always entails a chain of cause and effect that unfolds into the phenomenon being explained. If freewill could be explained, it would consist merely of the unfolding of causality, which contradicts the meaning of the word. Therefore, freewill is, *by definition,* something that can't be explained or modeled. The way in which I fit the notion of freewill into the membrane metaphor is, thus, coherent and consistent with its meaning. In fact, the metaphor even explains *how* it is that freewill can truly be *free,* making some sense of an otherwise slippery abstraction.

Self-imposed topographical/topological constraints

If what sets the membrane of mind in motion is the freewill of the one subject of all existence – that is, the membrane itself – it should then be able, in principle, to freely adjust its experiential reality according to its wishes, simply by vibrating in more suitable harmonics. Yet we, localized points-of-view of this one mind, mostly experience *limitation.* The hallmark of human life, more than the experiences we *can* have, seems to be the whole truckload of experiences we wish for but *can't* have. Or, worse yet, the experiences we are frightened of but cannot avoid. The patterns and regularities represented by the laws of physics also pose firm limitations on what experiences can unfold (you can't fly by flapping your arms) and even enforce other experiences regardless of our will (if you jump out of a window, you will fall). Somehow, out of unlimited flexibility to create experience, limitation arises.

Unlike what we discussed earlier, this isn't a paradox. It can be made sense of. As we've seen, there is only one active process in mind: *movement*. In order to understand this process, it is handy to divide it into *vibration* and *structural reconfiguration*. Now, when mind takes on a certain local structure in the form of a protrusion or a loop, this structure defines the particular *modes of vibration* supported by it. In other words, each local structure can vibrate according to certain patterns, *but not according to others*. There is, thus, a sense in which one aspect of the movement of mind – namely, structural reconfiguration – creates limitations and constraints for the other aspect of the movement of mind – namely, vibration. *When these two aspects are taken together as a single process of movement, there is no limitation. But taken separately, as different sub-processes, one sub-process limits the other.*

It is fair to say that, when mind reconfigures itself structurally, the corresponding *movement* of the membrane is indeed registered as an experience. But this must happen only very gently and slowly, since we don't see people and animals – the *partial images* of these mental structures – morphing into other shapes or getting older in an instant. The corresponding experience must be, therefore, practically imperceptible. However, once a certain structural configuration is in place, it limits the modes of vibration supported within it. Therefore, *most experiences in life are bound to the modes of vibration supported by particular structures of the membrane of mind*. Since our egos are nothing but such structures, our lives seem much more characterized by *limitation* than by experiential freedom.

Yet, this limitation is only an illusion generated by the localization of mind: it only exists from the perspective of the human psychic structure, not from the perspective of the unified, global process of mental movement. *By exploring its very freedom to move, mind at large ends up creating local structures throughout its surface. And then, as a direct consequence of this act of creative freedom, local limitations arise as far as the modes of vibration supported by each structure.* What appears to us as limitation is actually a *natural and necessary result* of the expression of creative freedom.

As a matter of fact, if the broader membrane of mind were to remain flat, its structure would only support limited patterns of vibration, analogous to those in Figure 10. It is precisely by contorting itself into multiple, local structural configurations that mind creates a limitless variety of localized patterns of vibration, far expanding the richness of experience that would otherwise be possible. Therefore, from the broader point-of-view of the membrane at large, the whole process is actually a means to create variety and diversity. *Local limitation is the expression of global freedom.* It's too bad, though entirely natural and probably unavoidable, that we, limited psyches, 'lose contact' with the broader view. Much sadness and anxiety could otherwise be spared.

Can the ego transcend its limitations?

Positing the primary cause – the energetic action of freewill – to be centralized somewhere or unevenly distributed over the membrane of mind would require unjustified new assumptions. Instead, we must take freewill to be a property evenly distributed throughout the membrane of mind. But then you might ask: 'If freewill is evenly distributed, then the ego has it. And since freewill applies to both vibration and structural reconfiguration, why can't the ego change its own structure at will?' If the ego could do that, the psyche would be able to transcend space, time, and empirical reality as a whole. Who wouldn't want that? Yet, not many of us seem able to do it. So what's wrong?

The first thing to consider is that the ego, whose partial image, as we've seen, is closed-cycle neural processes in the brain, is hosted by a larger structure – namely, the rest of the body – that is *not* under the full control of egoic will. You can move and use your body within certain limits but you can't, for instance, get taller or skinnier at will, or stop pain on command, or avoid all illness, etc. Indeed, *the rest of the body is a partial image of the 'personal unconscious' – that is, of the underlying protrusion – not of the egoic loop per se.* That's why we say that we 'have' a body, instead of saying that we 'are' a body. The fact that it is hosted by this body poses strong boundary constraints on how far the ego can go, even in principle, in altering itself through exercising its own egoic will. Furthermore, the body itself – including the ego – is hosted by a yet broader region of mind that we call the universe. This broader region operates according to patterns and regularities – that is, the 'laws of nature' – that are also outside the control of egoic will. So the scope of possibilities for the ego to change itself is limited to begin with, since it is inserted in a context that it cannot fully control, and which poses strict boundary constraints on the ego itself.

All this said, there is evidence that some people *can* develop psychic abilities beyond anything ordinary. There is evidence that some of us *can* achieve what the culture has come to call 'enlightenment': a state of mind that allows one to see a deeper reality, beyond ordinary egoic limitations. There is evidence that some of us *are able* to transcend the plague of egoic neuroses. And there is no doubt that very few of us wouldn't like to get there too. So why can't we all?

Here is my answer: the ego *is* the limited patterns of vibration entailed by a certain loop structure. It *is* the patterns of thought, feeling, and perception that arise within that particular structure. As such, it is fair to say that *the ego is the structure.* Therefore, from the ego's perspective, changing the structure too much means *dying,* insofar as it entails ceasing to be what it is. Although, in principle, it should have the freedom to carry out this action, the ego simply doesn't want to. *Precisely because it has freewill, it freely won't.* To avoid suffering, you may often think that you want to be 'different,' but that doesn't mean that your ego wants to become something else. In reality, what you *really* want is to stop suffering *as yourself,* not to abandon your current sense of identity. After all, it doesn't help if it is *someone else* who stops suffering!

Another point to consider is how much the egoic structure can be altered without this alteration turning into the process we call physical death. After all, we know empirically that the psychic structure – whose partial image is the body, including the brain – is a very delicate system. A significant change in the egoic structure would entail as a significant change in the image we call the brain. And we all know that too significant a change in that image – I will refrain from graphical descriptions here – correlates with physical death. In other words, large disruptions in the *partial image* that we call a brain reflect large disruptions in the 'whirlpool' of the psyche (remember?), perhaps to the point that it could no longer sustain itself and would dissipate instead.

So, does this all mean that most of us are condemned to the egoic prison, with all its trappings and grasping, until physical death? Not necessarily.

The ego has no problems using its freewill – its portion of the primary cause's mental energy – to try and improve its own feelings and thoughts. After all, we all want to have better feelings and higher thoughts *without ceasing to be who we are.* In the metaphor, this corresponds to choosing which ones, among the many modes of vibration supported by its loopy structure, the ego wants to vibrate in. No significant structural reconfiguration is entailed and, thus, no threat to the ego. All it is trying to do is to become the best version *of itself* that it can be. Your very reading of this book likely reflects an attempt by your ego to do just that.

But now an interesting and unexpected effect sneaks into the picture, outside the ego's radar screen: *vibrations can dramatically affect the configuration of the structures where they take place.* The original Tacoma Narrows Bridge is a clear example of this: after the resonant vibrations taking place in it did their job, the bridge ended up looking a little different. Theoretically, in fact, there are always resonant patterns of vibration that can change and even destroy any structure hosting them.[126]

Ordinarily, one disperses one's mental energy by exciting multiple, *interfering* modes of vibration within the egoic loop. The resulting vibrations, thus, never build up to disruptive levels: the different patterns partially cancel each other out. However, each egoic loop has the freedom and the potential will, *within the modes of vibration it is bound to,* to channel its energy into a single resonant pattern. When one focuses one's thoughts and feelings this way, there is no cancelation, but a *cumulative build-up* of vibration. The result is akin to continuously using all of one's power to push a swing at just the right pace: eventually something disruptive will happen (and you don't want a child to be sitting on the swing at that moment), just as it did with the original Tacoma Narrows Bridge.

Even though the ego is applying its freewill to excite vibrations alone – not structural reconfigurations – the process will end up disrupting the structure of the individual's psyche. And when it does, the psyche will have a *new* structure and, therefore, support *new modes of vibration!* Without really intending to do it directly, the ego will have transformed into something else. Whether this change is positive or not depends on the process. Mental energy can be focused on certain modes of vibration through, for instance, meditation. In this case, the changes tend to be positive *by design,* since the individual chooses where the focus goes. But in other cases, like in Obsessive-Compulsive Disorder (OCD), the reinforcement may not go in a desirable direction.

If these considerations are correct, our individual thoughts and feelings can potentially change our psychic structures and alter the set of constraints that our experiences are ordinarily bound to. Since brains are *partial images* of these structures, it is conceivable that our thoughts and feelings could change the anatomy and 'wiring' of our brains, an effect neuroscience has come to call 'self-directed neuroplasticity.' And indeed, there is strong empirical evidence that the effect happens. For instance, experiments have been performed in which patients suffering from OCD have been able to physically alter their own brain anatomy and neural 'wiring' – thereby curing themselves – simply by focusing their thoughts.[127] Several other studies have been done showing analogous results.[128]

As I elaborated upon in my earlier book *Rationalist Spirituality,* such results are difficult to make sense of under materialism, requiring contrived and promissory explanations. As Dr. Jeffrey Schwartz, of the UCLA Neuropsychiatric Institute put it, 'the demand that the data be understood solely from the perspective of brain-based causal mechanisms is a severe and counter-intuitive constraint.'[129] In contrast, the observed effect is natural and explainable in a very intuitive manner under the idealist interpretation described in this book.

The membrane and the laws of physics

We are now finally ready to take a major step: to try and reconcile our idealist membrane metaphor with our current leading-edge understanding of the laws of physics. After all, the patterns and regularities of nature captured by physics are empirical facts; they cannot be denied. Any idealist worldview must acknowledge and be able to integrate these patterns and regularities into its ontological framework in a coherent manner. In other words, physics must still make *good sense* under our idealism. And indeed, with the vibrating membrane metaphor we can make good sense of physics. Let us see how.

Physics today suffers from a kind of split personality

disorder: it entails two very different and conflicting models of nature. The first model, called the 'Standard Model' of particle physics, explains the microscopic world of molecules, atoms, and subatomic particles. The second model is Einstein's 'General Relativity,' which explains the macroscopic world of moons, planets, stars, and galaxies. Both models are verified to be correct in their respective domains, with an exquisite degree of confidence and precision. And our understanding entails that both should apply everywhere at all times. In other words, General Relativity should apply at the atomic scale, while the Standard Model should apply at cosmic scales.

The problem is that they contradict each other. They cannot be simultaneously true everywhere.[130] Therefore, there is obviously something wrong or incomplete about our current understanding of physics. Einstein himself died trying to solve this problem: trying to unify General Relativity with subatomic physics. He failed.[131] But at around the early 1980s, a promising new avenue was discovered.

As we have seen earlier, the Standard Model entails a bewildering variety of 'fundamental building blocks' to explain nature: dozens of fundamental subatomic particles, each considered an ontological primitive in its own merit. In other words, the fundamental subatomic particles in the Standard Model are irreducible; they are what they are because that's how nature is. The great insight achieved in the early 1980s was this: we can imagine that each fundamental subatomic particle is, in fact, an unimaginably small *vibrating string*. Particles that display different properties or behavior do so simply because *their underlying strings vibrate according to different modes.* Some modes of vibration create the property of mass, others the property of spin, electric charge, etc. This way, the only ontological primitive in nature is the strings themselves. Particles can all be reduced to strings vibrating in different modes.[132] *The entire universe is supposedly a kind of symphony generated by the vibration of funda-*

mental strings. Everything is vibration.

By 1995 problems and contradictions had arisen in the many mathematical attempts to make sense of this vibratory model of reality. But then a new breakthrough was made: a new theory postulated that, instead of countless identical but separate strings – one for each subatomic particle – our entire universe was, in fact, made of *a single membrane vibrating in ten spatial dimensions.*[133] The 'wiggle room' – that is, degrees of freedom – provided by these ten dimensions was required by the mathematical model in order to accommodate enough modes of vibration to account for the entire variety of phenomena in nature. Of the ten dimensions demanded by the mathematics, we can only see three. The other seven are postulated to be invisible. The original strings were now seen as small *sections* of this universal membrane, the vibrations of which give rise to all existence. The theory was called 'M-Theory,' where 'M' may stand for 'Membrane.' It is the very leading edge of physics today.[134]

The correspondences between M-theory and the vibrating membrane of mind are obvious. But we must not forget this: most physicists are realists and, therefore, *interpret* the membrane to exist objectively, outside and independently of mind. However, the mathematical model of M-theory does not imply such an ontological interpretation: it simply models the modes of vibration of the membrane. *I thus submit that the membrane of M-theory is nothing but certain aspects of the vibrating membrane of mind.* What M-theorists are doing is modeling the patterns and regularities of *some* of the dynamics of mind: those that we associate with the empirical world 'outside.' They miss the rest of the dynamics of the membrane of mind: the vibratory patterns corresponding to our inner-world of feeling, insight, passion, etc., as well as the sum-total of the personal and collective 'unconscious.'

As I argued before, a new worldview does not necessarily

need to entail new physics. It only needs to provide a framework for a new *interpretation* of existing physics. By taking the hyper-dimensional membrane of M-theory to represent aspects of *the medium of mind itself,* I trust to be doing just that.

A few observations need to be made at this stage. M-theory is not a complete theory, in the sense that its mathematical elaboration has not yet been fully worked out. The extra dimensions required compound the problem significantly and physicists need time to sort it all out. Another criticism often leveled against M-theory is that it is not a proper scientific theory. The point of contention here is *falsifiability:* any proper scientific theory must make *unique* predictions that can be verified empirically, and which can either confirm or falsify the theory. But most of the predictions of M-theory are identical to those of the Standard Model and General Relativity, *as they should be,* since the predictions of both the Standard Model and General Relativity have been abundantly confirmed experimentally. The few predictions that are specific to M-theory don't seem to fall within the possibilities of experimental verification in the foreseeable future.[135] So many scientists claim, with good reason, that M-theory is not falsifiable; that it can, at best, only be shown to be internally consistent.

Be it as it may, the point here is that M-theory offers an avenue to resolve a fundamental contradiction in physics. Whether it is a falsifiable theory or not, *it can potentially make sense of something that we know to be inconsistent today: the Standard Model and General Relativity cannot both be correct simultaneously.* One should not underestimate the importance of that. And, as it turns out, the most promising way to resolve this contradiction is to imagine that all empirical phenomena are *the vibrations of a membrane in ten spatial dimensions; an uncanny correspondence to the membrane of mind with which we can explain the ego and the 'unconscious.'*

M-theory focuses on modeling the patterns and regularities of the empirical world. In other words, it models only our *shared perceptions of a common environment: the modes of vibration of the broader membrane that resonate with all human egoic loops.* It ignores the idiosyncratic vibratory patterns arising within each ego, as well as the 'unconscious.' As such, the membrane of M-theory captures but some aspects of the vibrating membrane of mind. The mathematics of M-theory only models *a limited part of the dynamics of mind.* It leaves out the tapestry of emotion, passion, insight, etc. Although we *can* import all the mathematics of M-theory onto the membrane of mind, this does not solve the complete problem, only a part of it.

Perhaps one day physicists and psychologists will take a hint from the collaboration between Carl Jung and Wolfgang Pauli[136] and realize that they are both tackling different aspects of the exact same problem: physicists trying to model the movements of mind corresponding to the so-called 'outer world,' while psychologists try to make sense of the movements of mind corresponding to the so-called 'inner world.' *Both camps are working with different modes of vibration of the membrane of mind.* The day this realization dawns upon our intellectual elite will be the day that the 'hard problem of consciousness' disappears, for its artificiality will become self-evident.

The role of metaphors

You may be thinking now that, in the idealist worldview developed in this book, the vibrating membrane of mind is nothing but a metaphor. The membrane of M-theory, on the other hand, should be something real, concrete, and not just a metaphor.

Well, it is correct that the membrane of mind is just a metaphor. After all, as discussed earlier, the medium of mind itself cannot be known directly, for it is the knower. *But the membrane of M-theory is also just a metaphor!* The only reality we can observe is supposedly the oscillations of this membrane. The membrane itself is beyond empirical verification. Physicists talk about a membrane simply because they have found a *correspondence of form* – an isomorphism – between the patterns of vibration of an abstract, imaginary membrane wiggling in ten spatial dimensions and the phenomena observed in the laboratory. In other words, reality behaves *as if* underlying it all there were a membrane. This does not necessarily mean that there *literally* is a membrane out there. It is a modeling tool, a metaphor, even a convenient fiction.

More generally speaking, when physicists postulate entities or fields that are beyond direct observation they are just creating metaphorical models. In philosophy of science this general view is called *anti-realism,* and it is a fairly well accepted view.[137]

Setting the words right

To conclude this chapter let us finally define, with more precision, what different words mean in the context of the worldview now largely laid out in this book:

Mind: refers to the medium of all existence as a subjective phenomenon, as well as its inherent property of freewill. In this book, mind has been metaphorically visualized as a stream of water, an ocean of mercury and a hyper-dimensional tinfoil membrane.

Consciousness: synonym of mind.

Freewill: the primary cause and 'energy' that sets mind in motion. Freewill is an irreducible, uniformly distributed property of mind. It cannot be explained in terms of causality.

Experience: a particular movement of mind. The qualities of an experience are determined by the pattern of this movement. In this book, we have metaphorically visualized the movements of mind as undulations, ripples and vibrations.

Contents of mind: a set of experiences.

Information: synonym of experience. Information only arises out of a contrast between different states, like on and off, black and white, zero and one, etc. Similarly, experience only arises out of a movement of mind that creates a contrast between different configurations, like the upward and downward bulges of the string in Figure 9. The two terms, therefore, are isomorphic. Notice also how intuitive it is to equate them: if there is no information, what is there to experience? Indeed, philosopher David Chalmers once speculated that conscious experience might be intrinsically associated with information.[138] His extensive argument substantiates the equivalence proposed here.

Awareness: a self-reflective form of conscious apprehension. When you are aware of an experience, not only do you have the experience, you also know that you are having the experience. Naturally, awareness is itself a special form of experience, so you can be aware that you are aware ... that you are aware of something.

Thought: a particular type of experience arising autonomously within an individual psychic structure.

Perception: a particular type of experience within an individual psychic structure, but which originally arises outside the psychic structure. Perception is triggered and modulated by patterns of vibration arriving from the broader medium of mind. These broader vibrations inject similar information into multiple psychic structures.

The unconscious: does not truly exist. The word is a misnomer for contents of mind that are not (sufficiently) amplified because they fall outside protrusions or folded-in loops in the membrane of mind.

Notice that a choice of words in cases like this is always somewhat arbitrary. I could have chosen different words to label the concepts described above. *But what is key are the concepts, not my particular choice of labels.* For instance, you may feel that words like 'awareness,' 'mind,' or 'thought' should be used differently. After all, other authors assign different meanings to them. You may even – and perhaps correctly – think that my definition of these words doesn't do justice to their mainstream usage. Indeed,

I admit that my choice may not have been optimal, though I did my best to strike a balanced compromise. What I ask is that you do not judge the *concepts* on the basis of their *labels,* nor misinterpret my argument by implicitly assigning to the words a meaning different from what I intended.

Sometimes different authors may be trying to say the exact same thing but their respective choices of words lead to apparent contradictions. To give you just one illustrative example of the dangers of word usage, consider this: some Zen-leaning authors I respect may say that 'mind is unreal,' which apparently contradicts the core point of this book. However, given the meaning they seem to assign to the words 'mind' and 'unreal,' they may actually be trying to make the same point I am making. *What they call 'mind' I call 'thought':* a movement of mind arising autonomously within an individual psyche. And since there is no 'correspondence theory of truth' under idealism, no thought has any anchoring in a reality outside mind. As such, what my Zen-leaning peers may actually mean with the statement 'mind is unreal' is that 'no thought corresponds to a reality outside mind.' This is entirely consistent with the message of this book! Do you see how subtle and dangerous words can be when removed from their proper context?

I urge you to look beyond labels when you consider the ideas in this book in light of the broader literature.

Chapter 7

Re-interpreting Reality

The core of the idealist worldview developed in this book has been laid out in the preceding chapters. What is left to do is to re-interpret reality and the phenomena of life and nature in terms of what has been discussed. If all reality is in mind, does it still make sense to speak of a cosmological past and a Big Bang? What are life and death? If the body is an image of a process in mind, why does a corpse remain – at least temporarily – in consensus reality after physical death? What can we make of parallel realities, the idea of a soul, ghosts and apparitions, non-ordinary states of consciousness and psychic phenomena under our new worldview? These and other topics are addressed in this chapter.

The membrane awakens: a cosmological history

I like to imagine the cosmological history of mind in the following way:[139] in the very beginning, the membrane of mind was at rest. It didn't move or vibrate. Its topography and topology were as simple as possible: an entirely flat membrane without any bumps, protrusions, or loops of any sort. As such, not only was there no self-reflectiveness, but also no experience, since experience consists in the vibrations of the membrane. Only an infinite abyss of experiential emptiness existed; the deep, dreamless sleep of nature. Yet, such unending emptiness was not *nothing*, for there was inherent in it *the potential for something*.

At some point, some part of the membrane moved, like in an involuntary spasm. Instantly, this movement was registered by the one subject of existence as a very faint *experience*. There is a significant sense in which an experience concretizes – brings into existence – its very subject. The membrane realized, at that moment, that there was *something*. It is not difficult to imagine that such a realization could lead to a kind of surprise and agitation that immediately translated into more spasmodic movements, more experiences. Shortly the membrane of mind was boiling with vibrations. And the more vibrations there were, the higher the agitation, and the more vibrations, etc., in a chain reaction of rising experience. The metaphor of a great explosion and inflationary expansion – a 'Big Bang' – doesn't seem that inappropriate here.

But since there were still no loops in the medium of mind, there was no self-reflective awareness. Existence was still a confusing maelstrom of instinctive experiences in which the subject was completely immersed. The subject *was* its own uncontrollable flow of passions and images, with no ability to step out and ponder about what was going on; no ability to make sense of its own predicament. Like a startled man in the middle of a giant, precariously balanced domino field, the subject was unaware that it was its own instinctive thrashing about amidst the falling dominoes that caused them to fall in ever-greater numbers. The one subject of existence was still a prisoner of its own instinctive unfolding. Love, hate, bliss, terror, color and darkness were all morphing into each other uncontrollably, like a storm. But all was still one.

At some point, the thrashing about of the membrane caused a small part of its surface to fold in on itself, closing a hollow loop. Suddenly, there was a hint of self-reflective awareness. And it was enough: the idea of 'I am' arose in mind for the first time. And the questions 'What am I? What is going on?' followed suit. A fundamental *awakening* happened and a creod – a developmental path – was discovered: a path to self-reflective awareness. From here on, a still somewhat chaotic refinement and expansion of that creod was the name of the game. Folds and loops began to emerge elsewhere in the membrane in a precarious attempt to replicate and expand on the original event. And today, we may still be living through this process.

Critics of idealism often ask why minds would conspire to confabulate empirical evidence for the story of the Big Bang and for all cosmological history preceding the rise of consciousness, given that everything has supposedly always been solely in mind. This criticism, of course, is fallacious from the start by assuming that any kind of conspiracy or agreement between separate minds is necessary: there is only one medium of mind from which all empirical observations are ultimately derived. Another fallacious notion embedded in this criticism is the idea that mind *arose* at some point in our cosmological past. This quite literally begs the question: it assumes that mind arose in particular organizations of matter at some point in time, which is an axiom of materialism. Under idealism, however, it was matter that arose in mind as a particular modality of experience. Mind never arose, for it was always there. So the criticism is based on multiple fallacious premises. The question it asks makes no sense.

Nonetheless, it is still worthwhile to consider the basic intuition behind this malformed criticism. The intuition is this: why do the patterns and regularities of experience suggest, by extrapolation, a complex past that precedes self-reflective awareness? The answer could be the very cosmological history imagined above: there was indeed a past in which mind still had no loops or folds. The *abstracted partial image* of this cosmological past, as *reconstructed* by the human ego according to the preferred symbols of a particular culture or time, takes the form of a Big Bang, or a collision of hyper-dimensional membranes in M-theory,[140] or the pulling apart of father Sky from mother Earth,[141] or of many other creation myths.[142] Indeed, any historical account of a remote cosmological past is, fundamentally, a self-referential *symbol* in mind for the history of mind itself. It is a more or less useful *image* – a metaphor – constructed by the psyche based on its own *interpretation and extrapolation* of the patterns and regularities it can empirically observe.

Does anyone have all the answers?

A ubiquitous notion across many religions and spiritual traditions is the idea that, although we, human beings, are ignorant
and confused while immersed in the school of life, there are
higher beings who possess all the answers to the mysteries of
existence. These beings supposedly stand *outside* the game: they
look on, all-knowingly, as we go through the trials of education.
And – it is also believed – there is a *plan*, or curriculum, for all of
our tribulations. As such, the craziness of life is supposedly only
apparent, for underlying it all there is great order. When we
physically die, our souls are believed to be welcomed by these
beings and receive whatever answers we couldn't figure out
ourselves, during life, the hard way.

Clearly, this is a comforting and reassuring narrative. But is it
true? I cannot answer because I genuinely do not believe to know
the answer. What I can do is to offer some thoughts and considerations that are relevant in the context of the narrative.

It is conceivable that other ego-capable psychic structures in
the fabric of mind, corresponding to broader loops with a
perhaps more complex topography or topology, have already
accumulated insights and understandings that far transcend our
possibilities as human beings. As a matter of fact, simple proba-
bility shows that this is not only conceivable, but the most likely
possibility. However, it is an entirely different question whether
the existence of these beings implies that there are answers to all
the questions that *we* have. Our philosophy may be more comprehensive than that of whales or elephants, but do we have answers
to the questions that whales and elephants ask themselves? Can
we even grok their questions? Do our human insights render the
insights of whales and elephants redundant? Not knowing much
about the realities they live in, I do not dare answering 'yes' to
these questions.

The human psychic structure defines our experiential reality by determining what modes of vibration resonate with us. For the psychic structure of another ego-capable being to understand all of *our* questions, and formulate answers that make sense to *us*, it would have to support all natural modes of vibration that the human psychic structure supports, and then at least some more. The likelihood of this is not necessarily high. And if these beings somehow did exist, there is a sense in which they would render our existence redundant: whatever insights we could potentially add to mind, through our many tribulations, would already be in mind to begin with. Moreover, if these beings could communicate to us, why not just tell us all the answers? Why allow us to go through so much suffering while struggling to find out the answers the hard way?

I think we should not ignore the possibility that, at the current stage of universal unfolding, *nobody anywhere* has all the answers.[143] We are the expression of mind in its attempt to make sense of what is going on. That this attempt is still in a somewhat chaotic state seems clear from even a casual glance at contemporary history. We are the very process that we seek to understand and control. Maybe there are beings that know *more* than we do, but not necessarily beings that know *what* we know, so our contributions are original.

Life, death, love and evil are all part of the inherent potential of mind. That many of us revolt against certain aspects of existence is also part and parcel of mind trying to make sense of its own nature and potential. Why do people suffer and die? Why is there evil? Why is there so much inequality and injustice? Maybe nobody really knows. Maybe we are all still running around, knocking things over clumsily in our struggle, as the dominoes fall all around us. And it is possible that *we alone* have a shot at making sense of it as we go through life. In any case, what else can we do other than to try and understand what is going on?

But notice this: if this possibility turns out to be true, *then our lives are meaningful in the strongest way imaginable!* It implies that we aren't just students redundantly having to find out, the hard way, answers already known to others. Instead, *we are researchers at the leading edge of knowledge.* We aren't receiving knowledge, but generating it. Our suffering is not redundant: it is part of what happens when we try to figure out what is going on, because we *are* what is going on. We are like a desperate physician performing exploratory surgery *on himself* – without anesthesia – to find out how his body works and then, hopefully, be able to master it. But the physician *feels* every slice of his scalpel and every pinch of his tweezers. In his agony, his hands aren't steady and he sometimes – maybe too many times – slices more than needed.

We are the chaos, the mess, the bleeding and the injustice. We are the harmony, the bliss, the healing and the compassion. We are the whole works, but we still don't understand how and why it unfolds the way it does. We are an impersonal force of nature – like a volcano, or a supernova – revolving wildly in uneasiness as it wakes up to itself. As such, existence is bound to be messy for the same reason that you can fall off of bed if you revolve wildly in a semi-awakened state.

Life, soul, and body

According to the worldview developed in this book, there is no soul separate from the body. There are only the movements of mind. As such, *the body is a partial image in mind of a process of mind.* The process in question is a form of self-localization of consciousness, analogous to how a whirlpool is a process of self-localization of water. In ordinary language we call this process of self-localization *life*. The end of life thus entails dissolution of the whirlpool, dissolution of the body image. Consciousness does not cease to exist, but simply de-localizes and flows more freely. The body image disappears in exactly the same way that a whirlpool disappears when the water stops flowing in circles. No water ceases to exist; it simply begins to flow unconstrained.

But there is a small problem here. If the body is an image of a process of consciousness localization, then when that process stops the image should also disappear, just like the whirlpool. *But a corpse stays in empirical reality for a while after death,* this being the reason we have burials, cremations and other similar rituals. The body doesn't disappear instantly, like the whirlpool does. How come? Notice that the old dualist metaphor of the soul doesn't suffer from this problem: since the soul merely inhabits the body, there is no contradiction in the fact that a body stays behind after the soul leaves it, just like a house stays behind when its occupants leave. Does this mean that dualism is a better worldview?

Not really. The problem here is that, as usual, we inadvertently make realist assumptions in an idealist context. Yes, the body is merely the partial image of a process, just like the whirlpool. *But that image does not exist in some kind of objective reality outside mind. The image itself exists in mind.* So the right question to ask is: In which part of mind does the image of a body exist? When you see my body, *my body image exists in your psychic structure.* When I look at my own body, my body image exists also in *my* psychic structure. Upon my physical death, my psychic structure – at least the part corresponding to the ego – unravels, so my body image can no longer exist in it. *But nothing stops my body image from continuing to exist – for a while, that is – in your psychic structure and other parts of the medium of mind.*

Alan Watts spoke of a corpse as a residual *echo* of something that mind is no longer doing.[144] Indeed, as discussed in Chapter 4, the body image corresponds to undulations imprinted by a whirlpool of mind into the broader stream, which eventually penetrate other whirlpools. After the source of the undulations – that is, the original whirlpool – has vanished, the undulations that had already been imprinted still maintain some momentum, flowing in the broader medium of mind where they can continue to penetrate the remaining whirlpools. These undulations can no longer be renewed by new excitations from the original source, so they eventually fade out. The partial image of this fading out is bodily decomposition, putrefaction.

The analogy with the echo is nearly perfect: an echo persists as air undulations after the original source stops emitting sound, but its momentum slowly wanes in the absence of new excitations. It gets weaker, distorted, and eventually disappears, in the same way that a corpse slowly decomposes and eventually disappears. Attempts at preserving a corpse can be understood as techniques for maintaining the momentum of the echo. It is conceivable that one can try to keep existing undulations going in the broader medium of mind even after their original source has vanished. The partial image of this process in our ordinary perception is mummification, embalming, etc.

The corpse is just an echo, but the living body is inherent to the psychic structure in the same way that flames, as an image, are inherent to combustion. The living body is not a mere habitation of the soul, but a true – albeit *partial* – image of the conscious entity. It is not an artificial shell, or a distorting barrier concealing and cloaking an inner entity, but the authentic way in which the conscious entity manifests in consensus reality. As such, it is not invalid to think of a person according to her body image: the body image is as honest to the conscious entity as flames are honest to combustion. However, it is ludicrous to think of the body image as the *complete* story about a person, in the same way that is incorrect to think that flames are all there is to combustion. Let's explore this last point a little further.

Partial images

Throughout this book, I have insisted in qualifying our ordinary perception of the phenomena of nature as *partial* images. For instance, I have insisted above that the body is a *partial* image of the process of consciousness localization. The reason for this has already been discussed in Chapter 2: we have absolutely no reason to believe that evolution would have favored a nervous system capable of capturing a complete and undistorted view of the world; much to the contrary. In Chapters 4 to 6 this argument has been substantiated under an idealist framework: not all undulations or vibrations of the broader medium of mind can penetrate the psyche. Under the vibrating membrane metaphor, for instance, only the modes of vibration that resonate with the structure of the egoic loop are perceived by the ego. Everything else is filtered out.

Therefore, what we call consensus reality is but a partial view of what is actually going on. The ordinary constraints of space and time – that is, our inability to see across corners or relive the past – are themselves consequences of the filtering process. How much is filtered out? It is impossible to say. But it is entirely reasonable to expect that *most* of what is going on remains unseen by the ego. As such, the body we see may be just a small, flattened projection of something much more complex. This complex 'hyper-body' would correspond to the full pattern of vibration put out by a psychic structure into the broader membrane of mind; that is, the full set of undulations imprinted by a whirlpool into the broader stream. But we cannot see the full pattern ordinarily, because our egoic structures only resonate with certain modes of vibration.

With these considerations in mind, we should not expect to ever be able to find, in the human brain, specific and unambiguous neural correlates for each and every aspect of subjective experience. The patterns of brain activity that we can measure are, like the rest of nature, *partial* images of the mental processes they represent. When we look at a person's active brain, we will always find correspondences between what we see there and the subjective experiences reported by the person. But what we see is not the complete story. There is just no reason to expect that we will ever uncover a complete, detailed, one-to-one mapping between every quality of every experience and a specific parameter of measurable brain activity.

Behind every phenomenon we see – from brains to lightning, from fire to galaxies – there may be unfathomably more complex, rich and nuanced processes than the partial images we can apprehend. The ego cannot see empirical reality for what it truly is. If this is correct, then science – at least as we know it today – will never be able to find complete causal closure. In other words, science will never be able to explain every phenomenon of nature – not only in principle, but in explicit detail – on the basis of what we can ordinarily measure. As I argued in my earlier book *Meaning in Absurdity*, there will always be unexplained mysteries, missing pieces of the puzzle.

Non-ordinary states of consciousness

The discussion above raises interesting questions: Can we do anything in order to see more of what is *really* going on? Can we somehow alter our psychic structures so less of reality is filtered out? Can we somehow partially and temporarily de-localize our consciousness in order to transcend ordinary space and time constraints?

As we've seen in Chapter 6, the ego is unable to alter its own topographical/topological structure directly because it *is* that structure. It has a self-preservation reflex analogous to our inability to, say, hold our breath until we die or choke ourselves with our own bare hands. But not all changes to the structure of the egoic loop need to be initiated by the ego itself: the broader membrane of mind, corresponding to the 'collective unconscious,' is not identified with the ego and, therefore, is not bound to any egoic reflex of self-preservation. The same can be said of the protrusions corresponding to our 'personal unconscious' (whose partial images, except for the parts of our active brains that correspond to the ego, are the rest of our physical bodies).

Thus, the dynamics of the 'unconscious' can fundamentally alter the structure of anyone's ego, just like a storm can damage your house regardless of whether you like it or not. They are just impersonal manifestations of a force of nature. When this happens, the affected ego will perceive these changes not as its own doing, but as an external intervention imposed on it. Spontaneous mystical experiences, so-called 'alien abduction' experiences[145] and certain types of acute mental breakdown – for instance, some of those that psychiatrist Stanislav Grof has called 'spiritual emergencies'[146] – could be seen as instances of a sudden vibrational interference from the 'unconscious.' Some chronic psychic conditions – like certain types of dementia, neuroses, and psychoses – could perhaps reflect a more gradual raid by the 'unconscious.' Even mundane physical afflictions of the brain – like infections, inflammations, aneurisms, etc. – could be thought to originate in the 'personal unconscious.' In many of these cases, the alterations of the psychic structure can be seen, as a partial image, in the form of anatomical or functional changes to the brain.

There are also techniques for intentionally – albeit temporarily – altering one's psychic structure: think of psychoactive drugs, hyper-ventilation, ordeals, G-force centrifuges, Transcranial Magnetic Stimulation and other proce-dures discussed in Chapter 2. They allow an adventurous ego to bypass its own self-preservation reflex in order to temporarily weaken itself. I hesitate with the allegory that I am about to use, but it is the clearest and most evocative one: with these techniques an ego can partially choke itself with a noose, instead of trying in vain to do it with its own bare hands. The noose allows the ego to bypass its self-preservation reflex.

All these techniques have something in common: they weaken the egoic loop and, therefore, reduce self-reflectiveness. One could visualize it as a temporary and partial opening or loosening of the loop: the opposing mirrored surfaces no longer face each other optimally. The vibratory patterns are no longer optimally reflected and the corresponding amplification is reduced. *Less self-reflective amplification reduces the level of obfuscation and allows for otherwise 'unconscious' contents to become discernible; a kind of egoic eclipse that allows the stars to become visible at noon.* Under a functional brain scanner, as we have seen, the partial image of this process is a reduction of brain activity, which corresponds to the loosening of the egoic loop. Indeed, the psilocybin study mentioned earlier has shown that much of the observed reduction in brain activity takes place in the 'Default Mode Network,'[147] an area of the brain associated with the ego.

The examples of non-local, transpersonal experiences discussed in Chapter 2 can be explained as described above: a loosening or weakening of the egoic loop, which reduces obfuscation, and which in turn allows 'unconscious' contents to become discernible. Precognition, clairvoyance, telepathy, and all kinds of psychic phenomena could also conceivably be explained in the same manner.

What really happens after death?

The simple answer is: nobody alive knows. But we can make educated inferences from the little we know about life. Indeed, the metaphysics discussed in this book can be tentatively extrapolated towards the after-death state.

It is reasonable to assume that *the mental process we call physical death 'makes the unconscious more conscious,' because it eliminates a source of obfuscation; namely, the egoic loop.* After all, physical death is the partial image of the process of unraveling of the egoic loop. As such, it is reasonable to expect that it causes us to *remember* all that we already know but cannot recall. From the ego's perspective, this may seem like receiving all kinds of new answers. *But it won't fundamentally add any original insight to mind.* The sense of novelty here is merely the illusion of an ego going through dissolution. Once the ego is gone and all is remembered, the sense of novelty will disappear. One way to think of this is what happens when we suddenly awaken from an intense nightly dream: for a few seconds, we are astonished to remember who we really are and what is really going on ('Oh, it is a dream! My real life is something else!'). While still half in the dream, we register this remembrance as *novel* knowledge about ourselves and about what is *really* going on. But the sense of novelty quickly wanes once we settle back into ordinary conscious states. After all, we simply continue to know what we already knew anyway, but had just forgotten while in the dream. *The only true novelty was the experiences of the dream,* not what was remembered upon awakening. As such, maybe life and death are entirely analogous to dreaming and waking up, respectively.

The question, of course, is whether self-reflective awareness disappears completely upon physical death. This depends on the topographical and topological details of the human psychic structure, which are not known. If the ego is the only loop in the human psychic structure, then physical death indeed eliminates all self-reflectiveness. But it is conceivable that the psychic structure entails an underlying, partial, not-so-tightly-closed loop underneath the egoic loop. I say this because many Near-Death Experiences seem to suggest that a degree of self-reflectiveness and personal identity survive death.[148] In this case, the ego would be a tight loop perched on top of another partial loop. Assuming that physical death entails the dissolution of only the egoic loop on top, then our awareness would 'fall back' onto the underlying partial loop, preserving a degree of self-reflectiveness. The result would be more access to the 'unconscious' – due to less obfuscation – but we would still maintain a sense of separate identity. This, of course, is highly speculative.

Even if the ego is the only loop in our psychic structure, there is still another interesting avenue of speculation regarding the preservation of a form of identity in the after-death state. Carl Jung, towards the end of his life, compared the physical body to the visible part of a plant as it grows from the ground in the spring. He thought of the core of the individual as the root (rhizome), which remains invisible underground.[149] Jung's analogy can be mapped very straightforwardly onto the membrane metaphor: the root is the underlying protrusion that corresponds to the 'personal unconscious.' This protrusion, we can speculate, remains largely invisible in ordinary consensus reality because its vibratory 'footprint' on the broader membrane is largely filtered out by the ego. The physical body we see may correspond to just a small part of the protrusion, the majority of it remaining invisible. The ego is in the visible part of the plant, which rises in spring and dies in winter. Its partial image in ordinary consensus reality is closed-cycle neural processes in the brain.

Physical death, as such, doesn't necessarily entail the *complete* dissolution of the underlying protrusion, but perhaps only some peripheral parts of it, along with the egoic loop. Throughout life, egoic experiences could leak – through resonance – into the 'personal unconscious' and accumulate there. This way, our personal history – a key element of our identity as individuals – could largely survive death as well. If this is so, then physical death may bring us back to the world of the 'personal unconscious': the world of our memories and dreams. But it may eliminate self-reflective awareness, so we become immersed in the dream without being able to think critically about what is going on; without being able to ask questions like "What is happening? How did I end up here?" We may just re-live our memories and traverse our own dreamscape in a way that transcends time, space, and even logic.

Amid all these speculations, I think only one thing can be stated with very high confidence: physical death does *not* entail the end of consciousness, for consciousness is the fabric of all existence. In addition, it is reasonable to expect that physical death reduces self-reflectiveness and, thereby, increases our access to the contents of the 'unconscious' due to less obfuscation. This last point is another clue to the usefulness of ordinary life: it provides us with a heightened ability to self-reflect about existence and our condition within it.[150]

Ghosts and apparitions

The topic of ghosts and apparitions is a very delicate one. Any appropriate treatment of this subject requires a very precise definition of what one means with the words 'ghosts' and 'apparitions.' Many imagine ghosts as quasi-physical entities that can interact with matter in space-time in ways similar to a physical body: by pushing objects around, making noises, stepping on floors, etc. Under the worldview developed in this book, such a conception of ghosts is difficult – if at all possible – to support. Allow me to elaborate on this.

As we've seen earlier, the partaking of a psychic structure in consensus reality is a process that has an image: a physical body. As such, conception and birth are the images of the early stages of the process whereby a protrusion of mind alters its configuration so as to resonate with the broader vibratory patterns corresponding to consensus reality. Death is the image of the end stage of that same process. Therefore, to expect a psychic structure to partake in consensus reality without going through conception, birth, or having a correlated physical body is like expecting combustion without flames, atmospheric electric discharge without lightning, or coagulation without clots. *The body simply is the image of the partaking.* It is thus difficult to see how or why one should expect a different image – namely, a ghost or an apparition – to be associated with a psychic structure interacting physically within consensus reality.

This is not to say, however, that living entities cannot, in some way, communicate with differentiated structures in the fabric of mind that do not (anymore) partake in our consensus reality. After all, all communication is a process of resonance. A dead person might simply be a differentiated structure that no longer resonates with the patterns of vibration we call the empirical world. *But it will still resonate with other patterns.* The question, then, is whether a living person can, through non-ordinary states of consciousness, tune into the vibratory patterns put out by a deceased person. This doesn't seem impossible, though further speculation is only justified if there is enough empirical evidence to demonstrate that the phenomenon exists.

The notion that communication with the departed – if it happens at all – must take place through some form of mental resonance, as opposed to the (quasi-)physical manifestation of the deceased in consensus reality, is supported by the conclusions reached by one of the foremost experts in the subject: Professor Erlendur Haraldsson. In his book *The Departed Among the Living* Haraldsson says: 'There can hence only be a cognitive or telepathic connection between the living and the dead. The deceased person moulds the perception in the mind of the living person.'[151]

Traditional cultures

It is striking how traditional cultures around the world seem to have been consistently non-materialist. Native American Indians, the great civilizations of Central and South America, Amazonian Indians like the Zuruahã mentioned in Chapter 1, Australian Aboriginals, Siberian and African tribes, etc., all held – and most still hold – strongly to non-materialist worldviews. We casually explain this to ourselves today with the arrogant presumption that our Western civilization is philosophically superior and simply knows better. Traditional cultures – we like to think – were, and still are, plagued by superstition and ignorance. Yet, I suspect that this is too simplistic and easy an explanation. It dismisses the question rather than answer it. After all, if materialism really is true, it is difficult to see why human beings anatomically identical to us would, for thousands upon thousands of years, have insisted on basing their entire culture and society on beliefs that have never had any empirical basis.

I dare to offer a different explanation here. Unlike all traditional cultures, Western civilization has reached a degree of technological and social advancement that allows for unprecedented levels of physical health and comfort. We eat more than well; we live in heated houses; we move about in sheltered vehicles; we developed effective treatments for a variety of chronic diseases; etc. In contrast, members of traditional societies were often exposed to the weather, to malnutrition, to extreme physical exertion, and to chronic health conditions. I suggest that such level of exposure would have compromised brain function sufficiently to induce non-ordinary states of consciousness on a regular basis. To put it simply, traditional people would be regularly exposed to what they called 'the otherworld,' a part of reality otherwise filtered out by well-functioning brains. Their non-local, transcendent experiences wouldn't be merely personal and idiosyncratic, but validated at a collective level, since most members of the society would also experience them. Such sharing of transcendent experiences ensured that a non-materialist ontology became enshrined in most traditional cultures as the official worldview. Their ontology wasn't based on superstition, but on shared *empirical* observation recorded, thereafter, according to allegorical images and narratives peculiar to each particular culture.

In the West, spontaneous access to such transcendent experiences has become nearly impossible. Non-ordinary states of consciousness no longer have collective momentum, since our sheltered lives ensure optimal levels of brain activity and function. The isolated instances in which people do have non-local, transcendent experiences are comparatively few and far between; enough for them to be treated as dismissible anomalies. This is why it has become at all possible for us to adopt a materialist view of nature in the first place.

Notice that, even in the West, non-materialist worldviews were the norm before the technological and social advancements that so much improved our health and comfort. Medieval Europeans lived in a magical world populated by fairies, elves, angels, and demons. If one goes back in history to the time of the early Roman Empire, or even earlier, the prevailing worldview among Europeans was paganism, almost the antithesis of materialism.

Parallel realities and nested consciousness

The experiential reality we live in is a function of our psychic structures: the patterns of vibration of the broader membrane that resonate with our psychic structures determine our shared, empirical experiences. It is thus conceivable that there are ego-capable beings whose psychic structures are so different from ours that no pattern of vibration of the broader membrane could resonate with both their and our psychic structures. Our respective worlds would, thus, be entirely different and disjoint. Moreover, it is conceivable that none of the vibratory patterns that these beings put out into the broader membrane of mind would resonate with our psychic structures, and vice-versa. As such, we would not be able to perceive anything about their existence and neither would they perceive anything about us. For all practical purposes, these beings would not occupy the same framework of space-time that we do. In effect, we would be living in *parallel realities.*

It is fun to speculate whether there could be conscious beings whose world is disjoint from, but yet so close to, ours that, through a slightly altered state of consciousness, we could establish a degree of resonance – a form of communication – with them. The world's traditions are certainly full of mythological references that could conceivably fall under this scenario: fairies, elves, djinns, nixies, gnomes, sylphs, grey aliens, angels, demons, etc.

There is another way in which we could speculate about the existence of parallel realities under the worldview developed in this book. Imagine that a region of the membrane of mind differentiates itself in two steps: in a first step, a *large* area of the membrane protrudes according to a certain topography that supports specific patterns of vibration. Let's call this first protrusion a *base structure*. In a second step, *multiple* psychic structures – each corresponding to a conscious being – then protrude *from the base structure*. There is, thus, a sense in which the specific modes of vibration supported by the base structure determine the empirical reality – the physics – shared by the psychic structures protruding from it: whatever modes of vibration are not supported by the base structure cannot be part of the empirical reality of the respective conscious beings. It is conceivable that there could be countless base structures across the broader membrane of mind, each entailing a very particular parallel reality with its own distinctive, internal physics and logic. Our entire universe may be but one of myriad base structures.

It is interesting to notice that, like any protrusion, *a base structure is itself a conscious entity with its own 'unconscious.'* This way, there is a sense in which our entire universe may be the partial image of a conscious entity: an *Anima Mundi* or a Platonic Demiurge. Similarly, since the human body is a kind of micro-universe composed of trillions of individual living cells, the exact same rationale may apply at its own level: your body may be the partial image of a base structure from which trillions of microbial-level protrusions emerge. In this case, your brain may correspond to a segment of this base structure that has folded in on itself, giving rise to an ego 'attached' to the broader micro-universe of your body. Finally, what applies at both the cosmic and human levels may also apply at levels in between: take, for instance, James Lovelock's 'Gaia' hypothesis, under which our planet is seen as a self-regulating living organism.[152] Earth could be the partial image of a base structure from which all plant and animal protrusions emerge.

The general notion behind all these speculations is that membrane structures can emerge from membrane structures in a nested manner: protrusions rising from protrusions, which in turn rise from protrusions, and so forth, like fractals. The degrees of freedom with which the topography of mind can conceivably organize itself along these nested levels – the nuances, details, and complexities of the organization – transcend, almost by definition, our human ability to visualize them. As such, the membrane metaphor is formidable in its potential explanatory power.

Chapter 8

Final Musings

In this chapter I'd like to share some open thoughts with you about the worldview laid out in this work, the way it has been conveyed, and how it relates to the present state of our culture. There is a sense in which this chapter is a personal critique of the rest of the book. The points I will attempt to make are subtle and could be easily – as well as unfavorably – misinterpreted. The more intuitive tone of the chapter could also be misconstrued as loose and become detrimental to the book as a whole. Yet, I believe the potential benefits of doing this outweigh the risks. After all, I am not trying to win any beauty contest, but simply to convey ideas in as honest and open a way as possible. The judge, if there is any, is you alone.

Before we get to the more delicate and nuanced parts, let's start easy.

Split-off complexes

A core idea of this book is the notion that localized segments of mind at large can become immersed in the illusion of being separate from the rest of the broader membrane. The illusion originates from the self-reflective amplification of certain mental contents to the detriment of others. The ego becomes blind to the broader membrane of mind, identifying itself solely with the amplified contents in its own field of self-reflection.

Yet, talking about this with friends, I've heard from some that they were uncomfortable with the whole idea. To them, it was counter-intuitive that different segments of *the same mind* could really become convinced that they were separate entities. After all, we experience our own psyches mostly as single, unified mental spaces. It is hard for most people to imagine that their psyches could be broken up into seemingly separate and independent identities. Thus, how could that happen to mind at large?

But *we know empirically that the fragmentation of the human psyche into multiple and seemingly separate identities happens all the time.* Indeed, psychology informs us of countless cases of the phenomenon of 'Dissociative Identity Disorder,' in which a single person can display multiple and seemingly disconnected identities and personalities.[153] Each of these identities does not identify with the others, considering itself to be a separate entity, a separate center of consciousness. Yet, clearly they are all parts – *split-off complexes* – of a single, broader psyche. Somehow these complexes forget, through dissociation, what they are part of. And although they may 'take turns' manifesting themselves through the ego-body system, there is reason to believe that they exist concurrently in the psyche, at all times, living parallel lives.[154]

When I say that each conscious being is a segment of a broader membrane of mind that somehow becomes dissociated from its true identity, I am appealing to the same underlying process as split-off psychic complexes. There is nothing fundamentally unprecedented about it. All I am doing is extrapolating that well-known phenomenon to a transpersonal and even trans-species level. *I contend that each one of us is a split-off complex of the one medium of mind underlying all existence.* The feasibility of this basic idea does not require anything that is not already known to happen in mental space.

Here is an easy way to visualize all this: place your indicator finger upright just in front of your nose, almost touching it. Yes, go ahead and do it right now. You will see that its image is blurred and undefined even if you look at it cross-eyed. Now, try to close one of your eyes and look at it with the other eye only, without moving the finger. It looks a little sharper and better defined. Look at it now with the other eye, closing the first one.

You can swap eyes a few times. You will notice that each eye has a completely different view of the finger: one sees it from the left, while the other sees it from the right; two very different points-of-view on the same object. Yet, *both points-of-view are experiences of the exact same mind* – namely, your psyche. For emphasis: the experiences of each of your eyes, while different, are merely particular points-of-view of the same mind. Do you see where I am going with this?

You can clearly notice these different points-of-view by swapping them *in time;* that is, by alternating between left and right eye. Now imagine that this alternation could happen not only in time, but *in space* as well. This would be equivalent to a dissociation of your psyche so that one split-off complex would experience the point-of-view of your right eye, while the other split-off complex would experience the point-of-view of your left eye, *at the same time.* Each split-off complex would believe itself to be a separate entity observing the reality of an upright finger placed in front of a nose. In a way, this is what I believe our personal psyches are: particular points-of-view of one mind – just like each of your eyes is a particular point-of-view of your psyche – that become dissociated in the dimensions of space, instead of swapping perspectives in time.

The reason it is difficult for you to see your finger clearly when both of your eyes are open is that your psyche attempts to unite the different points-of-view of each eye into one single image. Give it a go again to experience this: if you pay attention, you can actually see two overlapping images of your finger, which generates confusion. When the object seen is far away enough, both your eyes see nearly the same image, so they can be easily reconciled by your psyche into one single, compound image. You can experience this if you slowly move the finger away from your face, swapping eyes as you do it, until the left- and right-eye images become nearly identical. But when the object is very close, the left- and right-eye images become very different and the reconciliation contradictory. That's why it's better to close one of your eyes at a time to more clearly see the finger in front of your nose: closing an eye by-passes your psyche's precarious attempt to reconcile very different points-of-view, thereby eliminating the apparent contradiction.

Metaphorically speaking – in fact, more metaphorically than before – when mind tries to 'look at itself' what it gets are these hard-to-reconcile, contradictory images on top of one another. After all, mind is very close to itself; it cannot take distance from itself in the way you can move your finger away from your face! But, by dissociating itself into separate egoic points-of-view, mind may end up getting a clearer, less contradictory – albeit more limited – view of itself in the same way that you get a clearer view of your finger if you close one eye at a time.

Substance dualism

Modern Western society seems to have converged to a highly polarized metaphysical dichotomy: while materialism is the dominant paradigm as far as its deep influence in society's values and organization, *substance dualism* is seen as the only mainstream alternative in the form of religious or spiritual worldviews. As discussed earlier, substance dualism is the notion that, apart from matter, there is also an immortal soul that interacts with matter in mysterious ways. Matter and soul are seen to be different and separate types of 'stuff,' irreducible to one another.

This polarization of the metaphysical debate between materialism and substance dualism is a cultural victory for materialism. After all, what empirical evidence is there for the existence of a ghost-like soul floating in space-time? Is it the simplest explanation to postulate another type of 'stuff' that fundamentally transcends all empirical verification? Moreover, notice that substance dualism also entails realism, therefore causing a key flaw behind materialism to go unquestioned. Indeed, according to substance dualism, both soul and body supposedly exist *objectively,* outside mind. Therefore, precisely because substance dualism is perceived as the sole alternative, materialism becomes perpetuated as the only coherent metaphysics from the point-of-view of the intellectual elite; a tragic social situation that reflects a profound lack of metaphysical imagination.

So, does substance dualism have no value at all?

I actually believe it has, despite everything I said above. There is a sense in which substance dualism is closer to reality than naïve materialism: it correctly predicts that consciousness does not end upon physical death and even provides a metaphorical framework for understanding an enduring 'personal unconscious' in the form of an invisible 'soul.' Under materialism, there is room for neither of these things. Moreover – and I am quick to admit this – substance dualism is much more straightforward to grok than idealism. This is why, in Chapter 2, I used a dualist metaphor to introduce the 'filter hypothesis.' So there clearly is social value in substance dualism, given the lamentable state of our metaphysics today.

I will go even further: substance dualism can 'run on top' of idealism as an easier-to-digest metaphor for idealist truths. In other words, there is a way to interpret the key points of the idealist formulation of this book with dualist analogies. One of these analogies has already been mentioned in the previous paragraph: the soul is analogous to an enduring 'personal unconscious.' But we can systematize the analogy further because, in fact, there is a certain form of duality built right into the worldview developed in this book. Allow me to elaborate on this.

As we've seen, freewill is a property of mind at large. It is distributed uniformly throughout the membrane. However, because of self-reflective amplification, we identify ourselves only with a very small part of mind. *Only the freewill at work within this small field of amplification is recognized by the ego as its own will.* The force – the primary cause – that puts the rest of the membrane of mind in motion is seen by the ego as foreign and utterly outside its control. This way, all patterns of vibration that come from outside the field of self-reflective amplification are seen by the ego as external phenomena: the 'world outside.' And here is where a duality is born: *I versus the world, inside versus outside, 'little me' versus the rest.* This is not a fundamental duality, in the sense that it does not entail different kinds of 'stuff,' like matter and soul. *But it is a duality of mental attitude.* When mind does not identify with parts of itself, it creates the entire illusion of an external world, which lies at the heart of realism, materialism and even substance dualism.

The body image, of course, compounds the illusion. The body is simply an image in mind of a process of localization of mind, just like a whirlpool is an image in water of a process of localization of water. The body doesn't imply anything other than mind and its movements, in exactly the same way that a whirlpool doesn't imply anything other than water and its movements. *But we can look down and see our own bodies.* Although the ego, corresponding to closed-cycle processes of information flow in the brain, does not identify itself with the whole body – we even say 'I have a body' instead of 'I am a body' – it does recognize the body as the *vantage point* and platform of its interactions with the world. So, in effect, everything happens *as if* the ego, like a soul, *inhabited* the body. A whirlpool that could look at itself and recognize its own boundaries would also fall prey to the same illusion of duality: it would see itself as separate from the rest of the stream, including other whirlpools seen at a distance but which clearly did not constitute its own platform and vantage point. Illusion as it may be, there is a strong sense in which this duality is true, even though not *ultimately* true. It is true in the sense that, on many levels, it provides an accurate metaphor for what is going on. Many things do happen *as if* we were conscious souls inhabiting physical bodies.

We can, thus, lay out the following correspondences between substance dualism and the idealist formulation of this book: the soul corresponds to the segment of the psychic structure that may remain differentiated after the egoic loop unravels at physical death; that is, the underlying protrusion of the membrane of mind from which the egoic loop arises. The freewill of the soul corresponds to the operation of the primary cause *within the psychic structure.* The 'external world' corresponds to the vibrations of the membrane of mind that are originally set in motion, by the primary cause, outside the human psychic structure and then penetrate it through resonance. The physical body is the partial image of the topological reconfiguration process by means of which the soul becomes (more) self-reflective.

With these correspondences in mind, I consider it fair to use dualist metaphors when one talks about the fundamental nature of reality and of human identity. As a matter of fact, my first book, *Rationalist Spirituality,* despite establishing my idealist position early on, goes on to use dualist metaphors to convey most of its ideas. In a strong sense, things work *as though* people had souls, separate from the body and the rest of the world, which survived physical death.

What is it that survives?

A question that is then immediately raised is this: fine, my consciousness will survive my physical death. But my ego won't. And I identify with my ego, not with the 'unconscious' segments of my psyche. Therefore, that which survives is not really me. For all practical purposes, I really will die. Isn't it so?

The key point here is to separate the ego from the sense of 'I' that underlies all of our experiences. Indeed, *experience intrinsically entails this sense of 'I'*: a subject that experiences. Therefore, the sense of 'I' is inherent to all points of the membrane of mind, regardless of topography or topology, since experiences can unfold anywhere in the membrane. The ego, on the other hand, corresponds to a narrative – a story – consisting of memories, projected self-images, values, attachments, conceptual constructs, explanatory models, etc. It corresponds to the particular set of vibratory modes that gets amplified within the egoic loop. But the *witness* of this story, who ends up mistakenly believing itself to *be* the story, is not the ego. It is that sense of 'I,' which is distributed throughout the membrane and is inherent to experience. We might call it the 'amorphous I,' because it exists even in the absence of all narratives from which form arises. It is a witness without identity, like a newborn.

There is a traditional thought exercise that illustrates this powerfully. It consists of asking yourself who you are and then systematically eliminating every answer you come up with. Am I my name? No, for I could legally change my name tomorrow and still have the same sense of identity. Am I my profession? No, for I could have studied something else, or get another job, and still be me. Am I my body? Well, if I lost a limb or had a heart transplant tomorrow I would still have the same sense of identity, so this can't be it either. Am I my genetic code? No, for I could have an identical twin with the same genetic code and I wouldn't be him. Am I my particular life history, as encoded in my brain? Well, wouldn't I still have the same sense of 'I' if I had made different choices or had had different experiences in the past? And so on. It is possible to eliminate every answer conceivable. The conclusion of this exercise is that our inner sense of 'I' is fundamentally independent of any story we could dress it up with. As such, it is entirely undifferentiated and *identical* in every person. It is formless. This undressed, naked, 'amorphous I' is inherent to the membrane of mind at large, the sole subject of existence. Not only does every person have the same inner sense of 'I,' I contend that every conscious being has it: cats, dogs, fish, etc. At the deepest, narrative-free levels, they must all feel exactly like us.

Another way to see this is to consider that you have always had the same sense of 'I' throughout your life, even though everything else has changed: your body has changed, your thoughts and opinions have changed, your memories have changed, your self-image has changed, the world around you has changed, etc. Even though very few – if any – atoms in your body today are the same as when you were a child, you still believe yourself to be that same person. This happens because there has been a *continuity* of the sense of 'I' from the time you were a child up until now. The formless witness has remained the same. It is this continuity of the 'amorphous I' that makes you think to be the same person, even though everything about you has become different.

And here is the key point: the metaphysics developed in this book implies that there is an uninterrupted preservation of the 'amorphous I' throughout the process we call death. After all, if this inner sense of 'I' is inherent to the membrane of mind, there is just no reason to believe that a change in the topography or topology of the membrane would eliminate or interrupt it. *There must be a continuity of your most fundamental sense of 'I' even as your ego is dismantled and the 'story of you' is no longer identified with.* Although you will realize, as physical death unfolds, that you aren't and have never truly been the narratives of your ego, you will never lose touch with the naked sense of 'I' that you feel right now. Therefore, *for exactly the same reason that you believe yourself to be the same person you were when you were a child, you will feel unambiguously that it is really you that survives physical death.* Moreover, because I speculate that the topography of mind corresponding to the 'personal unconscious' may be largely preserved, you will likely still *remember* your egoic narratives and personal history. You will know exactly who you thought yourself to be. In a sense, you will just wake up at 'home' without forgetting the dream you are having right now.

Do we need the word 'mind'?

Words are category labels. For instance, the word 'chair' is a label for a category of things that we sit on. Categories establish relative differences between things. For instance, it only makes sense to speak of the category 'chair' because there are countless other things that are *not* chairs: tables, trees, people, planets, stars, etc. If everything in nature were chairs, then there would be no sense in creating the category 'chair,' since it would establish no relative differences between things. Indeed, why even bother using the word 'chair' in that case? It would convey no information whatsoever. To put this more formally, *words are only useful insofar as they label discernible subsets of reality.*

And here is where a seemingly valid criticism can be made of my articulation in this book: since I am arguing that everything – absolutely everything – is mind, why bother with the word 'mind'? The word itself may be said to be useless. In a sense, it may be claimed that my articulation of idealism renders the very category 'mind' null and void. There are three answers to this, though.

The first answer is quite straightforward: materialists (in fact, all realists) have themselves invented an abstracted category of things that are *not* mind. As a matter of fact, they have invented an entire universe of things and phenomena that are, supposedly, *not* mind. Since I am arguing my case against theirs, it is entirely valid that I use the word 'mind' to differentiate my metaphysics from theirs. As such, my insistence in using the word aims at making clear that I *deny* their invented, abstracted, unprovable universe of things and phenomena outside subjective experience.

The second answer is a little subtler but more important, so bear with me. There is a sense in which I am incorporating an emphasis of realism into the framework of idealism: the patterns and regularities of empirical experience. Indeed, realists tend to think of mind as something voluble, unstable, and mostly under the control of egoic will. By being ignorant of the 'collective unconscious,' they fail to see that mind can also move according to strict patterns and regularities, entirely outside the control of egoic will. Now, by claiming that large expanses of mind do behave according to strict patterns and regularities, I am acknowledging and incorporating a key emphasis of realism. All the properties and characteristics that we ordinarily attribute to the world of matter – solidity, continuity, momentum, palpability, etc. – are not denied but brought into the dynamics of mind as acknowledged experiences. In other words, the idealist formulation of this book acknowledges the solidity, continuity, momentum, and palpability of matter insofar as these are *experienced*. What it denies is the notion that these experiences are caused by things and phenomena of an abstract world outside mind.

Therefore, it is fair to say that my worldview doesn't deny any of the properties or characteristics of matter that any human being has ever experienced with or without instrumentation. It doesn't really deny anything we know about matter. *As such, much more than a proclamation of the dominance of mentation, my metaphysics is an attempt to eliminate the artificial separation between mind and matter that has led to the 'hard problem of consciousness.'* Nonetheless, I still chose to label it 'idealism' and continue to use the word 'mind' in order to establish a clear contrast with the reigning materialist paradigm, particularly with regards to survival of consciousness beyond physical death. Let there be no ambiguity here: it is a direct and unavoidable implication of my worldview that your consciousness – your subjective experience of being, right now – will survive your bodily death. My use of the word 'mind' to characterize the underlying nature of reality helps to make this point clear.

Finally, the third answer: upon reading the above, some may think that I am endorsing certain streams of materialism that claim mind to be a fundamental, irreducible property *of material processes*.[155] After all, they also entail that matter cannot be separated from mind. But notice that these materialist streams of thought require panpsychism: the notion that inanimate material particles or arrangements thereof possess circumscribed, individual conscious points-of-view of their own. These streams of thought imply that there is something it is like to be an inanimate object in and of itself. However, as I argued earlier, there is simply no empirical reason whatsoever to adopt panpsychism.

Moreover, panpsychism very subtly takes matter to be more primary than mind: according to it, mind is a property *of* matter. *Matter is seen as the substrate of mind*, even though mind is considered intrinsic to matter. I, on the other hand, take the symmetrical position: I take matter to be a particular *modality* of the movement of mind. While my view renders matter equally inseparable from mind, *I take mind to be the substrate of matter, not the other way around.* This subtle but critical difference is another reason I chose to adopt the label 'idealism' and continue to use the word 'mind' even though, as discussed above, I do it with some reservation.

If my worldview is correct, everything we perceive, think, or feel is a vibration *of* mind. *But we have to stop looking for the 'stuff' that vibrates.* We won't find it, because there is no such 'stuff.' Ultimately, as discussed above, we should even drop the word 'mind' altogether, along with the concept it represents, for mind simply is what is. *The medium of mind is that which perceives.* Mind is not outside, but *is*, ourselves. The eye that sees can't see itself directly. The need to make sense of idealism by somehow measuring the 'stuff' of mind is understandable, but naïve and counterproductive. It arises from a throwback to realist delusions. To understand the underlying nature of mind one has to turn inward, toward introspection and away from measurement.

Realism is the culprit

Indeed, it is the unquestioned assumption of realism – reflected on an overwhelming focus on measurement – that leads the intuition of materialists astray. Case in point: materialist philosopher Daniel Dennett often states his strong intuition that, ultimately, there isn't really a 'hard problem of consciousness' at all. He doesn't see the need to create different ontological categories for brain and mind, instead intuiting that they are fundamentally of the same nature.[156]

Yes, he is right!

The problem is that, by implicitly assuming realism, Dennett is forced to extract an absurd conclusion from his correct intuition: if matter is really 'out there' and the 'hard problem' doesn't really exist, then consciousness can *only* be the matter 'out there.' In other words, consciousness must be an illusion! Dennett correctly rejects a fundamental split of categories between matter and mind, but he does this by postulating that mind is *nothing,* instead of contemplating the empirically obvious alternative that mind is *everything.* Both avoid the categorical split, but just one isn't absurd on the face of it. The problem is that only the absurd option is allowed by realism. Do you see the dilemma?

There is indeed no 'hard problem': the brain is in no way fundamentally distinct from mind. But instead of meaning that mind is nothing but the brain, what this means is that *the brain is nothing but mind!* It is mind that is the broader framework, encompassing the brain but also the rest of existence. Our heads are in mind, not mind in our heads. The brain is merely an image in mind of a process of mind.

There are many other aspects of the materialist worldview that are based on sound intuition, deduction and accurate empirical observation. It couldn't be any different, otherwise materialism would never have become consensus among the intellectual elite. But these same sound intuitions, deductions and accurate observations often force materialists into absurd conclusions because of the unexamined – yet all-pervading – assumption of realism.

For instance: materialists correctly deduce that processes obeying strict patterns and regularities continuously take place outside any individual ego. After all, when you close your garage door behind you in the evening, it's clear that some process *holds the pattern* of things you leave behind in the garage – including your car – while you are asleep, since you can come back to that same pattern in the next morning. There is no denying this. But, because of the assumption of realism, materialists must then associate the pattern with a universe *outside mind* itself. Drop the assumption of realism and the original deduction leads to a completely different, and much more parsimonious, conclusion: the process that holds the pattern is a *mental* process that happens to transcend egoic awareness, in the same way that the mental processes responsible for generating dreams or schizophrenic visions also transcend the ego. That a pattern can be held – and even develop – independently of the ego does not mean that such pattern isn't still purely mental. A whole phenomenal universe indeed unfolds outside the ego, *but not outside mind*. Such trans-egoic universe is still an experience, but the experience of a broad, non-personal, non-self-reflective segment of mind.

Materialism is a reasonable castle built on top of rotten foundations. Its proponents tend to be rational and intelligent people who happen to start their entire thinking process from a ludicrous premise: realism. It is that starting assumption – not their otherwise sound way of thinking – that forces materialists to bite the unappetizing bullets of their metaphysics. Take the premise of realism out and it is surprising how much of the materialist thinking would be conducive to a sound ontological interpretation of reality.

Reality as metaphor

Throughout this book I have endeavored to convey my ideas through metaphors. Indeed, metaphors are powerful tools to paint subtle, complex and nuanced mental landscapes that are difficult or even impossible to communicate literally. While literal descriptions seek to characterize an idea *directly*, metaphors do it *indirectly*, by borrowing an *essential, underlying meaning* from another known idea or mental landscape. For instance, I sought to characterize mind by borrowing the essential, underlying meaning of the imagery of vibrating membranes.

Metaphors use disposable vehicles – in this case, the imagery of a vibrating membrane – to describe a new idea gestalt. The vehicle itself is not to be taken literally: mind, of course, is not *literally* a vibrating membrane. It is only the *essential, underlying meaning* surrounding the imagery of a vibrating membrane that is useful to characterize mind. Once this essential meaning is conveyed, one must discard the vehicle as if it were disposable packaging, lest it outlive its usefulness and turn into an intellectual entrapment.

The vehicle of the metaphor may have literal existence: vibrating membranes do seem to exist literally. Yet, that is not needed or even important. Passages from many fantasy books and films are routinely used as powerful metaphorical vehicles, even though they do not have any literal existence. For instance, I could have alluded to the 2010 Hollywood film *Inception* to metaphorically illustrate my idealist view that the world is akin to a shared dream. This metaphor would have been a powerful one, as you will probably acknowledge if you've watched the film. Yet, *Inception* was 100% fiction and the events it portrayed never had literal existence. The literal existence of the metaphorical vehicle is unimportant for the evocative power of the metaphor.

With this as background, I invite you now to join me on a little thought experiment. *Since the eye that sees cannot see itself directly, mind can never understand itself literally.* A literal – that is, *direct* – apprehension of the nature of existence is fundamentally impossible, this being the perennial cosmic itch. The vibrations of mind – that is, experiences – can never directly reveal the underlying nature of the medium that vibrates, in the same way that one cannot *see* a guitar string merely by hearing the sounds it produces when plucked. Yet, the vibrations of mind do embody and reflect the intrinsic potentialities of their underlying medium, in the same way that valid inferences can be made about the length and composition of a guitar string purely from the sound it produces. The sound of a vibrating medium is a *metaphor* for the medium's essential, underlying nature. The medium obviously *isn't* the sound, but its essence is indeed indirectly *reflected* on the sound it produces.

As such, *consensus reality is nothing but a metaphor for the fundamental nature of mind.* Nothing – no thing, event, process or phenomenon – is literally true, but an evocative vehicle.[157] As we've seen above, not only is this sufficient for mind to capture its own essential meaning, it means that *only this essential meaning is ultimately true.* Everything else is just packaging: disposable vehicles to evoke the underlying essence of mind. The plethora of phenomena we call nature and civilization holds no more reality than a theatrical play. They serve a purpose as carriers, but they are not essential in and by themselves. 'All the world's a stage, And all the men and women merely players,' said Shakespeare.[158]

A metaphorical world isn't a less real place; on the contrary! *It is a world where only essential meanings are ultimately true.* It is a world of pure significance and pure essence. It is a world where there is no frivolity, where nothing is 'just so.' *All phenomena are suggesting something about the nature of mind.* Understanding this allows one to peel off the cover of dullness preventing us from developing a closer, richer, and more mature relationship with life. It forces us to try and absorb the underlying meaning of each development, each day, and each encounter. Life becomes compelling. The cosmic metaphor is unfolding before us at all times. What is it trying to say? A job loss, a new romantic relationship, a sudden illness, a promotion, the death of a pet, a major personal success, a friend in need... What is the underlying meaning of it all in the context of our lives? What are all these events saying about our true selves? These are the questions that we must constantly confront in a metaphorical world.

We must look upon life in the same way that many people look upon their nightly dreams: when they wake up, they don't attribute *literal* truth to the dream they just had. To do so would be tantamount to closing one's eyes to what the dream was trying to convey. Instead, they ask themselves: 'what did it *really mean?*' They know that the dream wasn't a *direct* representation of its meaning, but a subtle metaphorical suggestion of something *else*. And so may waking reality be. As such, it is this ineffable *something else* that – I believe – we must try to find in life. Do you see what I am trying to say?

In a metaphorical world, all the images of consensus reality are *symbols*, not literal facts. Goethe knew this, for he wrote in *Faust:*

'All that doth pass away
Is but a *symbol;*'[159]

What in life doesn't pass away? What in life isn't transitory? Goethe went on to say:

'The indescribable
Here is it done;'[160]

Yes. The indescribable is done – or reveals itself – through the transitory symbols of life. Think of the self-embracing double helix of DNA; the magical collapse of dualities during the sexual act; the melting away of parts of ourselves in the form of tears; the mysterious doorway of the eyes; the life-giving self-sacrifice of breastfeeding; the Faustian power of technology; the strange split of empirical experience into five different senses; the miracle of birth and the finality of death. What does it all mean? What are these images trying to evoke underneath their pedestrian literal appearances? *They aren't 'just so' phenomena but, instead, represent something ineffable; something that cannot be conveyed in any other way but through the metaphor we call our everyday reality.*

We cannot be told what it all means. We must live it and somehow 'get it.' There is no other way. We must *pay attention* to how these symbols get woven together in the mental narrative we call life. Therein, concluded Henry Corbin from his study of ancient Persian traditions, lies the ultimate meaning of it all. He wrote: 'To come into this world ... means ... to pass into the plane of existence which in relation to [Paradise] is merely a metaphoric existence. ... *Thus coming into this world has meaning only with a view to leading that which is metaphoric back to true being.*'[161]

Perhaps Lao-tzu, over 2500 years ago, put it best in his description of the *Dao*, which might as well be a description of the membrane of mind:

'There is something formless yet complete
That existed before heaven and earth.
  How still! How empty!
Dependent on nothing, unchanging,
All pervading, unfailing.
One may think of it as the mother of all things under heaven.
I do not know its name,
But I call it "Meaning."'[162]

Hong Zicheng made it clear where the meaning of the *Dao* can be seen and how it relates to mind. He wrote, in the 16th century: 'The chirping of birds and twittering of insects are all *murmurings of the mind.* The brilliance of flowers and colors of grasses are none other than the patterns of the Dao.'[163]

Clearly, we once knew with intuitive clarity that which we can no longer remember. In today's culture we take the package for the content, the vehicle for the precious cargo. We attribute reality to physical phenomena while taking their *meanings* to be inconsequential fantasies. By extricating 'reality' from mind, materialism has sent the significance of nature into exile. With the pathetic grin of hubris stamped on our foolish faces, we carefully unwrap the package and then proceed to throw away its contents while proudly storing the empty box on the altar of our ontology. What a huge stash of empty boxes have we accumulated! Idols of stupidity they are; public reminders of a state of affairs that would be hilarious if it weren't tragic.

The meaning of it all is unfolding right under our noses, all the time, but we can't see it. We don't pay any attention. We were taught from childhood to avert our gaze, lest we be considered fools. So now we seem to live in some kind of collective trance, lost in a daze the likes of which have probably never before been witnessed in history. We feel the gaping emptiness and meaning-lessness of our condition in the depths of our psyches. But, like a desperate man thrashing about in quicksand, our reactions only make things worse: we chase more fictitious goals and accumulate more fictitious stuff, precisely the things that *distract* us further from watching what is really happening. And, when we finally realize the senselessness of such reactions, we turn to 'gurus' doling out pill-form answers instead of paying attention to life, the only authentic teacher, who is constantly speaking to us. There is no literal shortcut to whatever it is that the metaphor of life is trying to convey. *There is no literal truth.* The meaning of it all cannot be communicated directly. There are no secret answers spelled out in words in some rare old book. The metaphor is the only way to the answers, if only we have patience and *pay attention.* Look around: what is life trying to say?

Universal telos

Questions such as this immediately raise another: is there a grand purpose – a telos – behind existence? Human beings have perennially wondered about the meaning of life. Could it all be just an accident? And if not, where is it all going? What role must we play in the unfolding of existence? I have elaborated on this myself in my earlier book *Rationalist Spirituality*. But here I'd like to frame those ideas in the context of the membrane metaphor.

To me, the idea that life and all of existence are a metaphor for something of crucial importance – yet unspeakable and non-literal – is sufficiently convincing that I try to live my own life according to this notion. I seek to understand what underlying, essential meaning the events of my life – the good and the bad ones, the major and the apparently insignificant ones – might have. Having said that, it is easy to see how a constant search for meaning behind daily events can, if one is not careful, drive one down the most misguided and preposterous paths. The human psyche is naturally prone to seeking patterns and often believes to find them where they aren't, like faces in the clouds. Another easy misstep is to try to uncover something transcendent but *literally* true behind the metaphor of life, a recurring fallacy in, for instance, the New Age movement. When we keep trying to find a *literal* essence behind the metaphor – be it the discrete interventions of space brothers from the Pleiades or the chance throw of the Neo-Darwinists' dice – we become blind to its underlying, ineffable, essential meaning.

But one should also not throw the baby out with the bath water: although the underlying meaning of events may be too subtle for literal, naïve, and culture-bound interpretations, *it exists and is important*. In recent history, I believe that Swiss psychiatrist Carl Jung and Nobel Prize Laureate physicist Wolfgang Pauli have come the closest to decoding the metaphor of empirical events.[164] Yet, I suspect that even Jung's analytical psychology remains a very long way away from unveiling the mystery in its completeness. Ultimately, the work of interpreting the metaphor is personal and up to each one of us individually.

Be it as it may, it is reasonable to state that the purpose of existence has a lot to do with our observing and trying to make sense of the underlying meaning of the metaphor of life, both at an intellectual and an intuitive level. Moreover, I believe that there is yet another important aspect to the telos of existence, one having to do with the cost of self-reflectiveness. As discussed earlier, the self-reflectiveness gained with the formation of the egoic loop comes at the 'loss' of everything that doesn't fall within the loop: it creates the 'unconscious' by obfuscation of mental contents. Nonetheless, *it is self-reflectiveness that gives us a chance of interpreting the metaphor of life at all.* Without it we would be simply immersed in the unfolding of experience, like instinctive animals. We would have no way of making sense of whatever is going on.

In a sense, *we have been deputized by mind at large to look back at itself and try to make something out of what we see.* For all we know, we're the only game in town as far as being able to do it. But what do we do instead? We look away! We don't like to be confronted with the darkness within ourselves, so we numb our psyches with every conceivable distraction, making sure that the 'unconscious' *remains* 'unconscious,' instead of being brought into the field of self-reflectiveness. We don't like to be confronted with the darkness we see in the empirical world either, so we tell ourselves 'That's not me!' And by disidentifying with it, we eliminate any chance we might otherwise have of making something out of all the suffering and evil around us. The tragedy we are faced with is that all this suffering might be for nothing, since the ones deputized to interpret it are looking away instead of trying to make sense of the metaphor. Instead of asking 'All this darkness is part of me too, so what does it mean?' we watch gossip shows on television. Clearly, thus, *in addition to creating the 'unconscious,' self-reflective awareness has another cost:*

the illusion of separation that arises from it prevents us from confronting our full nature and making something out of it.

These considerations point to a telos for the topology of the membrane: if the entire membrane could fold in on itself to form *one single loop encompassing all of mind* – a kind of cosmic sphere of mind – there would be no trade-off. Self-reflectiveness would be all-encompassing, in the sense that all vibrations of mind – all mental contents – would fall within the field of self-reflection. There would be no 'unconscious.' Moreover, there would be no illusion of separation either: this one loop of mind would identify itself with all good and all evil, all bliss and all suffering, all polarities and perspectives. The *full* nature of mind would *unavoidably* penetrate the field of its own self-reflective contemplation.

We can speculate that, through the evolution of life in all its known and unknown forms, mind at large is trying to find its way to this single global loop.

One might now ask: Why doesn't the membrane of mind simply use its freewill to form this single global loop at once? Why hasn't it happened yet? Why all the struggles? The answer here is rather simple: for mind at large to *know* that it should shape itself as a single loop *it would already have to have the global self-reflectiveness that only a single loop could provide.* Without it, self-reflectiveness is only present in localized egos, whose freewill cannot change the topology of mind beyond themselves. Do you see the chicken-and-egg situation? To put it more simply: mind at large does not know that it should form a single loop, even though it would have the power to do so if it knew. And local egos do not have the power to reshape the broader membrane, even though some of them know that a single loop is the goal to be pursued.

There is no shortcut for this dilemma. In fact, I am not even sure that it can be resolved at all. Mind at large, through us and other living beings, must try to find its way to this ultimate topology: a cosmic sphere of mind whose mirrored internal surfaces enable every thought and every experience in all existence to be recursively self-reflected. And, even if it reaches that stage, it would still be left with the challenge of interpreting its own metaphor for itself. If it somehow succeeds, it will know what it is and what is going on. While it doesn't, we are left with struggle and mystery.

Closing remarks

I will now – unashamedly – re-emphasize a point I have already made earlier, but which is extremely important. In my many metaphors, I have made analogies between brains and whirlpools; egos and membrane loops; photons and ripples of an ocean of mercury; etc. All these metaphorical images – whirlpools, loops, ripples – were *disposable vehicles*. The actual images of reality are brains, egos, and photons. I know of no brain that looks like a whirlpool! Whirlpools, loops and undulations *are just ways of thinking* about brains, egos, and photons; *ways of seeing* them. My metaphors did not aim at replacing the actual images of reality, but simply at conveying a certain *way of thinking* about them.

And since all of reality is a metaphor for an ineffable truth, we end up finding ourselves in the strange position of having to use metaphors to clarify a metaphor. Is this crazy? Of course not. First, it is no wonder that nature, simply by *being* what it is, would provide suitable metaphorical images – nightly dreams, whirlpools, liquid mercury, vibrating membranes, etc. – with which we, as parts of nature, could get our bearings. After all, as discussed earlier, nature is a metaphor for itself. And second, if the goal is to understand the primary metaphor of reality, we absolutely need to use all means at our disposal to get rid of the mad interpretations of it that have obscured our view for so long. What chance do we have to make something out of the primary metaphor while living under the astonishing abstraction that reality is outside mind? By denying all the meaning of reality, materialism has made it impossible to find meaning in reality. This isn't a sustainable state of affairs. Therefore, it is my hope that this book makes a contribution – small as it may be – to remedying the appalling cultural state we find ourselves in. We need to outgrow the lunacy of our present condition.

Do I believe that the *way of thinking* laid out in this book nails down the truth? Do I believe that my metaphysics is complete? Of course not. Such a belief would be of exceptional hubris and naïveté. What I do believe is that *the worldview discussed here is a concrete and sound step forward when compared to the reigning paradigm. As I hope to have demonstrated, it explains all aspects of reality that materialism claims to explain, and then many more.* As such, I'm absolutely convinced that my formulation of idealism is significantly closer to the truth than the madness of materialism. It is a more complete, reasonable, parsimonious and skeptical worldview. Therein lies the value of this book, as far as I see it. To nail down the complete truth is, to say the least, a very-long-term project, if at all feasible. All we can hope to accomplish are baby steps in the right direction. We do not know how long the road is or what challenges and dangers lie ahead. We do not even know whether the road really leads anywhere. But what else can we do other than to try and fix our errors once they become glaringly obvious?

It is time that the materialist fairytale were exposed for what it is. Its attractiveness stems from the fact that it *guarantees* that all of our problems and suffering will, *inevitably*, come to a *permanent end* eventually. It provides us with a reliable way out when things become unbearable; a kind of panic button. It spares us the weight of all responsibility, insofar as it implies that life is devoid of meaning *anyway*. It gives us permission to be stoic. And, as if all this weren't enough, society still portrays us as tough guys and girls, courageous and candid enough to stare the difficult facts in the face, if we simply declare our belief in such a comforting little tale! Go figure.

Let us be honest: the fairytale of materialism has served a valid purpose during a more naïve and childish age, but has now far outlived its usefulness. We no longer live in the reality of the 19th century. The collective experiences of modern humanity in the early 21st century demand a mature, adult worldview.

Afterword

'Knowledge and love are thus revealed as the two cosmic forces which are apparently separate in nature but which spring from the same potency and source.'
Giordano Bruno, 1548 -1600

When Bernardo graciously asked me to write an Afterword for this book, he was still in the process of writing the last chapters, polishing and annotating the manuscript and preparing it for presentation to his publisher. Our conversations started in August of 2012 and have continued to unfold into one of the more remarkable relationships I have experienced in my entire professional and personal life. Bernardo was interested in speaking with a transpersonal, Jung-influenced psychotherapist and I was interested in sharing ideas with this remarkable, intellectually diverse and energetic thinker, over a generation younger than myself.

I received my undergraduate Baccalaureate degree in general history studies during the late 1960s, at a time of tumultuous social and cultural change. This opening up to an expanded worldview was amplified by my passion for understanding other times and other places in which mankind was engaging the world in similar ways through different metaphors, cultures, and languages. Despite these differences, most 'enlightened human beings' in history were essentially in agreement with what Aldous Huxley named the 'perennial philosophy,' the philosophy of 'mind at large,' the esoteric wellspring that ran deep below the world of superficial appearances.

The perennial philosophy is an inspired convergence into remarkably similar and parsimonious spiritual truths or cosmologies of mind that have remained up-to-date and vital from century to century, right up to the latest quantum cosmologies of the 21st century. Today's scientists, 'shutting up and calculating' the quantum foam, seem curiously blind to this. It is clear and obvious to me that mainstream science has no clue about the nature of consciousness. Nor can current scientific methodology even ask the basic questions needed to even begin to study the nature of consciousness. The standard scientific story is that 'obviously' mind is produced by the brain and that all aspects of consciousness can be reduced to electrochemical events between neurons. Anyone who dares to suggest otherwise is 'obviously woo-woo,' a fraud, or a pseudoscientist. Yet, no one – no scientist, no philosopher, no self-appointed guardian of media 'truth' – can even begin to explain how purely physical brain events could ever 'squirt out' subjective experiences. In this 'century of the brain,' apparently the only acceptable way to talk about consciousness or mind is in the language of materialist cognitive science or neuroscience. The mere whiff of any alternative attracts suppression.

It was in the context of my own personal and professional journey, during which I pondered the issues above, that I made the decision to contact Bernardo. This decision was based primarily upon what felt like an impersonal impulse on my part. As a practicing transpersonal psychologist, I will take the liberty to use Jungian terminology at this point: my reaching out to Bernardo was an archetype seeking to actualize, within the constellation of my own journey, the validation, mentoring and encouraging of a younger, metaphysically-inclined scientist who was undergoing the agony of the collapse of appearances. His rational, personal self was beginning to encounter the deeper, arational, impersonal unconscious forces that were welling up from his inner depths.

My intuition was that Bernardo was experiencing a transformation, a shedding of his former personal self and an encounter with a powerful, unconscious inner realm. Like the shaman's agonizing inner journey, the personal self experiences a form of death or annihilation as the powerful, impersonal, unconscious Self emerges. This is a disconcerting experience. One can feel alone as one crosses an ontological boundary away from the familiar world and the language describing that familiar reality becomes lost. 'Being' unfolds impersonally and one experiences life as a mystery. All former belief systems become dysfunctional. Anchorless and with no life support, one loses the sense of being in control, realizing that one was never in control to begin with. One awakens and discovers that one is simply the space where the story of life and identity is dreamt. One goes through the death throes of a hell realm that slowly gives way to subjective awareness without a personal story and then, eventually, to the liberating feeling that we are the space of interconnected human experience, driven by unconditional love and compassion. The language of the 'Otherworld' arises in dream-like metaphors.

I felt a strong impulse to reach out to Bernardo and, with hindsight, I can see it as an unconscious wish to validate his work and encourage him to participate in the 'metaphysics of the third scientific revolution.' This revolution is not likely to occur within the establishment universities and research institutions that require conformity in thinking. This radical turnabout in the way scientists conceive and interpret natural phenomena requires new interdisciplinary thinkers like Bernardo. It requires a change in focus from analysis to synthesis. It requires freedom from institutional restrictions and an ability to pursue a wide range of horizontal knowledge. From all this, a new conceptual basis will emerge to explain the origin of life, the evolution of increasing complexity, and the miraculous organizing potency of nature that have led to self-aware sentient life, consciousness and the astounding mystery of 'I am.' Everything points to an immanent order that Gregory Bateson calls 'the larger mind.'

This Afterword, in some fashion, rounds the circle from the ancient philosophy of 'as above, so below' to Bernardo's concise, updated metaphors for the nature of consciousness, the human mind and the brain. He has brought a brand new way of seeing the ancient idea of 'infinite mind.' Although written in a personal and breezy tone, this book is a vast philosophical endeavor. It captures 'big picture' ideas in a manner accessible to a wider audience. My contribution here has been to try and relate this 'big picture' back to Bernardo's remarkable interior life as he wrote this book.

The quote that opens this Afterword is from Giordano Bruno, born in Nola, Kingdom of Naples. Bruno had a tragic life that ended on February 17, 1600, in the *Campo de' Fiori,* a central Roman market square. He was burnt at the stake after Pope Clement VIII declared him a heretic. The numerous charges against Bruno included heresy in matters of dogmatic theology, involving some of the basic doctrines of his philosophy and cosmology. Bruno claimed that Copernicus and Galileo had not gone far enough by merely replacing a geocentric cosmology with a heliocentric one. He believed in an 'infinite, acentric universe holding perhaps an infinitude of earth-like planets.' His great strength and eventual horrific death were the result of his vociferous belief in freethinking, his extraordinary memory, keen intellect and ability to grasp a wide diversity of ancient philosophers, mathematicians and cosmologists.

His once-heretical cosmology is now indispensable to contemporary science. It links the immeasurably large to the infinitesimally small. Indeed, Bruno's cosmology united Eastern and Western thinking by precisely formulating three of the key assumptions of contemporary cosmology: the unity of the universe; its uniformity, homogeneity and isotropy; and the universal applicability of its laws. I share Bruno's story in this Afterword for obvious reasons.

Bernardo has just begun his journey across the ontological boundary. He directly experiences the apprehension of the heart, or the movement from 'doing' into infinite 'being.' My encountering him has given me hope for our future as human beings who must find a way back to the meaning and enchantment of direct experience.

Peace and out,

Rick Stuart, Ph.D.
State College, Pennsylvania.
May 2013.

Notes

1   Poz (2005).

2   I consistently write the words 'subconscious' and 'unconscious' between quotes because, as I will explain and substantiate later in the book, I do not believe that any content of mind falls *truly* outside consciousness.

3   Kuhn (1996).

4   Russell (2007).

5   Even in the case of String Theory (Davies and Brown 1992), according to which subatomic particles can be explained in terms of vibrating strings, it is still *the relative differences between the modes of vibrations of these strings* that explain nature. The fundamental nature of the strings themselves is left unaddressed.

6   Professor Austin Hughes wrote cogently about this (Hughes 2012).

7   Hawking has made statements like: 'Because there is a law such as gravity, the universe can and will create itself from nothing' (Hawking and Mlodinow 2010, p. 227). This is incoherent, since the law of gravity is *not* nothing. There has been plenty of critical deconstruction of Hawking's claims. For instance, physicist Paul Davies wrote: 'The multiverse comes with a lot of baggage, such as an overarching space and time to host all those bangs, a universe-generating mechanism to trigger them, physical fields to populate the universes with material stuff, and a selection of forces to make things happen. Cosmologists embrace these features by envisaging sweeping "meta-laws" that pervade the multiverse and spawn specific bylaws on a universe-by-universe basis. The meta-laws themselves remain unexplained – eternal, immutable transcendent entities that just happen to exist and must simply be accepted as given.'

(Davies 2010).

8 In this book, I use the word 'material' in a modern physicalist sense that incorporates the insights of quantum physics; not as in 19th-century billiard-ball materialism.

9 Zee (2010), p. 29.

10 Chalmers (2003).

11 Levine (1999).

12 Miller (2005).

13 Oerter (2006), chapter 10.

14 This is called 'weak emergence' (Chalmers 2006).

15 See the definition of 'strong emergence' in Chalmers (2006).

16 See, for instance, Daniel Dennett's verbose but irremediably failed attempted (Dennett 1991).

17 Strawson (2006), p. 5.

18 Strawson (2006).

19 For simplicity, I am not making a distinction between panpsychism and 'panexperientialism,' which is a slightly more moderate version of strict panpsychism. For clarity, I take the term panpsychism to encompass panexperientialism.

20 Chalmers (1996), pp. 293-297.

21 This is related to what David Chalmers has called 'type-F monism' (Chalmers 2003).

22 Strawson (2006), p. 5.

23 Eagleman (2011), pp. 44-51.

24 Ibid.

25 Lehar (1999).

26 The argument I am about to make here is, in a restricted sense, analogous to Plantinga's evolutionary argument against naturalism (Plantinga 1993, chapter 12). However, it does not touch on supernatural entities and further elaborates on Plantinga's basic notion with the idea of reality-distorting sensory preprocessing.

27 Kastrup (1997) and Seixas et al. (1995).

28 Dennett (1991).

29 In an interview, Koch said: 'I take the point of view that ultimately ... consciousness is something real; it's ontologically distinct. It's different from the brain that gives rise to it. So when my tooth hurts I have a feeling of pain. That is different from the neural mechanism that gives rise to pain. Those are two different things. They're not the same. They relate to each other and the way they relate to each other is through this idea of information.' But later on, he continues: 'We have many, many instances of [this] beautiful, very specific, sometimes even causal relationship between the ... biophysics ... of the brain and our conscious perception. ... As far as I know, when I die that's it. ... once my brain dissolves, my consciousness dissolves. It's an unfortunate fact of life.' (Koch and Tsakiris 2012)

30 For more details, I recommend Eric Kandel's comprehensive tome on neuroscience (Kandel et al. 2012, parts II and III).

31 In reality, it is an oversimplification to say that neurotransmitters are either excitatory or inhibitory. There are more nuances. But, for the purposes of this book, this simplification is fair and sufficient.

32 Christof Koch wrote extensively about the neural correlates of consciousness (Koch 2004).

33 Metzinger (2000).

34 Pascual-Leone et al. (2002).

35 Tononi (2004a).

36 Ibid.

37 See, for instance: Gross (2002).

38 Keim (2013). Italics are mine.

39 Dresler et al. (2011).

40 Hameroff (2006).

41 Chalmers (2006).

42 Shermer (2011).

43 Koch made this claim during a talk (Koch 2011).

44 Tononi (2004b).

45 Ibid.

46 Krebs and Weitzman (1987).

47 Oerter (2006).

48 Gröblacher et al. (2007).

49 Bergson (1912).

50 Jung (1991).

51 Jung (2009).

52 Jung (1991), pp. 50-51.

53 Ibid.

54 Journal of Transpersonal Psychology.

55 Neal (2008).

56 Shuman (2007), p. 80.

57 Whinnery and Whinnery (1990).

58 Rhinewine and Williams (2007).

59 Taylor (1994).

60 Retz (2007).

61 Strassman et al. (2008).

62 Carhart-Harris et al. (2012), p. 1.

63 Ibid. p. 2.

64 Ibid. p. 1.

65 Blanke et al. (2002).

66 Taylor (2009).

67 Urgesi et al. (2010).

68 Piore (2013), Lythgoe et al. (2005), Treffert (2006), and Treffert (2009), p. 1354.

69 Lammle, R. (2010).

70 Lythgoe et al. (2005).

71 Lammle, R. (2010).

72 Miller et al. (1998) and Miller et al. (2000).

73 Treffert (2009), p. 1353.

74 Peres et al. (2012).

75 DiSalvo (2012).

76 Alexander (2012), Moorjani (2012), and Sudman (2012).

77   Kelly, Greyson, and Kelly (2009).

78   Ustinova (2009).

79   Lilly and Gold (1996).

80   Eliade (2009).

81   See, for instance: Koch and Tsakiris (2012). Since some of Dr. Koch's points were critiques of statements I had made in an earlier interview, I wrote a rebuttal to his comments (Kastrup 2012).

82   Persinger (2010).

83   See, for instance: Shermer (1999).

84   Carhart-Harris et al. (2012).

85   Jung (2002), p. 7.

86   Okasha (2002), p. 58.

87   Ibid.

88   This is not as black-and-white as I portray here, since different formulations of idealism can be more nuanced. But, for simplicity, I will stick to this definition of idealism as a metaphysics entailing that all reality is solely in mind.

89   Fogelin (2001).

90   Boswell (1820), p. 218. Original italics.

91   Gröblacher et al. (2007).

92   Kuhn (1996), chapter 4.

93   Gröblacher et al. (2007).

94   'Occam's razor' is a heuristic best-practice in science. It states that the best explanation for a phenomenon is that which requires the fewest new assumptions. It is often loosely interpreted to mean that the best explanation is the simplest one.

95   This is a serious notion in philosophy, known as 'philosophical zombies' or 'p-zombies' (Kirk 2011).

96   Watts (2009), p. 16.

97   Roberson et al. (2005) and Roberson et al. (2006).

98   Jung (1991).

99   Iacoboni, Rayman, and Zaidel (1996).

100 Strictly speaking, the screen displays *measurements* – representations – of the neural processes. But for the sake of argument, let's imagine that the neuroscientist can *directly* see the *actual* neural processes, not just representations.
101 Dennett (1991).
102 Ffytche (2011), part 3.
103 Augusto (2010).
104 Hofstadter (2008).
105 Chalmers (2003).
106 Gordon (1999).
107 Boly et al. (2011).
108 Ibid., p. 858.
109 Peck (2011). Italics are mine.
110 Tononi (2004b).
111 Here I mean 'active imagination' in the Jungian sense (Jung and Chodorow 1997).
112 Gebser (1986), p. 2.
113 Read (1995), pp. 7-15.
114 Jung (1991), p. 3.
115 Gebser (1986), p. 3.
116 Ibid., p. 18.
117 For more technical details, see Tongue (2001).
118 See, for instance, Sheldrake (2011).
119 See, for instance, Chalmers (1996), pp. 266-274.
120 Carl Jung himself clearly saw this correspondence. He wrote: 'So far as we can see, the collective unconscious is identical with Nature to the extent that Nature herself, including matter, is unknown to us. I have nothing against the assumption that the psyche is a quality of matter or matter the concrete aspect of the psyche, provided that "psyche" is defined as the collective unconscious.' (Jung and Sabini 2002, p. 82)
121 Adyashanti (2006).
122 Physicist Paul Davies speaks of this potential as 'meta-laws'

(Davies 2010).

123 Zee (2010), pp. 17-25.

124 Ibid.

125 Jung (2001), pp. 17-37.

126 Douglas Hofstadter, in his magnificent book *Gödel, Escher, Bach*, told a little tale titled *Contracrostipunctus* that wonderfully illustrates this point (Hofstadter 1980, pp. 75-81).

127 Schwartz and Begley (2004).

128 A discussion of many of these studies can be found in Schwartz, Stapp, and Beauregard (2005).

129 Schwartz, Stapp, and Beauregard (2005), p. 1311.

130 Greene (2003), chapter 5.

131 Folger (2004).

132 Greene (2003), chapter 6.

133 Ibid., chapter 12.

134 Ibid.

135 See, for instance, Smolin (2007).

136 Jung and Pauli (2001).

137 Okasha (2002), chapter 4.

138 Chalmers (1996), chapter 8.

139 What follows should be taken as an 'educated myth,' part philosophy and part art, but in any case entirely speculative in nature. It has been inspired by an essay one of my readers, Michael Larkin, wrote about the membrane metaphor. The essay is titled *Of the Universe and Loops* and is available online at www.bernardokastrup.com.

140 Musser and Minkel (2002).

141 Leeming (2010), volume 2, pp. 346-347.

142 Leeming (2010).

143 In his autobiography, Carl Jung described a dream that one of his pupils, a woman of sixty, had two months before dying. In her dream, the woman had already died and, in the afterlife, was expected to give a lecture to others who had passed away before her. The other dead were anxious

to hear about the experiences and insights that she, the newly deceased, was bringing with her from life (Jung 1995, p. 336). As the rest of his text makes clear, Jung took this dream to be a sign that human life produces original, unique, but universally relevant knowledge. Somewhat echoing this view, and probably without knowing of Jung's work, Natalie Sudman, in the metaphorical description of her Near-Death Experience, also suggested that non-physical entities eagerly await the insights we will bring to them after having gone through life ourselves (Sudman 2012, chapter 4).

144 Watts (2009), p. 79.
145 Mack (1999).
146 Grof and Grof (1989).
147 Carhart-Harris et al. (2012), pp. 4-5.
148 Alexander (2012), Moorjani (2012), Sudman (2012), as well as Kelly, Greyson, and Kelly (2009).
149 Jung (1995), p. 18.
150 Carl Jung, through more than 50 years of clinical experience studying the 'collective unconscious,' believed that only through life – that is, through egoic self-reflectiveness – could we arrive at certain answers to the mysteries of existence (Jung 1995, pp. 338-340 and p. 343).
151 Haraldsson (2012), p. 67.
152 Lovelock (2005).
153 American Psychiatric Association (2000), pp. 526-529.
154 Jung (2001), p. 113.
155 These streams of materialism can be classified under Chalmers' 'type-F monism' (Chalmers 2003).
156 Dennett (2003).
157 Patrick Harpur has written a wonderful book (Harpur 2009) about the nature of non-literal truth and reality as metaphor.
158 Quoted from Act 2, Scene 7, of William Shakespeare's play *As You Like It*.

159 Goethe and Bernays (1839), p. 207. Italics are mine.

160 Ibid.

161 As quoted in Cheetham (2012), p. 59. Italics are mine.

162 As quoted in Jung (1985), p. 97. Italics are mine. The translation used by Jung is slightly changed to account for Richard Wilhelm's reading of the term 'Dao' (which is often also spelled 'Tao').

163 Zicheng, Aitken, and Kwok (2006), p. 105. Italics are mine.

164 Jung (1985), as well as Jung and Pauli (2001).

Bibliography

Adyashanti. (2006). *Emptiness Dancing, 2ⁿᵈ Edition.* Boulder, CO: Sounds True, Inc.

Alexander, E. (2012). *Proof of Heaven: A Neurosurgeon's Near-Death Experience and Journey into the Afterlife.* New York, NY: Simon & Schuster.

American Psychiatric Association (2000). *Diagnostic and Statistical Manual of Mental Disorders-IV (Text Revision).* Arlington, VA: American Psychiatric Publishing, Inc.

Augusto, L. M. (2010). Unconscious knowledge: A survey. *Advances in Cognitive Psychology,* 6, pp. 116-141.

Bergson, H. (1912). *Matter and Memory.* London: George Allen & Co.

Blanke, O. et al. (2002). Stimulating illusory own-body perceptions: The part of the brain that can induce out-of-body experiences has been located. *Nature,* 419, pp. 269-270.

Boly, M. et al. (2011). Preserved Feedforward But Impaired Top-Down Processes in the Vegetative State. *Science,* 332(6031), pp. 858-862.

Boswell, J. (1820). *The Life of Samuel Johnson, LL. D., Volume 1.* London: J. Davis, Military Chronicle and Military Classics Office.

Carhart-Harris, R. L. et al. (2012). Neural correlates of the psychedelic state as determined by fMRI studies with psilocybin. *Proceedings of the National Academy of Sciences of the United States of America,* 23 January 2012. [Online]. Available from: www.pnas.org/content/early/2012/01/17/1119598109 [Accessed 14 February 2013].

Chalmers, D. (1996). *The Conscious Mind: In Search of a Fundamental Theory.* Oxford: Oxford University Press.

Chalmers, D. (2003). Consciousness and its Place in Nature. In: Stich, S. and Warfield, F. eds. *Blackwell Guide to the Philosophy of Mind.* Malden, MA: Blackwell, pp. 102-142.

Chalmers, D. (2006). Strong and Weak Emergence. In: Clayton, P. and Davies, P. eds. *The Re-Emergence of Emergence.* Oxford: Oxford University Press, pp. 244-254.

Cheetham, T. (2012). *All the World an Icon: Henry Corbin and the angelic function of beings.* Berkeley, CA: North Atlantic Books.

Davies, P. and Brown, J. eds. (1992). *Superstrings: A Theory of Everything?* Cambridge: Cambridge University Press.

Davies, P. (2010). Stephen Hawking's big bang gaps. *The Guardian,* 4 September 2010, London. [Online]. Available from: http://www.guardian.co.uk/commentisfree/belief/2010/sep/04/stephen-hawking-big-bang-gap [Accessed 14 February 2013].

Dennett, D. (1991). *Consciousness Explained.* London: Penguin Books.

Dennett, D. (2003). Explaining the "Magic" of Consciousness. *Journal of Cultural and Evolutionary Psychology,* 1(1), pp. 7-19.

DiSalvo, D. (2012). When You Inject Spirit Mediums' Brains with Radioactive Chemicals, Strange Things Happen. *Forbes,* 18 November 2012. [Online]. Available from: http://www.forbes.com/sites/daviddisalvo/2012/11/18/when-you-inject-spirit-mediums-brains-with-radioactive-chemicals-some-really-strange-things-happen/ [Accessed 15 February 2013].

Dresler, M. et al. (2011). Dreamed Movement Elicits Activation in the Sensorimotor Cortex. *Current Biology,* 21(21), pp. 1833-1837.

Eagleman, D. (2011). *Incognito: The Secret Lives of the Brain.* London: Canongate.

Eliade, M. (2009). *Rites and Symbols of Initiation: The Mysteries of Birth and Rebirth.* New York, NY: Spring Publications.

Ffytche, M. (2011). *The Foundation of the Unconscious: Schelling, Freud and the Birth of the Modern Psyche.* Cambridge: Cambridge University Press.

Fogelin, R. (2001). *Routledge Philosophy GuideBook to Berkeley and the Principles of Human Knowledge.* London: Routledge.

Folger, T. (2004). Einstein's Grand Quest for a Unified Theory. *Discover Magazine,* 30 September 2004. [Online]. Available from: http://discovermagazine.com/2004/sep/einsteins-grand-quest#.USMxz0petJF [Accessed 19 February 2013].

Gebser, J. (1986). *The Ever-Present Origin, Part One: Foundations of the Aperspectival World and Part Two: Manifestations of the Aperspectival World.* Athens, OH: Ohio University Press.

Goethe, J. W. (author) and Bernays, L. J. (translator) (1839). *Goethe's Faust, Part II.* London: Sampson Low.

Gordon, D. (1999). *Ants At Work: How An Insect Society Is Organized.* New York, NY: The Free Press.

Greene, B. (2003). *The Elegant Universe: Superstrings, Hidden Dimensions, and the Quest for the Ultimate Theory.* New York, NY: W. W. Norton & Company.

Gröblacher, S. et al. (2007). An experimental test of non-local realism. *Nature,* 446, 871-875.

Grof, S. and Grof, C. eds. (1989). *Spiritual emergency: When personal transformation becomes a crisis.* New York, NY: Tarcher.

Gross, C. G. (2002). Genealogy of the "Grandmother Cell." *Neuroscientist,* 8(5), 512-518.

Hameroff, S. (2006). Consciousness, neurobiology and quantum mechanics: The case for a connection. In: Tuszynski, J. A. ed. *The Emerging Physics of Consciousness.* Berlin: Springer, pp. 193-241.

Haraldsson, E. (2012). *The Departed Among the Living: An Investigative Study of Afterlife Encounters.* Gildford: White Crow Books.

Harpur, P. (2009). *The Philosopher's Secret Fire: A history of the imagination.* Glastonbury: The Squeeze Press.

Hawking, S. and Mlodinow, L. (2010). *The Grand Design: New Answers to the Ultimate Questions of Life.* London: Bantam Books.

Hofstadter, D. R. (1980). *Gödel, Escher, Bach: An Eternal Golden*

Braid. London: Penguin Books.

Hofstadter, D. R. (2008). *I Am a Strange Loop*. New York, NY: Basic Books.

Hughes, A. L. (2012). The Folly of Scientism. *The New Atlantis, 37,* pp. 32-50.

Iacoboni, M., Rayman, J. and Zaidel, E. (1996). Left brain says yes, right brain says no: Normative duality in the split brain. In: Hameroff, S. R., Kasniak, A. W. and Scott, A. C. eds. *Toward a Scientific Basis of Consciousness*. Cambridge, MA: MIT Press, pp. 197-202.

Jung, C. G. (1985). *Synchronicity: An Acausal Connecting Principle*. London: Routledge.

Jung, C. G. (1991). *The Archetypes and the Collective Unconscious*. London: Routledge.

Jung, C. G. (1995). *Memories, Dreams, Reflections*. London: Fontana Press.

Jung, C. G. (author) and Chodorow, J. (editor) (1997). *Jung on Active Imagination*. London: Routledge.

Jung, C. G. (2001). *On the Nature of the Psyche*. London: Routledge.

Jung, C. G. and Pauli, W. (2001). *Atom and Archetype: The Pauli/Jung Letters, 1932-1958*. Princeton, NJ: Princeton University Press.

Jung, C. G. (2002). *The Undiscovered Self*. London: Routledge.

Jung, C. G. (author) and Sabini, M. (editor) (2002). *The Earth Has a Soul: C. G. Jung on Nature, Technology & Modern Life*. Berkeley, CA: North Atlantic Books.

Jung, C. G. (2009). *The Red Book: Liber Novus*. New York, NY: W. W. Norton & Company.

Journal of Transpersonal Psychology. Palo Alto, CA: Association for Transpersonal Psychology.

Kandel, E. et al. eds. (2012). Principles of Neural Science, 5th Edition. New York, NY: McGraw-Hill Professional.

Kastrup, B. and Seixas, J. M. (1997). A Single-Neuron Weighting

Technique for Classifiers. *Proceedings of the 5th European Congress on Intelligent Techniques and Soft Computing*, 1, pp. 480-484.

Kastrup, B. (2012). Response to Dr. Christof Koch. *Metaphysical Speculations*, 7 February 2012. [Online]. Available from: http://www.bernardokastrup.com/2012/02/response-to-christof-koch.html [Accessed 15 February 2013].

Keim, B. (2013). Consciousness After Death: Strange Tales From the Frontiers of Resuscitation Medicine. *Wired Magazine*, 24 April 2013. [Online]. Available from: http://www.wired.com/wiredscience/2013/04/consciousness-after-death/all/ [Accessed 22 May 2013].

Kelly, E. W., Greyson, B. and Kelly, E. D. (2009). Unusual Experiences Near Death and Related Phenomena. In: Kelly, E. D. et al. *Irreducible Mind: Toward a Psychology for the 21st Century*. Lanham, MD: Rowman & Littlefield, pp. 367-421.

Kirk, R. (2011). Zombies. *Stanford Encyclopedia of Philosophy*. [Online]. Available from: http://plato.stanford.edu/entries/zombies/ [Accessed 16 February 2013].

Koch, C. (2004). *The Quest for Consciousness: A Neurobiological Approach*. Englewood, CO: Roberts & Company Publishers.

Koch, C. (2011). The Neurobiology and Mathematics of Consciousness. In: *Singularity Summit 2011*. [Online video]. Available from: www.youtube.com/watch?v=6i9kE3Ne7as [Accessed 14 February 2013].

Koch, C. and Tsakiris, A. (2012). Dr. Christof Koch on Human Consciousness and Near-Death Experience Research. *Skeptiko podcast*, 160, 7 February 2012. [Online]. Available from: http://www.skeptiko.com/160-christof-koch-consciousness-and-near-death-experience-research/ [Accessed 15 February 2013].

Krebs, H. A. and Weitzman, P. D. J. (1987). *Krebs' citric acid cycle: half a century and still turning*. London: Biochemical Society.

Kuhn, T. S. (1996). *The Structure of Scientific Revolutions, 3rd*

Edition. Chicago, IL: The University of Chicago Press.

Lammle, R. (2010). The Amazing Stories of 6 Sudden Savants. *Mental_floss,* 29 June 2010. [Online]. Available from: http://mentalfloss.com/article/25048/amazing-stories-6-sudden-savants [Accessed 15 February 2013].

Leeming, D. A. (2010). *Creation Myths of the World: An Encyplopedia, 2nd Edition.* Santa Barbara, CA: ABC-CLIO.

Lehar, S. (1999). Gestalt isomorphism and the quantification of spatial perception. *Gestalt Theory,* 21, pp. 122-139.

Levine, J. (1999). Conceivability, Identity, and the Explanatory Gap. In: Hameroff, S., Kaszniak, A., and Chalmers, D. eds. *Toward a Science of Consciousness III, The Third Tucson Discussions and Debates.* Cambridge, MA: The MIT Press, pp. 3-12.

Lilly, J. and Gold, E. (1996). *Tanks for the Memories: Floatation Tank Talks, 2nd Edition.* Nevada City, CA: Gateways Books & Tapes.

Lovelock, J. (2005). *Gaia: And the theory of the living planet, 2nd Edition.* London: Octopus Publishing Group.

Lythgoe, M. et al. (2005). Obsessive, prolific artistic output following subarachnoid hemorrhage. *Neurology,* 64, pp. 397-398.

Mack, J. E. (1999). *Passport to the Cosmos: Human Transformation and Alien Encounters.* New York, NY: Three Rivers Press.

Metzinger, T. ed. (2000). *Neural Correlates of Consciousness: Empirical and Conceptual Questions.* Cambridge, MA: The MIT Press.

Miller, G. (2005). What Is the Biological Basis of Consciousness? *Science,* 309(5731), p. 79.

Miller, B. et al. (1998). Emergence of artistic talent in fronto-temporal dementia. *Neurology,* 51, pp. 978-982.

Miller, B. et al. (2000). Functional correlates of musical and visual ability in fronto-temporal dementia. *Br. J. Psychiatry,* 176, pp. 458-463.

Moorjani, A. (2012). *Dying To Be Me: My Journey from Cancer, to*

Near Death, to True Healing. Carlsbad, CA: Hay House, Inc.

Musser, G. and Minkel, J. R. (2002). A Recycled Universe: Crashing branes and cosmic acceleration may power an infinite cycle in which our universe is but a phase. *Scientific American,* 11 February 2002. [Online]. Available from: http://www.scientificamerican.com/article.cfm?id=a-recycled-universe [Accessed 20 February 2013].

Neal, R. M. (2008). The Choking Game. In: *The Path to Addiction: And Other Troubles We Are Born to Know.* Bloomington, IN: AuthorHouse, pp. 310-315.

Oerter, R. (2006). *The Theory of Almost Everything: The Standard Model, the Unsung Triumph of Modern Physics.* New York, NY: Pearson Education Inc.

Okasha, S. (2002). *Philosophy of Science: A Very Short Introduction.* Oxford: Oxford University Press.

Pascual-Leone, A. et al. eds. (2002). *Handbook of Transcranial Magnetic Stimulation.* London: Hodder Arnold.

Peck, M. E. (2011). Signal for Consciousness in Brain Marked by Neural Dialogue: Brain areas send signals back and forth to generate conscious thoughts. *Scientific American Mind,* November 2011. [Online]. Available from: http://www.scientificamerican.com/article.cfm?id=a-conversation-in-the-brain [Accessed 17 February 2013].

Peres, J. et al. (2011). Neuroimaging during Trance State: A Contribution to the Study of Dissociation. PLoS ONE, 7(11), e49360.

Persinger, M. et al. (2010). The Electromagnetic Induction of Mystical and Altered States Within the Laboratory. *Journal of Consciousness Exploration & Research,* 1(7), pp. 808-830.

Piore, A. (2013). The Genius Within. *Popular Science,* March 2013, pp. 46-53.

Plantinga, A. (1993). *Warrant and Proper Function.* Oxford: Oxford University Press Inc.

Poz, J. D. (2005). *Zuruahã: Cosmology and Suicide.* [Online].

Available from: http://pib.socioambiental.org/en/povo/ zuruaha/989 [Accessed 14 February 2013].

Read, S. (1995). *Thinking About Logic: An Introduction to the Philosophy of Logic*. Oxford: Oxford University Press.

Retz (2007). Tripping Without Drugs: experience with Hyperventilation (ID 14651). *Erowid.org*. [Online]. Available from: www.erowid.org/exp/14651 [Accessed 14 February 2013].

Rhinewine, J. P. and Williams, O. J. (2007). Holotropic Breathwork: The Potential Role of a Prolonged, Voluntary Hyperventilation Procedure as an Adjunct to Psychotherapy. *The Journal of Alternative and Complementary Medicine*, 13(7), pp. 771-776.

Roberson, D. et al. (2006). Colour Categories and Category Acquisition in Himba and English. In: Pitchford, N. and Bingham, C. eds. *Progress in Colour Studies*. Amsterdam: John Benjamins, pp. 159-172.

Roberson, D. et al. (2005). Colour categories in Himba: Evidence for the cultural relativity hypothesis. *Cognitive Psychology*, 50, pp. 378-411.

Russell, B. (2007). *The Analysis of Matter*. Nottingham: Spokesman Books.

Schwartz, J. M. and Begley, S. (2004). *Mind and the Brain*. New York, NY: HarperCollins.

Schwartz, J. M., Stapp, H. P. and Beauregard, M. (2005). Quantum Physics in Neuroscience and Psychology: A Neurophysical Model of Mind-Brain Interaction. *Philosophical Transactions of the Royal Society B*, 360(1458), pp. 1309-1327.

Seixas, J. M. et al. (1995). Reducing Input Space Dimension for Real-Time Data Analysis in High-Event Rate Environment. *Proceedings of the International Conference on Artificial Neural Networks*, 2, pp. 203-208.

Sheldrake, R. (2011). *Dogs That Know When Their Owners Are Coming Home: Fully Updated and Revised*. New York, NY: Three Rivers Press.

Shermer, M. (1999). Out of Body Experiment. [Online video]. Available from: http://www.michaelshermer.com/1999/09/out-of-body-experiment/ [Accessed 15 February 2013].

Shermer, M. (2011). What Is Pseudoscience? *Scientific American*, 15 September 2011. [Online]. Available from: http://www. scientificamerican.com/article.cfm?id=what-is-pseudoscience [Accessed 5 April 2013].

Shuman, G. D. (2007). *Last Breath: A Sherry Moore Novel*. New York, NY: Simon & Schuster.

Smolin, L. (2007). *The Trouble with Physics: The Rise of String Theory, The Fall of a Science, and What Comes Next*. Boston, MA: Mariner Books.

Strassman, R. et al. (2008). *Inner Paths to Outer Space*. Rochester, VT: Park Street Press.

Strawson, G. (2006). Realistic Monism: Why Physicalism Entails Panpsychism. *Journal of Consciousness Studies*, 13, pp. 3-31.

Sudman, N. (2012). *Application of Impossible Things: A Near Death Experience in Iraq*. Huntsville, AR: Ozark Mountain Publishing.

Taylor, J. B. (2009). *My Stroke of Insight*. London: Hodder & Stoughton.

Taylor, K. (1994). *The Breathwork Experience: Exploration and Healing in Nonordinary States of Consciousness*. Santa Cruz, CA: Hanford Mead.

Tongue, B. H. (2001). *Principles of Vibration, 2nd Edition*. Oxford: Oxford University Press.

Tononi, G. (2004a). Consciousness and the Brain: Theoretical Aspects. In: Adelman, G. and Smith, B. eds. *Encyclopedia of Neuroscience, 3rd Edition*. [CD-ROM]. Elsevier.

Tononi, G. (2004b). An Information Integration Theory of Consciousness. *BMC Neuroscience*, 5(42). [Online]. Available from: www.biomedcentral.com/1471-2202/5/42 [Accessed 14 February 2013].

Treffert, D. (2006). *Extraordinary People: Understanding Savant*

Syndrome. Omaha, NE: iUniverse, Inc.

Treffert, D. (2009). The Savant Syndrome: An Extraordinary Condition. A Synopsis: Past, Present, Future. *Philosophical Transactions of the Royal Society B*, 364(1522), pp. 1351-1357.

Urgesi, C. et al. (2010). The Spiritual Brain: Selective Cortical Lesions Modulate Human Self Transcendence. *Neuron*, 65, pp. 309-319.

Ustinova, Y. (2009). *Caves and the Ancient Greek Mind: Descending Underground in the Search for Ultimate Truth.* Oxford: Oxford University Press.

Watts, A. (2009). *The Book: On the Taboo Against Knowing Who You Are.* London: Souvenir Press.

Whinnery, J. and Whinnery, A. (1990). Acceleration-Induced Loss of Consciousness: A Review of 500 Episodes. *Archives of Neurology*, 47(7), pp. 764-776.

Zee, A. (2010). *Quantum Field Theory in a Nutshell, 2nd Edition.* Princeton, NJ: Princeton University Press.

Zicheng, H. (author), Aitken, R. (translator), and Kwok, D. W. Y. (translator) (2006). *Vegetable Roots Discourse: Wisdom from Ming China on Life and Living: The Caigentan.* Berkeley, CA: Shoemaker & Hoard.

BOOKS

ACADEMIC AND SPECIALIST

Iff Books publishes non-fiction. It aims to work with
authors and titles that augment our understanding of the
human condition, society and civilisation, and the world or
universe in which we live.
If you have enjoyed this book, why not tell other readers
by posting a review on your preferred book site.

Recent bestsellers from Iff Books are:

The Fall
Steve Taylor
The Fall discusses human achievement versus the issues of war,
patriarchy and social inequality.
Paperback: 978-1-90504-720-8 ebook: 978-184694-633-2

Brief Peeks Beyond
Critical Essays on Metaphysics, Neuroscience, Free Will,
Skepticism and Culture
Bernardo Kastrup
An incisive, original, compelling alternative to current
mainstream cultural views and assumptions.
Paperback: 978-1-78535-018-4 ebook: 978-1-78535-019-1

Framespotting
Changing How You Look at Things Changes How
You See Them
Laurence & Alison Matthews
A punchy, upbeat guide to framespotting. Spot deceptions and
hidden assumptions; swap growth for growing up. See and be
free.
Paperback: 978-1-78279-689-3 ebook: 978-1-78279-822-4

Is There an Afterlife?
David Fontana
Is there an Afterlife? If so what is it like? How do Western ideas
of the afterlife compare with Eastern? David Fontana presents
the historical and contemporary evidence for survival of
physical death.
Paperback: 978-1-90381-690-5

Nothing Matters
A Book About Nothing
Ronald Green
Thinking about Nothing opens the world to everything by
illuminating new angles to old problems and stimulating new
ways of thinking.
Paperback: 978-1-84694-707-0 ebook: 978-1-78099-016-3

Panpsychism
The Philosophy of the Sensuous Cosmos
Peter Ells
Are free will and mind chimeras? This book, anti-materialistic
but respecting science, answers: No! Mind is foundational to all
existence.
Paperback: 978-1-84694-505-2 ebook: 978-1-78099-018-7

Punk Science
Inside the Mind of God
Manjir Samanta-Laughton
Many have experienced unexplainable phenomena; God,
psychic abilities, extraordinary healing and angelic encounters.
Can cutting-edge science actually explain phenomena
previously thought of as 'paranormal'?
Paperback: 978-1-90504-793-2

The Vagabond Spirit of Poetry
Edward Clarke
Spend time with the wisest poets of the modern age and of the
past, and let Edward Clarke remind you of the importance of
poetry in our industrialized world.
Paperback: 978-1-78279-370-0 ebook: 978-1-78279-369-4

Readers of ebooks can buy or view any of these bestsellers by clicking on the live link in the title. Most titles are published in paperback and as an ebook. Paperbacks are available in traditional bookshops. Both print and ebook formats are available online.

Find more titles and sign up to our readers' newsletter at http://www.johnhuntpublishing.com/non-fiction

Follow us on Facebook at
https://www.facebook.com/JHPNonFiction
and Twitter at https://twitter.com/JHPNonFiction